ALSO BY ELLEN HANDLER SPITZ

Inside Picture Books

Museums of the Mind

Image and Insight

Art and Psyche

The Brightening Glance

The Brightening Glance

*

IMAGINATION AND CHILDHOOD

Ellen Handler Spitz

PANTHEON BOOKS, NEW YORK

Pantheon Books and colophon are registered
trademarks of Random House, Inc.

Some of the material in Chapters 1 and 5 was
previously published in *Michigan Quarterly Review.*

Owing to limitations of space, all acknowledgments for
permission to reprint previously published material
may be found at the end of the volume.

Library of Congress Cataloging-in-Publication Data

Spitz, Ellen Handler, [date]
The Brightening Glance: imagination and childhood /
Ellen Handler Spitz.
p.   cm.
Includes bibliographical references and index.
ISBN 0-375-42058-4
1. Imagination in children. 2. Aesthetics. 3. Awe. 4. Wonder.
5. Child development. 6. Child psychology. I. Title.
BF723.I5S65 2006   2005050943

www.pantheonbooks.com

Printed in the United States of America
First Edition
2   4   6   8   9   7   5   3   1

FOR JOANNA

O body swayed to music, O brightening glance,
How can we know the dancer from the dance?

—WILLIAM BUTLER YEATS,
"Among School Children"

Contents

A Note to My Reader

As a writer on the arts, I have often felt curious about the role of imagination and of early aesthetic experience in shaping the lives of those who work in fields of special interest to me and in far-flung disciplines as well. I know the beginnings lie in childhood, when nothing can be taken for granted. For nearly all my adult life I have had the good fortune of being close to certain children. This book, inspired by them and by countless writers and artists only some of whose works are acknowledged in these pages, takes that curiosity as a springboard for eight chapters, eight leaps. Yet ever since, as a Brownie scout growing up in New York, I defied my diminutive size to compete in a track event known as the running broad jump, there's been a bit of the daredevil in me, and perhaps this book could be seen as an intellectual adult equivalent of that once beloved sport. Then as now, the pleasure comes from trying rather than winning.

As a fellow at the Sterling and Francine Clark Art Institute in the Berkshire hills during the summer of 2004, I was blessed with a tranquil, verdant refuge in which to write. One day, in conversation with several colleagues, over a glass of wine, I began to muse about you, my unknown reader, and to wonder how you might take to the pages that follow. Very soon, you will know that I have written about what I love. I have made an effort to open gates to a land without borders. Just kick up your heels and sprint in meadows spangled with clover and devil's paintbrush, where invisible frogs burp and sunbeams glint on the Queen Anne's lace. Let's imagine; I'll be with you.

The Brightening Glance

The Magnifying Gaze of Children

It is hardly worth the effort to try to grow up into—
and live fully within—a world that is not full of
wonder.

—Bruno Bettelheim, "Children and Museums"

Brooding, she changed the pool into the sea, and
made the minnows into sharks and whales, and cast
vast clouds over this tiny world by holding her hand
against the sun, and so brought darkness and desola-
tion, like God himself, to millions of ignorant and
innocent creatures, and then took her hand away suddenly and let the sun stream down.

—Virginia Woolf, *To the Lighthouse*

Spaceman Spiff and Rapunzel at the Ballet

As childhood recedes in time, it steals in closer and feels more palpable.
Like a lost toy that has slipped into a cranny, it suddenly turns up. You
want to hold on to it again. Thus, my own childhood intrudes sometimes into these pages. Because of this stealing back of memory, you
will find, in this book, impressions, recollections, even an occasional
bit of exhortation. My wish is to take you back to moments in your
own childhood as well as to invite you to consider matters that confront young children today. For childhood is, after all, not only the

start of life; it stays with us, follows us, and continues to survive as a realm to which we return. Perhaps, moreover, the artists are right, and returning purposefully to it from time to time can inspire us to continue to grow.

Throughout my life as artist, dancer, writer, parent, and scholar, a deep undertow has always pulled me back to childhood. Not only to my own but to all manner of stories, objects, images, plays, songs, films, and even theories that touch on childhood. I want to consider the ways in which children grow and learn in the realms of the *aesthetic* or, to put it more precisely, in their sensory, perceptual, and *imaginative* lives, and the ways in which this growing and learning intersects with their emotional lives and with the feelings of those dear to them. Although we tend conventionally to make a distinction between the notions of imagination and perception, I shall, in these pages, treat these terms as very close, rather like an intimate dyad, because this is the way they function in early childhood. Normally, we conceive of imagination as an inner, mental activity (daydreaming in the dark, for example) quite separable from perception, which we take to be directed toward outward stimuli (listening to sounds, discriminating between colors, inhaling fragrances); yet, in early childhood, these modes work in close harmony. Children's wishes, dreams, and fantasies feed into their immediate sensory perceptions, and their aesthetic lives in turn shape the contours of their fantasies. This interdependence is so pronounced in early childhood because during those brief years the aggressively occupying armies of compartmentalization have not yet fully colonized our mental landscapes.

Other authors have challenged the dichotomy between aesthetics and imagination. The scientist Alan Lightman, for example, in *A Sense of the Mysterious*, wonders how we can possibly picture what we have never, in some sense, seen, and he reminds us of how helpful and even necessary it is to form mental pictures to accompany abstract ideas so that, to understand scientific discoveries, one reverts to terms and images familiar "from daily life—spinning balls, waves in water, pendulums, weights on springs," and he quotes Einstein's poetic statement that " 'the universe of ideas is just as little independent of the nature of our experiences as clothes are of the form of the human body.' " Italo Calvino, too, coming at it from the other side in his bewitching *Mr. Palomar,* reveals the lunacy of our quixotic attempts to make our abstractions, our maps, match living experiences that always exceed them. I especially treasure his memory of waiting on a long queue in a busy *fromagerie,* where each aromatic cheese on display evokes, as he gazes at it and whiffs it, a different bucolic landscape dotted with cows or sheep or goats so that by the time he has reached the counter, he has become so engrossed in his fantasies that he cannot decide which cheese he wants to buy. Children dwell in just such a universe, and they disclose it to us moment by moment when we watch and listen to them.

Our discussion in these pages will range far beyond any traditionally limited view of children's aesthetic lives. Although I started out with the idea of writing a book about first experiences in the traditional arts such as dance, theater, music, literature, and visual art (and you will find traces of that agenda still), I quickly came to see that children do not separate these out subjectively from other aspects of their lives—from their ordinary excursions, their living and play spaces, their holidays. We will not be principally concerned, for example, with teaching the practice of any of the conventional arts to young children, nor will we focus exclusively on the subject of taking them to museums and concerts. This is because, just as perceiving and imagining go hand in hand in early childhood, so do the various aspects of their aesthetic lives. To a child, these realms feel seamless. After all, it is not they but we who have been trained to think in categories. What I want to urge is that we stop and reconsider these boxes; for only when we broaden our horizons on the artistic and imaginative possibilities in children's lives can we begin to perceive the aesthetic potential in myriad aspects of their daily routines. Thus, although I am passionately interested in the complexities of teaching and learning in the arts, my principal focus here is on the aesthetic dimensions of children's everyday lives. I will ask you to reconsider the ordinary and the apparently mundane: looking out at and listening attentively to the world, playing imaginatively, living in an assigned space, celebrating a birthday, waiting for a parent in an international airport, feeling lost, being found, seeming different from others and misunderstood, as well as occasions when a child's experience does intersect with the arts (attending a music class for toddlers and mothers, getting ready for an opera, becoming afraid during a movie, watching a television show, peering curiously at works of visual art in a museum or gallery). In each instance, I invite you to ask yourself how such formative experiences proliferate and feed into later encounters with the arts and life. Likewise, how do the arts—visual (including film, television, video), musical, dramatic, and poetic—serve to determine the forms of children's imaginative lives, their play, symbols, ideals, and dreams? The arts exert a powerful force not only directly but also indirectly, for they portray childhood in ways that influence our adult views of children, which we then pass along to them. Above all, I am fascinated by the close mingling of psychological and aesthetic factors. This mingling will serve as a constant leitmotiv throughout these pages.

Several large questions have intrigued me and serve as a continuing springboard for my work: What can we learn about beauty and aesthetic pleasure from young children? How do children's aesthetic and emotional lives intersect? Can we as adults enhance young children's aesthetic experiences without imposing our own prejudicial templates and classifications?

I want to give priority to the fluidity of children's inner and outer lives. Few have illustrated this flow more tellingly than the brilliant graphic artist Bill Watterson in his delightful *Calvin and Hobbes* comic strips. With charm, wit, and wisdom, he reveals how young children slip back and forth between their private worlds of imagination and the domain of shared cultural experience. In one strip, Watterson draws six-year-old spikey-haired Calvin, with goggles on, thoroughly absorbed in one of his favorite daydreams, in which he assumes the role of the intrepid commander Spaceman Spiff. We don't know it right away, but Calvin is actually in school. As Spiff, with his rocket ship hurling toward destruction, he counts down backward, in terror, from ten. His second-grade teacher, Mrs. Wormwood, quietly approaches his desk and sets him an arithmetic problem. "SEVEN!" Calvin blurts out, lost in his fantasy countdown; that turns out to be the right answer to his teacher's question. It is *this* exchange I am after: namely, the many-splendored ways in which individual children come to experience their worlds imaginatively and aesthetically—an exchange that also, importantly, involves their hearts. In a scene from ordinary life, I recently observed the following: At the Lyric Opera House in Baltimore, a well-dressed lady with her six-year-old grandson emerged in a crush of children and adults after a fanciful holiday performance of *The Nutcracker* ballet. Suddenly, from an adjoining staircase, there appeared in front of them a woman with shimmering blond hair that cascaded down her back practically to her knees. The boy clutched his grandmother's hand and announced in a stage whisper: "Look, Nana! That lady looks just like Rapunzel."

A word about my methodology. In no way do I mean all the anecdotes and illustrations in these pages to be generalized into overarching principles. Each story is offered to indicate a strand in the web of children's aesthetic lives—a strand that seems valuable in and of itself and worth pondering—but I have no wish to claim any part for them in a universal theory of aesthetic development. Nor do I attempt exhaustive analyses or believe that any amount of statistical research could accomplish such a goal. My chapters intersect and overlap. To get at the origins of imaginative and aesthetic experience, I have used the testimonies of adults as well as my own and others' direct observation of and interactive engagement with young children. Children, even passing by quickly, "like a bird, bullet, or arrow," as Virginia Woolf once put it, appear as main characters here; yet they have supporting casts and have not been divided into categories of age and stage, as is routine for texts in psychology and education. Their ages are offered only in passing in most instances, and although my focus is on the early years, my examples include children ranging from less than two years up through early adolescence. When a story has seemed helpful, I have adopted it. I have drawn freely on my own life and on the lives of my colleagues, friends, and family, on oral communications as well as published works, and on the theoretical and empirical studies of others, all of which are acknowledged directly in the body of this text or in its references. In many instances the names of children and parents—who hail from many parts of the globe, not solely from the United States—have been altered to protect their privacy. Perhaps, in fact, the stories themselves, like the experiences of which they speak, should be treated as ends in themselves. *Moments in the woods . . .*

What Do We Mean by *Aesthetic?*

If you were to ask a child to tell you what an *anesthetic* is, chances are you would hear something like: "Oh, the stuff they give in hospitals or dentists' offices to make you numb so you won't feel anything." Many children know that an anesthetic blocks sensation. But what about something *aesthetic?* What does *that* mean and do? Most children would not be able to tell you. In fact, many adults wouldn't either. Yet, *aesthetic* has a lot to do with *anesthetic,* for one is the opposite of the other. If I am under anesthesia, either concretely, in the medical sense, or metaphorically, in the sense of shutting myself off from potential pain, I not only avoid the anticipated unpleasantness, I also fail to feel much of anything else. Not only that, but when the anesthetic wears off, chances are I won't remember what has happened to me. Yet, although it may seem strange, if we give it a moment's thought, we can see that, for a variety of reasons, many people live for long periods each day as if they were under the effects of just such an anesthesia.

Aesthetics, on the contrary, has to do precisely with *not* being numb. Aesthetics has to do with feeling, sensing, perceiving, and imagining. It has to do with a heightened rather than a diminished receptivity, with the deployment of our senses—especially of sight and sound, but also of touch, taste, and smell—and of our abilities to conjure and suppose, to go beyond the given limitations of space and time. In aesthetic moments, our sense receptors get turned up, not off; they work harder, rather than shutting down. In aesthetic moments (at the opera, a poetry reading, a ballet, or an art exhibition, or while viewing a mountain landscape, turning the pages of a novel, strolling in late-autumn sunlight, looking up at a stormy sky, daydreaming), we awaken to kaleidoscopic worlds of sensation and stimulation. The aesthetic pulls us in and dares us to be fully present even at the risk of feeling some pain. In return, it offers us chances to discover new aspects of the world into which we have been thrust. It gives us intense pleasures. It arouses our ever-dormant proclivity for fantasy; it sharpens our powers of discrimination; and it expands, sometimes, our capacity for empathy. Occasionally, in its intensity, it momentarily blinds us to everything else and can, therefore, seem (as Plato taught) dangerous.

Aesthetic Judgments and Hierarchy in a Child's Vision of the World

Beyond openness to sensation and an embrace of the world, aesthetics has to do with making judgments. One may prefer Handel to Verdi; Rembrandt to Vermeer. Such judgments entail taste and preference, and they often seem like solemn verdicts about which we cannot argue productively with others: *De gustibus non disputandum est.* When it comes to children's television, for example, my editor and I disagree about the relative merits of *Mister Rogers' Neighborhood* and *The Simpsons,* even though, of course, they are aimed at children of different ages. Puzzled by the tenacity of such judgments, philosophers, notably David Hume and Immanuel Kant, explain that the subject baffles them because it requires two theses that appear mutually contradictory but true. On the one hand, our own aesthetic judgments seem so clear, right, and genuine to us that we instinctively feel they must be based on universal principles. Yet, surprisingly, we find that they are not; for we are neither able to persuade others by reasoned arguments to relinquish their own aesthetic preferences in favor of ours nor are we susceptible to persuasion by others on the basis of their reasoned arguments to give up our aesthetic preferences and adopt theirs. Aesthetic judgments, therefore, seem both based and not based on principles. Stout Timmy Willie, as Beatrix Potter implies, in spite of all his good reasons, cannot convince high-strung Johnny Town-Mouse that country life is preferable to dwelling in the city; each mouse is sure his way is best. Hence, the dilemma known to philosophers as "the antinomy of taste."

Let us consider children's aesthetic judgments. To do so is to see immediately that, like those of adults, children's tastes possess an intrinsic "rightness," a *non disputandum* of their own, even when they rub against the grain of our more sophisticated sensibilities. I know one dramatic five-year-old girl, for instance, who is unwaveringly partial to the color turquoise, although neither she nor her parents, despite much head scratching, can come up with any plausible reason why. Likewise, in the realm of the gustatory, infants indicate clear preferences for specific flavors and textures long before any symbolic meaning could be in place. Yet one cannot be sure. Mothers and fathers do, as we know, subtly betray their prejudices. A small girl named Sally never cared for milk. She did, however, love the taste of orange-flavored sodas and juice. This preference, observed by her mother, imposed on that devoted parent a hazardous daily task—that of flavoring Sally's milk (in order to provide her with sufficient calcium) with just the right amount of orange flavor to disguise it and yet not enough to curdle it. Another child categorically refuses to eat potatoes; he jokes about them, especially at restaurants when he sees others having French fries. Neither of his potato-eating parents can alter or explain his bias. As for shoes, which are the one garment children wear that they can actually *behold* all the time, have you noticed how fierce even the mildest children become in a shoe store when aesthetic choices are to be made ("No, Mommy, no! I ONLY want THESE!")?

Clearly, even the youngest members of society express their aesthetic tastes and preferences with no less vehemence and with no greater susceptibility to rational persuasion than adults. Thus, it is doubtful that anything we discover in these pages will resolve the philosophers' dilemma. However, later on, in the chapter on children's rooms, we will explore this topic at some length and consider not only the origins of certain tastes but also optimal ways in which adults might react to them. In general, however, I would plead that, whenever possible, we not summarily override their choices. This does not mean, of course, that we abandon any hopes for aesthetic education but merely that we realize (with tongue-in-cheek apologies to John Locke) that we are never starting from tabula rasa.

"Am I Still Your Favorite?"

Hierarchy, as I will discuss later in the chapter on scary experiences, seems inevitably built into children's early perceptions as they come to notice, say, the relations between body size and power, but language plays a decisive role in determining just how such templates function in individual cases. In the following anecdote, we see how the favored modes of linguistic expression within a child's family can be carried over into surprising new contexts.

Colin's family lives in Scarsdale, New York, and the highly educated parents of this three-year-old boy talk regularly and unproblematically about "favorites." Their world is imbued with rank and hierarchy—specifically, the best, and everything else. Until recently an only child, Colin has a well-established favorite color, a favorite food, and a favorite song, and whenever he is taken to a cultural event, he is asked to report afterward on his "favorite" aspect of the experience. Upon being presented, for example, with a videotape about Paul Bunyan, he is, after watching it, immediately pressed to name his favorite episode. Imitatively, as we might guess, Colin also routinely questions other people concerning *their* favorite things. How fascinating but not entirely unpredictable, then, to observe his first reaction at being taken to the hospital on the occasion of the birth of his baby sister. Looking into the crib at the tiny creature asleep, he immediately turns to his parents and asks them worriedly: "Am I still your favorite?"

Here we see the template given by the family utilized by the child to voice feelings that probably lay latent in any case but that, because of a linguistic structure and a value system established and reinforced by the family, may now prove troublesome. The parents' answer—that there will be no favorites among the children in the family—may prove just a bit harder for Colin to accept right away and to believe than for another child because it does not jibe with everything that has gone before. In transferring the mode of assigning value from the aesthetic realm to another quadrant of experience, this little boy has made a move that philosopher Gilbert Ryle might call a species of "category mistake." In Ryle's famous example, a visitor to the United Kingdom who is being shown the various colleges, libraries, and playing fields of a famous university admires them but then asks his host where the university is. Here the little boy, who believes there are favorite colors and foods, fears that there must also be a favorite child in the family. But, of course, as categories shift, meanings may evaporate altogether. Still, just as with the naïve visitor to England, Colin's anxious question in the maternity ward reveals a certain poignancy from which we can learn much about the oddities and quirks of our taken-for-granted linguistic practices. And try, perhaps, to be more mindful.

Autumn Leaves and Birdsong

Let's consider further what may happen between the generations with respect to children's burgeoning aesthetic lives. What do even the youngest children show us when we pay attention to them? How available are we to moments of value in their ordinary lives? On what bases do we make aesthetic judgments for them as well as with them?

Here are two brief anecdotes, both told to me by newly minted grandparents. One, a distinguished art historian on the eve of retirement, describes the enchanting experience he had one fall while visiting his almost-two-year-old grandson in Seattle. For nearly an hour he and his grandson simply rested together on the floor, in complete silence, watching through a set of French windows as the multicolored autumn leaves fell from the branches above and fluttered softly to the ground. My colleague cherishes this memory, and he insists that he cannot remember any comparable moments in the early lives of his own two sons, who are now in their thirties. Little Jason, he proudly claims, is an entirely different kind of child.

A new grandmother telephones me from an island in Chesapeake Bay. She reports a series of incidents with her seven-month-old grandson that astonishes her. Wonder giving an extra lilt to her voice, she reports that this tiny child actually listens each day with intent concentration to the songs of birds. Can such a thing be possible? Despite its improbability, she feels convinced it is the case because, as she says, while she watches, little Brian repeatedly turns his head in the direction of the birdsong while a peculiar expression creeps over his small face—a look that seems to her like awe. It is the look of someone completely enthralled. Like the art historian, she is persuaded that her grandchild is extraordinary. She, too, contrasts his behavior with that of her own, now-adult children. *They,* she says, never paid attention to such things; they focused on what was close by and essential.

I retell these stories because, as you can probably guess, I want to propose a somewhat different slant on them from what was offered by their tellers. My take is that these children are not as unusual as their doting grandparents believe. On the contrary, it is the tellers who are different; it is they who are unusual. In both cases, for reasons having to do very likely with a quantum of newfound leisure and the freedom from primary-caretaking responsibilities, these new grandparents are able to take note of phenomena that they had been too preoccupied to observe with their own children. What strikes me dramatically is that it is the adults who have changed. Young children's endless fascination with visual cues and with auditory and tactile stimuli is, in these stories, suddenly being noted and actually being shared by important adults in their lives—adults who are currently valuing it and marveling at it. "We haven't time, in this world of ours," as Gaston Bachelard says in *The Poetics of Space,* "to love things and see them at close range, in the plenitude of their smallness." But these two grandparents have made the time to do so and have consequently been rewarded.

I wish, in these pages, to advocate for exactly this sort of adult attention and to exhort you, my reader, to emulate these new grandparents. The task, however, will not be easy because parents and teachers, and indeed all adults who are directly responsible for children's welfare and safety, tend, understandably, to careen from one practical task to the next and in so doing often fail to notice what is catching the side glances of their charges. I want to suggest, however, that the consequences of a narrowly instrumental, goal-oriented focus may prove deleterious. By limiting ourselves to what a child obviously needs or to what we feel a priori he must attend to, we risk our child's growing less sensitive to ambient colors and sounds, to lights and shadows, to all the imaginative play and fantastic possibilities these phenomena awaken, and to a sense of unmeasured time that expands human life rather than consuming it. We betray what matters and what does not matter to us. Children learn to emulate our co-option by the mundane and the mindlessly adaptive. By relentlessly conveying that our primary concerns are pragmatic, we risk over time the erosion of a precious birthright. Training them, moreover, to focus on the task at hand and to skip down fast to the proverbial bottom line is to shortchange not only their sensibilities but our own.

By contrast, when significant adults pay close attention to what is capturing the eyes and ears of young children, when we allow the rustlings and cracklings of leaves or the warbling of summer birds to become focal points of delight, then youthful aesthetic proclivities are nourished. Budding sensitivities can blossom. Children's inborn wishes to discover the world and their native impulses to repeat an experience so as to refine their perceptions of it and be able thereafter to respond with increasing discrimination and nuance to it are encouraged. To describe this process and to advocate for active adult participation is, in part, my mission. As John Dewey has written in *Art as Experience*, "Perception that occurs for its own sake is full realization of all the elements of our psychological being."

How Do Adults Make Aesthetic Choices for Children, or What About *Bambi*?

Consider for a moment how you have made decisions as to a child's readiness for specific experiences in the visual, literary, or performing arts. Often such decisions pose a dilemma. Each situation requires reflection. In general terms, the dilemma might be expressed metaphorically: On the one hand, you yearn to offer a young person new vistas, to fling the doors of her mind wide open, so to speak, and push her gently through into landscapes that teem with wonders—panoramas, dizzying heights, bucolic meadows, precipitous ravines, churning waters that swirl and plummet. But, on the other hand, you cannot evade your responsibility to protect her, to be sure she has been prepared with hiking boots, camping gear, mosquito repellent, a life preserver, and athletic skills before you permit her to sally forth and take the plunge. We have no rules for such decisions in the realms of the aesthetic, but my desire is to leave you, by the end of these pages, somewhat better equipped than before to arrive at your own flexible guidelines. I want to add that several colleagues have pointed out to me that in this regard there exists a divide between adults who are and who are not parents. The latter, they aver, tend to feel less protective, less worried, and therefore less conservative than the former and are better able to tap in uncomplicatedly to their own venturesome years. Perhaps so. But each position has its possibilities and its limitations.

For now, let's consider an actual parent and invoke a young mother who is approaching term in an exceptionally high-risk pregnancy that is expected to culminate (this would be the best-case scenario) in an equally high-risk delivery. One day she is asked by a friend whether she would permit her verbally precocious, highly imaginative four-year-old son to watch a videotape of Walt Disney's *Bambi* with another boy of his age who has invited him over. She responds that she would not. Why? While deeming the film artistically beautiful, she says she feels it would be unwise to confront her boy at this juncture with the scene of Bambi's mother's death, a scene she remembers as being extremely frightening. It might prompt in him, she worries, a flood of questions, anxieties, and forebodings that could overload his already full plate of uncertainty about the new baby and her impending absence when she enters the hospital. Thus, the young mother tries carefully to take into account what she considers relevant psychological factors; she makes a judgment call. Moreover, from our perspective, we can speculate that even more is at stake in her decision than she realizes. While sensitive to possible risks to her child's psyche and eager to protect him, she herself clearly needs protection, too, and she may unknowingly be attempting to shield herself by keeping her son from watching *Bambi*. In other words, her own fears over the outcome of her pregnancy may also play a role in making this decision about her son's aesthetic life. If so, this would, surely, be understandable.

Salient, then, in this example of concerned mothering is the intersection of the aesthetic with the psychological, an intersection that takes place, I warrant, whenever choices about experiences in the arts are made by adults, whether seriously reflected on or not, on behalf of young children. In a later chapter we will return to *Bambi* and to the scene of his mother's death and to other examples of cases where aesthetic percepts and judgments can be seen as reflecting the immediate needs and desires of adults or children rather than factors purely extrinsic to them. We will, furthermore, devote an entire chapter to the question of cultural experiences that children themselves find frightening and how decisions about them can be framed.

Co-imaginative Response: Modulating from One Key to Another

Much sensitive and creative responsiveness to young children comes from an adult's uncanny ability every now and then to grasp a specific need or wish that arises in a child's psyche and to respond to it even when it is not only unarticulated by the child but unformulated.

Recently visiting at the home of a two-year-old, I heard some intermittent twanging sounds and discovered that the little boy was playing with a toy that resembled a wooden lap harp. I had never seen such a thing before, and it struck me as a highly original toy. I asked his mother about it, and she told me that she had searched for such a toy and had found it on the Internet. The reason, she said, was that for several weeks running she had noticed that her son had developed a habit of searching in the kitchen drawer for her wire egg slicer. Once he found this tiny instrument, he would pull it out and then, plopping himself down on the kitchen floor, become absorbed in experimenting with it musically by striking its wires with his fingers and listening to the sounds it made. Enchanted by this behavior, his mother decided to get him a "real" harp.

Fascinated, I probed further. Where, I asked her, did she think he had gotten the original idea for "playing" the egg slicer? She pondered my question and told me that, in his toddler music class, the teacher often accompanies the children's singing with an autoharp and has occasionally allowed them to pluck its strings themselves. This, perhaps, is whence the idea sprang. I was overjoyed, for this is precisely the sort of collaborative creativity that can be recognized and emulated. It involves, importantly, what I would call a *co-imaginative* process. Tuning in to the child, the adult meets and matches (as the British pediatrician and psychoanalyst Donald Winnicott would say) the child's moment of hope. The little boy, of course, was much too young to know about harps, but his mother wasn't, and when she saw his enthrallment with the kitchen gadget, she instantly made a leap into the cultural arena and gave him just what he was looking for without knowing it. Margaret Wise Brown's classic picture book *The Runaway Bunny* offers another exquisite example of this kind of aesthetic collaboration between an adult and child. The bunny in that book keeps coming up with ever more ingenious fantasies of evading his mother, who matches his wits so that they both become involved in an escalating game of the imagination, picturing themselves in a series of fantasied scenarios. Eventually, they realize that the game has run its course and the time has come to snuggle and share a carrot.

Collaborations of this sort can occur verbally and in both directions. At the *Nutcracker* performance mentioned above, the same little boy was overheard being told by his delighted grandmother that he was "cracking her up." He giggled and then retorted: "No, Nana. I am actually *nut*-cracking you up!" The process requires an attunedness, an alertness, an acute sense of timing, and an ability to know how and when to shift from one mode or state to another, to span disjunctive feelings, spaces, activities, moods, or persons. It has both an aesthetic and a psychological valence. Frequently, it involves a playfulness that spills over into humor. Fred Rogers, the television personality (whose work we will discuss later), possessed an uncanny gift for this process, which also involves intuitive empathy, and he expressed it once in musical terms. It is like modulating, as he put it, from one key to another. To move from one key to another, " 'you want to find as many notes in the new key that are the same as the notes in the old key. And you play with these notes and almost imperceptibly get into the new key.' In the modulation from C to F, he says, only the B-flat is new. 'There are a lot of notes you can play as if you were playing in both keys. So little by little you get to F' " (quoted by Roderick Townley in *Mister Rogers' Neighborhood*, ed. Collins and Kimmel).

An illustration of this modulation occurred recently when six-year-old Noah was dropped off at his Hebrew class in Newton, Massachusetts, by his great-aunt. Standing at the door to observe, the curious lady watched as a young Israeli teacher, Morah Bracha, invited each child in the group to stand up in front of the others and step successively on rectangular patches of color painted on the floor while reciting the names of those colors in Hebrew. It was a fine cross-modal exercise in that each child, while speaking and hearing the name of the color, was also both seeing it and experiencing his or her body placed directly on it, so that memory was being laid down in auditory, visual, and kinetic registers. One little boy, however, felt shy, as did a little girl seated as far away from him as possible. Neither child budged. What would the teacher do? Hesitating not a split second, Bracha swooped with her arms akimbo, like a mother bird, bent down, embraced both children, gathered them up, and led them to a square together. "Sometimes," she whispered softly, "it's easier to do things with a friend," and she encouraged them to help each other remember so that, as the first faltered, the second, standing right there on the same square, could fill in until at length the names of all the colors had been recited. By the end of the exercise, the children looked relaxed; everyone had completed the lesson with feelings of success. Now Bracha, with uncanny sensitivity, modulated to music and led the children in singing a Hebrew song. Picking up on their elation at having succeeded in the lesson, she enabled them to celebrate, all the while teaching them Hebrew words, and continuing to use the colors they had just learned, thus still functioning in the cognitive realm in which she and the class were principally engaged. Riveted by this stunning display of a teacher's ability to follow currents beneath the surface, tap into them, and match them, the aunt finally tore herself reluctantly away. "Each one of those children," she said to herself, "even the ones least endowed with language aptitude, will learn, because this teacher has made her class into an aesthetic experience."

When moments like this occur because of the intuitive understanding that allows them to do so, children relax and feel, on many levels, comfortable with themselves and with the world. We have all seen children make such transitions from anxiety into serenity, from inattention to concentration. Not infrequently, in situations where this kind of empathic responsiveness holds sway, children prove capable of taking risks with self-expression and with novelty and appear over time less frightened of failing because, to use a term offered again by Donald Winnicott, they feel themselves to be emotionally "held." Morah Bracha understood that notion intuitively. She knew that, for two children in her group, language learning would require a bit of extra support, and she responded to their unspoken need. Another teacher, also tuned in, might have reacted differently but with equally salutary results. What matters is not the specifics of any one solution but the richness and quality of the intuitive empathy that is kept in play so that children's inner lives are not left to wither from neglect.

When we, as adults, discover within ourselves an ability to grasp what a child is experiencing, even momentarily, we can draw upon our own inner resources to "meet and match the moment" of that child's hope. On the spot, we simply invent our own way of responding, and at such times we require no advice or assistance. Co-imagination, as we have seen it function in these examples, forms the *fons et origo*, I propose, of work with children in the realm of the aesthetic. What matters lies not principally in the arena of *knowing how to do* (which is the approach of many texts and manuals) but rather in the arena of *becoming acquainted with* and understanding, as in the French distinction between *connaître* and *savoir.* I advocate for a strong rededication to *connaître.* When, little by little, we find ourselves transported into children's worlds, even just briefly, we can meet them ever so much more richly in the fullness of their joys and passions, their frustrations, reluctance, anxiety, curiosity, and in their outbursts of merriment, indignation, or sorrow.

Mashed Potatoes, Cookies, and Seashells

Trying now to get even closer to the direct perspective of a child and secondarily to the observation of an adult who is dealing with that child, let's consider little Ricky, who is barely two years old. He is seated in his high chair with a plastic plate in front of him and a small mound of mashed potatoes, at which he is gazing intently. He is not making any attempt to eat them but keeps looking at them and repeating two syllables that sound like "Tuh-tuh." Baffled by his behavior, his mother cannot understand what he is trying to communicate. She proposes everything she can think of without success, but the little boy grows more and more agitated, desperate to get her to understand. Finally, in a flash of inspiration, she comes up as close as possible to his high chair and stands right behind him. Trying to see from his perspective, she stares at the mashed potatoes on the tray. "Turtle!" she suddenly exclaims, pointing. The mashed potatoes had indeed taken the form of a little shelled creature with head and feet protruding. "Turtle! Turtle!"

"Tuh-tuh!" Ricky answers, beaming with pleasure. His aesthetic and imaginative moment has been shared.

In a well-known book dealing with subject matter not altogether dissimilar to mine here, *The Arts and Human Development*, psychologist Howard Gardner describes a similar incident involving his twenty-month-old daughter who, after taking a bite out of a cookie, looked at it and declared it a boat. When her father looked at it, he, too, could see the prow of a ship. Then, when she picked up the rest of the cookie and took it apart, she said, "The boat broke." Once again, her father followed right along with her creative process and later wrote: "Her behavior was analogous to that of a painter or writer who seizes upon an idea or percept in his environment and then embodies and transforms it in an available symbolic medium." Later on, however, when she was two years old and they went to the seashore, Gardner pointed out to her the loveliness of a particular seashell. Instead of looking at it, he reports, she simply picked it up and put it into her mouth. He reprimanded her, and she promptly threw it away. Gardner analyzes this behavior in an interesting way. He does not feel that his daughter failed to experience the shell aesthetically but rather that her mode of doing so was to taste rather than to look. He interprets that, because she was a toddler, she was not yet ready to take the necessary distance from the object to admire it visually. She wanted to have it up very close and actually inside her mouth. I thoroughly concur with Gardner's way of understanding this moment, and I especially like the way he points out that, although the child missed *his* aesthetic experience of the shell, he also missed *hers.*

Nevertheless, it seems important to notice that she *was,* in fact, able to look at the cookie, albeit *after* she had tasted it. In that case, however, the aesthetic noticing was initiated by her; whereas, with the shell, the initial observation was made by her father. To me, these factors are not insignificant. Very young children, in my experience, often do best when they are the launchers of their own perceptual and imaginative pre-art adventures. This does not mean, of course, that we should refrain from pointing things out to them but merely that we need, very keenly, as Gardner and the young mother did, to follow their lead. To do so is to recover what Bachelard has called "the enlarging gaze of a child."

Skinny-Dipping and Barrettes

Here are two vignettes that bespeak ways in which slightly older children entwine their inner fantasy lives with what is encountered aesthetically and culturally in the world around them and that also reveal interesting aspects of children's subjectivity. Both stories concern the theme of sexual difference and the lengths to which both children and adults sometimes go in their efforts to come to grips with and to tame these differences. (I am indebted for the drift of these stories to the distinguished Parisian psychoanalyst Dr. Joyce McDougall, who told versions of them informally at a professional gathering in northern California in the late 1990s.) In them, we see how the most common-place of cultural artifacts, namely, the gendering of everyday clothing, can be co-opted to reinforce elements of a child's inner world of fantasy. We see that, although the purpose of gender-coded clothing is ostensibly to enable everyone to distinguish male from female, it turns out that this very difference, as it is elaborated by the culture in terms of colors and styles, can sometimes be used by children—if they feel it necessary—to obtain the very opposite result and, in fact, to deny the anatomical difference it proclaims. For our purposes here, what we see above all is that when children are anxious, they may close off their own perceptions and limit their access to the richness of the world around them.

A grandmother asked a small boy, after his summer vacation, what he had done at camp. He replied that it had all been great fun and that on the last day they had gone swimming in the nude.

"Oh, really," was the lady's somewhat taken-aback reply. "Was it the girls and the boys all together?"

"I don't know," he answered nonchalantly. "I couldn't tell."

Perplexed, the grandmother pressed him: "But why not?"

Dismissively, the little boy replied, "Silly! How could I tell if they were girls or boys with their clothes off?"

Of course, our first reaction to this as adults is to laugh, but the child was not quite joking. He was demonstrating in fact what very powerful defenders the cultural markers can be. Clothes, he revealed to his startled grandmother, can be used by young children not only to impart information (that is, in this case, to announce gender) but also, perversely, to bolster disavowal and to reinforce, in this instance, an early-childhood fantasy, namely, that all bodies are actually alike and that they all look like "mine." We see the child, then, taking himself as the norm against which all else is measured.

Recall, if you will, a rhyme by Robert Louis Stevenson, "Foreign Children," in which the poetic speaker, implicitly a small boy, asks rhetorically:

Little Indian, Sioux or Crow,
   Little frosty Eskimo,
   Little Turk or Japanee,
   Oh! don't you wish that you were me?

    .   .   .   .

You have curious things to eat,
I am fed on proper meat;
You must dwell beyond the foam,
But I am safe and live at home.
   Little Indian, Sioux or Crow,
   Little frosty Eskimo,
   Little Turk or Japanee,
Oh! don't you wish that you were me?

While I do not mean to equate colonialist condescension with the omnipotently masked gender worries of the little boy who went skinny-dipping, I *do* want to suggest that in both examples we see child characters representing themselves as being at the very center of the universe and the measure of all things. Each represents an effort to bolster the self so as to ward off feelings of vulnerability and insignificance. What we can learn here is how, when children are concerned (for personal reasons or because the fears are social), they may close off perception and co-opt or distort the aesthetic for protective purposes.

In the second story, another little boy, this one in England, is being brought up, along with his older sister, in a liberal-minded family by parents who encourage the siblings to play with each other's toys. One day the boy says he wishes to go to school wearing his sister's barrettes. His parents and his sister acquiesce without a murmur, but once the child arrives at school, he is mercilessly teased by a boy his age who repeatedly taunts: "You're a girl!"

Drawing himself up to his full height, the little fellow replies: "No, I'm not. I'm a boy."

"Ha, 'I'm a boy,' " mimics his schoolfellow. "Prove it!"

"I am a boy," replies the first child, nonplussed, "because I have a penis."

"Ha," pooh-poohs the second one. "*Everybody* has a penis, but only girls have barrettes."

Here, once again, we see how the enormous power of the aesthetic and the cultural may be used to express and at the same time to cover up a child's deep-seated wish to deny the anatomical differences between the sexes. Ironically, this wish is kept underground precisely by our strict adherence to different styles of dress for boys and girls. As grown-ups, we react to dialogues like this with humor and condescension but also, if we are truthful, with a certain measure of deeper feeling, of empathy, compassion, and unease, for the fantasies and confusions they bring to the surface cannot, even in adulthood, be fully expunged and laid to rest.

Concern over such a close meshing of cultural mores with psychological agendas in the arena of gender and its puzzlements was recently made the subject of a tender French film, *Ma vie en rose*, which tells the story of a seven-year-old boy named Ludovic Fabre who believes he is actually a girl. When the action begins, this boy, with his three older siblings and their parents, has moved into a manicured Parisian suburb right next door to the home of his father's boss, who, as it turns out, has a little boy exactly Ludo's age and who has suffered the recent death of his other child, a daughter. Fascinated and attracted by the aesthetic aspects of femininity, Ludo, with dark bangs and bobbed hair, tries his best to be a girl, acting and dressing and behaving like one. What appeals to him are the colorful costumes he associates with femininity, the graceful dresses and jewelry, the makeup, high-heeled shoes, and pageantry; of course he understands little else about what it might mean to be female. One day, while playing with the boss's son, he opens the door of the deceased girl's bedroom and, dressing up in her loveliest clothes, he persuades his friend to stage a pretend wedding with him. Passing by the open door, the boss's wife happens upon their play and faints dead away.

In a series of sensitive and reflective scenes, the film subsequently recounts the manifold ways in which each member of Ludo's beleaguered family, that of the other little boy and his mortified parents, the bewildered neighbors, the angry school community, a therapist, and

Ludo's grandmother react to his aberrant behavior and desires. Scenes with human actors and actresses alternate with radiantly animated sets that portray Ludo's rosy-colored fantasy life, dominated by a curvaceous golden-haired doll called Pam. Thus, the aesthetic mingles with the psychological to create a complex picture that explores themes and questions still vividly alive for many young children. To engage with this film as with the anecdotes reported above is to draw closer to the fluidity that characterizes children's imaginative lives and to confront the potency of their wishes. Later on, in the chapter on scary experiences, we will continue to explore this theme.

Looking Back

Let's turn away now from actual children and from child characters in order to revisit our own pasts and ask ourselves what we can still remember about our first aesthetic experiences. What happened to those moments? What was their fate? They matter because our understanding of young people depends not only on observing them, playing with them, and listening to them but also on being able to reanimate our own childhood selves and, through memory and reflection, form bonds that defy the barriers of age and historic time. Support for this view comes, in part, from the fact that so many of the notable writers for and about children have drawn principally on their own early lives rather than on their contacts with the young people around them. A prime example of this phenomenon is Hans Christian Andersen, who clung tenaciously and ambivalently to his youth and who mined it throughout his life to create such masterpieces as "The Ugly Duckling," "The Ice Maiden," and "The Little Match Girl," stories that speak with equal force to children and adults.

In visiting the reminiscences of childhood, we might ask how it is that some early aesthetic moments turn out to be pivotal starting points that develop into lifelong passions and even careers, whereas others lead off into related areas, and still others prove abortive even though their initial power refuses to diminish in our memories. Part of the answer surely has to do with adult awareness, support, and encouragement. But it also may require a certain judicious measure of laissez-faire.

In his essay "Children and Museums," Bruno Bettelheim stresses the value for children of visiting spaces in which objects are allowed to appear sui generis—that is to say, marvelous, strange, and wonderful. Impatient with laboriously detailed informational texts that accompany so many systematically organized museum exhibits, Bettelheim argues that objects should not be deprived of their sense of awe; we should not seek constantly to explain them (to children), for in so doing, we reduce them merely to the stuff of the mundane. By way of contrast, he recounts that, when he was a small boy, he habitually wandered the halls of the palatial museums of Vienna's Ringstrasse with his mother and was at liberty to gaze at whatever attracted his eye and to reject whatever did not.

The Voices of Mothers and Uncles

As for me, words and stories shaped the contours of my childhood, and from the start they mattered, even before I knew what they meant. An elderly cousin told me about a child who was bundled up in a fur-trimmed white hood, strapped into a perambulator, and wheeled ceremoniously back and forth on frosty mornings in Riverside Park on New York's Upper West Side. The granddaughter of immigrants on her father's side, she would astonish passersby with impromptu renditions of the Preamble to the U.S. Constitution. At bedtime, she heard poetry, not just stories: Robert Louis Stevenson, Eugene Field, A. A. Milne, Rudyard Kipling, Robert Frost.

I waited for the effect of my mother's voice. Modulated and mellifluous, it filled me with sounds, images, and wistful longings. It made me sad and happy all at once. Even now sometimes, reading to children makes me cry, and one of my daughters, when she was small, would cast furtive glances at me during long pauses in my reading—silences that gave me away.

Lying perfectly still beside my mother with her voice in my ears, I floated off to lands where pastel-colored gumdrops cascaded from silvery trees and turreted stone castles rose out of landscapes carpeted in the deepest of green. Witches cackled and grimaced; shy boys gave their knitted caps to princesses. Ogres menaced me with gaping mouths and guttural roars. Stalwart toy soldiers perished, their paper hats askew. Flowers with human faces erupted into bursts of tinkling laughter. Rocking horses teased their riders. A delicate lady in black rescued an elephant that had lost its mother. Another elephant asked a crocodile what it ate for breakfast on the banks of a great gray-green greasy river all set about with fever trees. A woman gave birth to a mouse. I shivered when Carabosse, the uninvited fairy, cast her hundred-year spell and tasted the drops of blood that fell from Sleeping Beauty's finger. Lonely and shy, I longed to be cared for, like the Darling children, by a furry Nana or to have a fairy godmother or a turbaned genie of my own.

Words determined my childhood loves. My father's oldest brother, Nathan, was my favorite uncle. I begged to sit next to him at family dinners because of his prodigious vocabulary. He specialized in arcane polysyllabic words and was fond of quoting as he launched into complex sagas with Homeric flourishes. He was never condescending to children. After dinner, he would indulge in aromatic cigars, the traces of their scent clinging to his scratchy tweeds. When my direct gaze met his, he responded with a knowing twinkle. Seated beside him, I felt enveloped not only by his mysterious words but by his bulk, his aroma, and by my primitive sensation that he was, because of his linguistic gifts, a font of limitless mental adventure.

My second-favorite uncle was Phil, who hailed from England and was actually named Lazarus, an eerie appellation to me long before I heard the story from which it came. Uncle Phil had an odd, clipped way of speaking and an impediment that made him sound as though he were hissing. Taking my beribboned sister on one knee and me on his other, he would regale us with cunningly crafted renditions of the great European fairy tales. Especially thrilling was his retelling of "Rumpelstiltskin." Astonishingly inventive, he could make the terrified queen guess dozens of names, each more exotic than the one before. Streams of names poured effortlessly from his lips until finally in the end when the dwarf simply had to be recognized by the queen, Uncle Phil would pronounce "RUMPELSTILTSKIN" in stentorian tones, enunciating the sibilants with his irrepressible hiss, and then let go suddenly, dropping us from his knees to the floor below, where we collapsed in a heap (falling down like the dwarf himself), only to plead for a repeat performance.

What about you? As you mull over your own childhood, why not try to recall the arts experiences that mattered to you. Recently, I polled my fellow scholars at the Clark Art Institute in Williamstown, Massachusetts, and they gave evocative replies. One, who grew up in Paris and travels regularly to Greece, works today in the field of classical archaeology. After only a moment, he was able to describe a book he had been given as a prize when he was six years old. It was Homer's *Odyssey*, and its front cover displayed a striking image of the prow of a trireme ship with the hero, Odysseus, his arms crossed, proudly stationed at the helm. My colleague treasured the book for years and believes that somewhere, in a box, he possesses it still. He feels it played a key role in determining his profession and the focus of his subsequent writing and research.

A Renaissance art historian who grew up in Argentina recalled without hesitation the terror and fascination that came over him each time he beheld his parents' edition of Dante's *Inferno*, with its engraved illustrations by the incomparable Gustave Doré. He does not know his exact age when he first encountered this book. Because of his trepidation, however, it was hidden from him by his parents; nevertheless, he always searched for it purely in order to relive the intoxicating blend of horror and attraction its black-and-white figures induced.

An accomplished quiltmaker who studies the art of Native Americans, the history of quilts, and the iconography of Guatemalan fabrics said she was brought up in a devout Catholic family in New England where several of her nearby aunts were nuns. When she was a little girl, these aunts gave her her own small Infant of Prague statue (which depicts Jesus as a little boy). The cherished icon stood in her bedroom, and each year on special occasions the aunts would jointly present her with hand-sewn garments they had fashioned for her to adorn it with.

Tenderly, she described to me how she loved to dress and drape her statue with the different robes and vestments and said she believes the experience was formative, over several years, in shaping her predilections and her choice of career.

Fishing Boats and Ribbons of Blood

In a book called *Reading Pictures,* Alberto Manguel describes his first encounter with an image he recognized was actually fabricated by human hands. He was ten years old. Unlike the pictures in his storybooks that were made to illustrate characters or scenes of action, the image that arrested his attention—Van Gogh's fishing boats at Saintes-Maries—appeared before him simply as an image. It was not supposed to go with anything. Nothing explained it. It simply existed and dared him to make of it what he could. He stared at it for hours, taking in its hulls and masts, its water and sand, its mesmerizing red and copper and blue. He never forgot it. Words of interpretation came much later, after the shapes and colors and lines and salty air were firmly fixed in his mind.

For me, the first images of art were printed on richly colored pages in heavy oversized books that crowded the bottom shelves of my parents' mahogany bookcases. Sitting cross-legged on the carpet all alone in what always felt to me like *their* cavernous living room, I spread these gold-tipped, leather-bound volumes open, gazing furtively but with intense fascination at fourteenth- and fifteenth-century images of the Crucifixion. Knowing nothing as yet of Christianity, I found them terrifying and uncanny. They filled me with anguish. Even today I can draw their details from memory—the writhing red curlicues of blood, the twisted fingers and ashen feet impaled by nails, a tilted, angular head, the unintelligible letters INRI. Nothing I studied later, in all my years of art history, has altered their impact.

Chapter Two

Between the Generations

It is on the plane of the daydream and not on that of facts that childhood remains alive and poetically useful within us. Through this permanent childhood, we maintain the poetry of the past.

—Gaston Bachelard, *The Poetics of Space*

For one's children so often gave one's own perceptions a little thrust forwards.

—Virginia Woolf, *To the Lighthouse*

What will we see, and what can we learn from children, as we observe their spontaneous imaginative and aesthetic responses to the world? Some authors criticize adult efforts to interpret children's inner worlds and imply that such efforts are little more than projections, political manipulations, crude reductionisms, or wild speculations. To me these protests seem, except in the most obvious cases, counterintuitive. They constitute merely a variation on a theme: the canonical philosophical problem of "other minds." We know, after all, that despite everything one might adduce (barriers of culture, history, geography, race, gender, and, yes, age), human beings *do* often manage to feel empathy for and comprehend one another to an astonishing degree and to communicate with and interpret one another's behavior. The father of Govinda, a five-year-old boy in Chennai, India, is a scientist and engineer; one day the question came up between the two of them as to whether there was a number larger than a million and what it would be. Govinda asserted: "Zero."

When his astonished father asked him how that might be, the little boy replied: "Because zero is far away, like you put a 'one' here, and then zeroes all the way to the sky; that would be a much bigger number than a million."

His father, enchanted by this response, smiled and nodded, thinking to himself: "The child has stumbled upon infinity."

The aesthetics of this moment have to do with the way the child imagined the scene; when his father, Srini, reported it to me, I immediately saw a soap-bubble wand waving and the long line of bubbles disappearing into the wind.

Waving Good-bye to Grandma

A young couple living in Bethesda, Maryland, decides to go out for dinner on a Saturday night; they stop at the home of the wife's mother to leave Bobby, their eighteen-month-old son, with his grandmother. The little boy plays happily on the floor with some scattered toys while the grown-ups chat and catch up for a few minutes. Then the grandmother scoops Bobby up, sits down on the sofa with him, and carefully explains to him that he must now wave good-bye to his mommy and daddy because they are going away for a short time, and he will remain there with her. Bobby wriggles out of her grasp, crosses the room, climbs up into his mommy's lap, and then, turning back toward his grandma, waves good-bye to *her.* Can anyone doubt what this toddler is wordlessly communicating? What Bobby has enacted makes perfect sense. We do not require a theoretical gloss, such as: "Eighteen-month-olds act out their separation anxiety." The child's behavior possesses its own transparent truth, deeply resonant and communicative in its own right, not to mention humorous, and from that behavior we can instantly infer his wish and his intent.

Contra those who prefer to think of childhood as a mystified realm beyond the pale to which none of us can return, I would argue that the reason we so instantly grasp the meaning of Bobby's performance is that his wish to remain with his mommy and daddy is a fantasy none of us entirely relinquishes. Thus, insofar as we retain feelings from our own childhood, we are able to relate to children even though we have become adults. Naturally, this does not mean we can understand everything or that understanding requires no effort, but it means that we surely do understand *something*, and that we can seek to understand more. Art historian Ernst Gombrich, in his celebrated essay "Meditations on a Hobby Horse," invokes the metaphor of an angel with a flaming sword who bars the way back to childhood. Appreciating his essay very much, I nonetheless resist that final metaphor, for in fact, if I accepted it, I would not have written this book.

Thus, even here, where the focus is on children's actual aesthetic experiences, reminiscences intrude and cannot be avoided. While I recount the experiences of contemporary children, memories return, and I find myself making use of them to analyze the material at hand and to offer suggestions as to how adults might participate more fully in children's aesthetic lives, especially how we might better recognize and seize upon moments ripe for unique types of shared learning.

Buying a New Mommy at Wal-Mart

The symbolic, the playful, the imaginative, and the aesthetic are always linked with our emotional lives and with more broadly psychological factors. Take, for example, the fantasy of a little boy whose mother is roundly pregnant and who, at four and a half, is just beginning to have apprehensions about the future and to comprehend that he will no longer be the only child in his family.

"Mommy," he proposes meditatively to her one day, "when the new baby comes, couldn't we just get another mommy? That way you can go on being *my* mommy, and the *other* mommy can be for the baby."

Astonished by this inventive solution to his impending dilemma, his mother replies, "Well, hmmm. But don't you think that might be a bit difficult? I mean, after all, where would we *get* another mommy?"

The child ponders briefly and then brightly answers, "I know. We can buy one at the store!"

Now, I don't know how the interchange actually proceeded from that point, but on hearing about it, my own imagination took off. I begin to fantasize about store-bought mommies. What would they look like? My mind conjures them up—phalanxes of mass-produced mommies all lined up in a discount warehouse. Picture them: row upon row of "Mommies for Sale," all waiting to be taken home, their smiles permanently painted on, their variously colored hair nicely coiffed, their outfits spiffy—jogging togs, blue jeans, tennis dresses, business suits— all equipped, of course, with pocketbooks containing Band-Aids, Kleenex, juice boxes, Scotch tape, baby wipes, safety pins, and even, in a few pricier models, mobile phones, picture books, and a set of well-chosen washable Magic Markers. Thus the aesthetic and the emotional lives of children and adults ignite each other, with sparks that fly in all directions.

Here, then, are some stories about children's early experiences in the realms of the aesthetic.

Royal Blue

One Sunday afternoon, accompanied by her parents and her two older siblings, five-year-old Sarah is visiting her octogenarian grandfather, who lives in an apartment on the twenty-sixth floor of a Manhattan skyscraper. Just as the family is congregating in the dining room to seat themselves for dinner, Sarah suddenly grabs her mother's hand and pulls her over to a large picture window that looks out over Central Park. Pointing urgently, she exclaims: "Mommy, Mommy, look at the sky! It's *royal blue*."

Her mother, following the child's gaze, allows herself to peer out over the trees below and at the almost silhouetted buildings etched in overlapping rectangular shapes against the horizon. She is moved by the vivid chromatics of the scene. Busily talking with her father and the other adults, she hadn't noticed the sky until that instant. What she feels now is a complex mixture of gratitude and pleasure, pleasure not only in the vision itself, to which the child has awakened her, but in the fact that her daughter is capable of responding with so much passion to such an unadulterated aesthetic vision and so eager to share it with her, and gratitude for the mutuality that this moment has produced.

I see this as a typically small but strikingly pure, nonreducible aesthetic moment. It is noteworthy that young children rarely use abstract words, such as "beautiful," to indicate an experience like this. They tend rather to gesture, point, pull, or push. Importantly, they seek to communicate and to confirm their perceptions by sharing them with the significant adults in their lives. In this case, the aesthetic moment evokes both a burst of appreciation and an active attempt to draw the mother in, and it is clear that the mother who reports it is equally enriched by her daughter's sight. Yet, all too often children's efforts like this turn into abortive sallies and thwarted ventures. In contrast to this example, where the mother responds with alacrity to her excited child, preoccupied or impatient adults brush children off at similar moments. To describe what might be deemed the optimal response to children's moments of wonder and aesthetic pleasure, we return to Winnicott's "meeting and matching the moment of hope." When this happens, benefits accrue to both parties; they are lifted out of the ordinary and taken into what Bachelard has called a confrontation with the strangeness of the world. Enlightenment and enchantment flow in both directions, between the generations.

In Stone and Concrete by Henry Moore

The notion of enlightenment flowing back and forth between child and adult is especially valuable, I propose, for the realm of the aesthetic, where each one of the pair has different gifts to contribute. From the child, we get a fresh and acutely sensitive apparatus as yet unsullied by wear; from the adult, the child receives a more refined, nuanced, and schooled capacity to perceive and to interpret. I am reminded of a series of sculptures by Henry Moore that can be seen as illustrating the stages in a child's perceptual development relative to his mother. They interest me in this context because the scene we have just "witnessed," so to speak, in the previous anecdote, is implicitly included.

First, let's picture an eight-inch stone sculptural study. A mother cradles her infant in her arms, the baby's globular head placed just below her spherical left breast so that it might almost be mistaken for an extra bodily protrusion, an oddly emergent third breast. All a live infant could possibly see from such a position would be its mother's belly and breast. On the other hand, the mother, with her bald head and impassive expression, is able to look out into the distance and does in fact gaze at the world beyond. *Her* perception is paramount.

A second, larger stone piece, about thirty-one inches high, shows the baby more detached now from the mother's body, its right arm placed against her torso as if to demarcate a boundary between them, but at the same time, it looks at her. Questioningly, it scans her face. The mother does not look back at her child but turns out toward the world as before, with a mildly apprehensive expression. In both of these works, the infant's perceptual role is entirely limited to focusing on its mother's body and face as if they were the sole source of all safety and knowledge. The mother, by contrast, once again faces the world, testing its temperature, so to speak, in order to interpret it to her child. It is her perception of the external world that counts. (In a later chapter, we will note how this phenomenon is portrayed in Walt Disney's film *Bambi*.)

A third stone piece depicts the baby grabbing its mother with both its arms and legs so that she is no longer the one doing all the holding. Their heads are now on the same level. Still, however, the baby's face is turned toward its mother. Picture it: You are able to see only one of the baby's eyeholes (indicating that its head is in profile), whereas the mother's two eyes are visible because she looks out toward the world and toward us. Again, enlightenment is a one-way street. Again, the task of the child is not to interpret the world for itself but to scan its mother's face as she surveys the world for both of them.

A fourth piece (made of carved concrete, about seven inches high) finally gives us the change that signals the kind of interaction I am endorsing here for aesthetic moments. Here the mother supports her child on her right hip with her right arm while, with her left hand, she clasps the right hand of the child—a hand-holding that itself betokens a new relation of mutuality and companionship rather than absolute dependence. Although the mother's head reaches above her child's, they are gazing out at the world together. They are looking in the same direction; clearly, they have found something out there that is of interest, and we are made to understand that it is the same something, although we have no way of telling who saw it first, which would of course be interesting. And we don't know whether or not it is royal blue!

Henry Moore, as far as I know, did not do so, but if *I* had been the sculptor of a series like this, I would have added another piece in which we see the child clearly turning his mother's attention toward something of interest to *him* and, perhaps, vice versa. Such pieces, if they were clearly conceived and wrought, might be able to illustrate the two-way street that aesthetic communication between parent and child can, as I am urging, ideally take. (For a further discussion of Henry Moore's mother-child sculptures, see Laurie Schneider's essay "The Theme of Mother and Child in the Art of Henry Moore.")

Spinning at the Guggenheim

Alla, almost six years old, has been taken to the Guggenheim Museum on Fifth Avenue in New York City for the first time with her older sister Anya. Rather than riding the elevator to the top floor and then gradually descending, which is the preferred way to view exhibits in this space, the mother and daughters have decided to do it in reverse, to climb upward through the spiraling galleries. During their gradual ascent, Alla manifests no outward response to the unique interior space of the building. Attracted by assorted paintings, drawings, and sculptures, she is especially delighted by Franz Marc's *Yellow Cow*, at which she laughs, and by what she calls her "favorite picture," Fernand Léger's grand mural *Le Cirque*. From time to time she stops to look back at people and at paintings she has already seen on the way up, and finally they arrive at the very top of the Guggenheim's spiral ramp.

After looking around, they decide to retrace their steps and walk down. Little Alla now begins to do something quite surprising. Keeping her body as close as possible to the railing, she starts spinning round and round as she slowly descends the ramp. Why is she doing this? What is she thinking? Watching her in puzzlement, her mother takes just a few moments to realize that, with the movements of her own body, the little girl is now recapitulating her kinesthetic experience of the entire architectural space created by Frank Lloyd Wright in the museum's interior. Round and round she twirls until her mother asks her gently to be careful so that she won't become dizzy and fall down.

In this example, we can see the way a child's aesthetic response need not be verbal at all but can take, instead, a form that engages the energy of her whole body. Although on the way up Alla looked at the pictures on the walls and seemed unconscious of her spatial surroundings, it was clear that the architecture of the museum had been working its subtle magic on her all the while, and she demonstrated this by repeating in her own small circular movements the larger spiral loops described by the structure on the way down. I see this also as a pure aesthetic response on the part of a young child, but not one of the sorts we would normally find recorded in most academic studies. Nevertheless, it accords with the findings of Daniel Stern, who for many years has conducted pioneering research on the cross-modal forms of attunement that develop spontaneously between infants and mothers, and who has also related his work to synesthetic experimentation in the arts.

It is noteworthy that Alla's mother, while grasping the deeper significance of the little girl's movements, did not share this insight with her but kept it to herself. I wonder whether or not it might have been valuable to ask Alla to look around herself at the building while spinning, so that by combining her visual perception with the motion itself she might have been able to make the cross-modal connection conscious. But, on the other hand, I am dubious about how valuable such an interpretation might be at such a time. Perhaps the mother's intuitive silence was based on greater wisdom, for sometimes, in order to preserve the spontaneity of a response, we must tread lightly with our interventions. To quote Winnicott again, this time from his writings on children's play, "Interpretation outside the ripeness of the material is indoctrination and produces compliance." Here I am going beyond his point to question the value of an interpretation that, were the mother to have made it, might have stayed within the ripeness of the material but nonetheless have been intrusive. Bachelard too addresses this point when he writes, "Images that are too clear . . . block the imagination. We've seen, we've understood, we've spoken. Everything is settled." To give explanations, therefore, or even to ask leading questions that call forth explanations, can serve to foreclose further exploration. In this case, had the mother spoken as soon as she made her interpretation of the twirling, she might have prevented the child from continuing to create what was in fact a protochoreographic statement. Alla, I am told, parenthetically, loves to dance and to draw but has not expressed any desire so far to become an artist when she grows up.

After relating this anecdote recently to a colleague of mine who studies Japanese art, she delightedly reported a similar incident. While visiting the Whitney Museum of American Art in New York City to view its special exhibit of the sculptures of Isamu Noguchi, she stood in a gallery contemplating his famous *Black Sun* of 1969, a granite work that resembles the shape of an enormous upright truck tire with protuberances and indentations. As she gazed at it, she noticed a little boy who, in perfect silence, was perambulating it, circling round and round at a steady pace, reiterating its shape kinesthetically. Entranced by his behavior, she thought that with his small body in locomotion, he was experiencing the work of art far more profoundly than she was with all her erudition and her stationary, well-trained eyes. He seemed in his orbit like a small planet drawn by the gravity of that dramatic sun.

Hannah and the Mayonnaise Jar

Let's conjure now a typical suburban kitchen in order to visit a little girl who is almost four years old. Here we will find another illustration of what Bachelard has called "the magnifying glass of the imagination." Hannah is sitting at the kitchen table while her mother makes a sandwich for her lunch. Watching her mother, Hannah begins to talk, but not to her mother. She is addressing a large, partly empty mayonnaise jar on the table.

"I love you, Mayonnaise Jar," she says.

Her mother, smiling, might have waited to see what would transpire next. Instead, she immediately enters into the spirit of her daughter's play. She responds spontaneously in the persona of the mayonnaise jar, so that a dialogue springs up between the child and the jar. With the gender of the mayonnaise jar as yet unfixed, the child repeats, "I love you," and then goes on to say: "I want to marry you."

"Well, I'm afraid you can't marry *me*," replies the mayonnaise jar, "because actually I am a mommy, already married. In fact, I have lots of little baby mayonnaise jars on shelves in the market."

"Oh," giggles Hannah. Then, looking at the jar more carefully, she observes: "You are almost empty, Mrs. Mayonnaise Jar. There's not much left in you. What will happen to you when you're empty?"

Remembering at this point, perhaps, that Hannah's father has taken her several times to the town recycling bin to toss away their empty glass vessels, her mother replies, "Well, it's very sad about me when I'm empty. They wash me out and put me into a box. Then, one day, they take me to the glass disposal and throw me away. I break into a million smithereens, and that's the end of me."

Hannah looks sad. After a pause, she ventures, "And what happens to you after that?"

"I don't know," replies the mayonnaise jar. "I'm all broken in pieces, smashed, and as far as I can tell, that's the end of me."

Suddenly, the game is over. The little girl's lip begins to quiver; tears fill her eyes, and she doesn't feel like eating her sandwich. Right away, a corresponding shift occurs: The mayonnaise jar vanishes, and a real mother reappears, asking softly, "What's the matter, Hannah?"

"I'm sad," she says, sobbing. "I'm sad about the mayonnaise jar."

Now her mother takes her on her lap, and soon they begin to laugh; the boundaries between reality and fantasy reinstate themselves, and the little girl is able to resume her lunch.

Much could be said about this incident, especially if we had a wider context for interpretation, but I want to stress the way in which the aesthetic element here entails the mutual creation of a transformed space that involves fantasy. What we have is a little playlet, a minidrama that centers on an external, apparently neutral object that Hannah transforms magically into a character, much in the same way Hans Christian Andersen did when he created his fairy tales. He, you will remember, was prone, just like a child, to turn whatever was at hand—a fir tree, a spinning top, a playing card, or a pen and inkstand—into characters in his stories.

In our anecdote, both mother and child participate. Only when Hannah's tears break the frame does her mother disengage as well. This fascinates me. I believe that it is the mother's heightened capacity for fantasy, her being swept up in her daughter's game, that provides a key to why the drama becomes so palpably real for the child. Indeed, perhaps the mother's failure to come up with anything soothing to say *while* they are playing stems not from a lack of inventiveness on her part but from her own susceptibility to being caught up in the drama. At that moment she was as completely lost in her role as Hannah was and thus unable to behave in a conventionally maternal way. She was truly experiencing and describing her own destruction as the mayonnaise jar. My reading of the anecdote, then, is that, in effect, Hannah's mother, assuming the guise of the character, ceases, as it were, to *be* Hannah's mother. Her gift for morphing so totally into an imaginary self is what intensifies the child's pleasure *and* what eventually frightens her and propels her out of the game.

Hannah's mother could easily have reassured Hannah during their play that after the jar had been recycled it might one day be made into another jar and thus enjoy a whole new life. One thinks of the ending of *Charlotte's Web*, which, admittedly, does often bring tears all the same. Yet Hannah's mother does not offer this happy ending. Her own submergence in the drama does not permit her to think of it at the time. It is, nonetheless, important to note that the moment the little girl begins to cry, her mother is able to return to *being* a mother (to switch roles and shed her costume, so to speak). She quickly sweeps away all the clouds of fantasy. This matters enormously. In so doing, she models for Hannah the possibility and indeed the necessity for emerging from fantasy and returning to the realm of the real.

Play States

The topic of adult participation in children's play is delicate, complex, and controversial. Every child's innate proclivity for experiences in the realm of the imagination is subject to influence on the part of the significant adults who surround her—the influence not only of parents but also of grandparents, teachers, counselors, and other relatives and friends. I am deliberately avoiding any mention in this context of the influence of the media on children's imaginative lives because it is a topic addressed by so many other authors. But of course these days even the youngest children learn not only from live human beings but also from the surrounding culture as it appears through the ubiquitous auditory and visual channels to which they are increasingly exposed. And we must not forget the impact of their first play spaces—their rooms—to which we will turn later on.

With its collaborative child-parent fantasy and abrupt breakdown, the story of Hannah's mayonnaise jar affords an opportunity to reflect more generally, too, on the topic of play itself and its vicissitudes. Recently, during an afternoon visit to the home of four-year-old Jake, I conversed with the boy's mother for over an hour while he, completely absorbed, played in a recreation area adjacent to the kitchen. Eventually, he made an appearance, laboriously pushing a contraption he had been concocting out of various toys, a chair, some scraps of ribbon, and string, which he proudly introduced to us as his "Tyrannosaurus rex." With this dramatic entrance, he made his first bid for maternal attention. Strikingly, however, during our entire preceding hourlong conversation, he had been lost, as it were, in a world of his own. We had seen neither hide nor hair of him.

This state of absorption in play has been studied in children and described by many authors, including Winnicott, who views it as a state closely allied to adult experiences in the realm of the aesthetic. Winnicott's theory is that play states, whether or not they include other human beings (as in the story of Hannah's mayonnaise jar), are satisfying, absorbing, pleasurable, and occasionally but not always inclusive of the elements of excitement and even anxiety. But play states can cease abruptly when they build toward peaks of arousal so that children can stop only by reaching a climax or a failed climax—that is, when mental anguish or physical pain, confusion, fear, frustration, or anger become sufficiently overwhelming that some form of external intervention is required. In such cases, the play stops. The curtain, as it were, comes down. We saw this happen in our mayonnaise jar story. We observe it routinely, moreover, in the day-care center, nursery school, or kindergarten. One child may be absorbed quietly with blocks or crayons until some implement he is using fails to work properly and frustrates him, or until another child comes along and interferes. The first child, thrown off balance, falls out of his play state, so to speak, and begins to complain, object, or cry, and adult assistance becomes necessary.

Play states are framed, rather like paintings or staged performances (as I have discussed in my writing on picture books). They occur in their purest form in secure time-spaces where fantasy and reality can freely blend, where clock time is suspended, and where an implicit sense of safety grounds the child's experience. I am reminded of a song by Fred Rogers that goes: "I can stop when I want to, / Can stop when I wish, / Can stop, stop, stop any time . . ." (Mister Rogers' Songbook), lyrics I interpret to suggest both self-control and the comfortable mood of a child who is playing in an emotionally secure state confident that he has the ability to move in and out of his games in an untroubled way.

Keats's Lady and the Risks of Fantasy and Art

At the same time, however, it is important to affirm that play states are inherently precarious, ever vulnerable to slipping over into nonplay states that can involve pain. Furthermore, to depart the real world, if you will, and enter the realm of fantasy entails an element of risk, even if it is principally psychic risk. I would like to offer a soulful ballad by Keats, "La Belle Dame sans Merci," as an extended metaphor for this concept of psychic risk. In this poem, a knight is enchanted by an ethereal fairy maiden whom he encounters one evening in the cold mists by a lake. Spellbound, he follows her deep into the surrounding woods, where she offers him kisses, wild honey, and "roots of relish sweet," and then, lulling him tenderly to sleep, she vanishes forever. As a consequence of his enchantment by her, the knight when he awakens cannot find his way back to his former life and is doomed to spend the rest of his days wandering in search of her. Pale and wan, he loiters listlessly in the marshes on the bank of the silent lake.

To me, the fairy maiden has always stood for the poet's muse, the knight for the poet; and the tale itself, a parable that warns of the dangers inherent in art and fantasy and of the magnetism of the imagination. Keats's source—a well-known medieval French legend—tells of an errant knight who, bewitched by an enchantress, is led willingly to his doom. It stresses the irresistible lure of beauty and of desire that draws one on to an unknown place and into a dangerous altered state of consciousness that quells all wishes to return.

In a similar fashion, writers, artists, daydreamers, and playing children are prone to giving themselves over completely. Absorbed, they become temporarily lost in worlds beyond the cyclone, the looking glass, or the rainbow. Or, finding themselves upon an island of wild things, they forget that they will eventually need to find their way home. Before the tragic drama starts, before the poet finds her first word, before the painter sullies a pristine canvas, before a page of the novel is turned, anticipatory anxieties may arise and counterwishes surface to keep the experience at bay. This poorly understood phenomenon probably figures, I warrant, not only in play disturbances but also in many artists' difficulties with beginning new work or with plunging back into their work after stopping for a while. As Virgil writes:

> The way down is easy from Avernus,
> Black Dis's door stands open night and day.
> But to retrace your steps to heaven's air,
> There is the trouble, there is the toil.

I am proposing that an element of risk is therefore inherent in all authentic aesthetic experience, from children's play to what has been called "high art," and this is a topic we will revisit in subsequent chapters.

Green Cows and Alligators

Returning now to the role of adults in children's imaginative play and in their aesthetic lives more generally, we see clearly that with every benefit come corresponding liabilities or dangers. As in the story of Hannah and the mayonnaise jar, highly imaginative adults afford children the boon of mental stimulation, energetic participation in their games, and creative role modeling, but there may be a negative side to this as well. The most original, dramatic, playful adults often find it necessary to doff their parental hats from time to time and, in effect, to abandon their children emotionally while they, too, inhabit those "other" worlds. On the other hand, persons of this ilk are such a rarity that we may be inclined to cherish them for their eccentricity and welcome their presence in the lives of our children. I think of Jacques Tati's film *Mon oncle,* in which a little boy oppressed by his absurdly prim bourgeois parents is occasionally released to spend afternoons with his delightfully whimsical and permissive oddball uncle. Pertinent are recent books by Carol Loeb Shloss and Robert Polhemus, on the Joyces and the Brontës respectively, which describe the complex imaginative negotiations that occur in the lives of parents and children with kindred artistic or literary sensibilities.

After all, the vast majority of American (and European) adults have been squeezed through the wringer of educational systems that prize neither aesthetic nor imaginative growth, and some of us have, as a consequence, lost touch with or marginalized these parts of ourselves. Yet, even if we cannot fly to Neverland ourselves, we ought not to belittle children's forays there. In an instance I observed recently, a mother criticized her three-and-a-half-year-old daughter's crayoned image of a green cow by pointing out to the deflated child that, for heaven's sake, cows are *not* green. Humor, incidentally, can serve a rescue function in such situations. This mother might have laughed appreciatively *with* her child over the picture, thus assuming (no doubt correctly) that both she and the little girl were perfectly well acquainted with the true colors of cows. Even beyond this, if she had been art-history-minded, she might have informed her daughter that there was once upon a time a real artist called Franz Marc who liked to paint his horses *blue*. And we have already mentioned the appeal of Marc's yellow cow.

Here now is an example of humor actively invoked to create and expand upon the imaginative possibilities that so often present themselves in the wake of small children's linguistic naïveté. Riding in a campus elevator, I was surrounded by a small crowd that included a toddler strapped into his stroller. The little fellow was trying valiantly to pronounce the difficult word *elevator* and kept coming out with something that sounded like *alligator*. As we ascended, his mother, irritated and apparently slightly embarrassed, kept correcting him by repeating: "*NOT alligator*, el-e-va-tor!" Just then, the big doors of the car retracted to reveal a broad gaping space in front of the child as we arrived at a new floor. An imaginative adult lady, presumably a stranger, leaned down over the stroller and whispered to the child, "But they *both* open their mouths v-e-er-r-y wide, don't they?"

Indeed, it may be difficult for most people to wear their artistic and parental hats at the same time. I am persuaded of this not only by virtue of my personal experience but because such a large number of artists, writers, and performers (even those whose works are directed to child audiences) admit to having been reluctant or ineffective parents themselves or remained childless for various reasons (in addition to Hans Christian Andersen, one could cite Beatrix Potter, Margaret Wise Brown, and Maurice Sendak, among others). However, children do have, optimally, two parents, or else several adults involved in their care, and one happy scenario might involve a thoughtful collaboration between them regarding their child's aesthetic life, each taking turns as it were, according to native predilections and gifts, each contributing to the child's growth in specific areas of his own greatest proficiency and pleasure. In one family I know, the father is a trained singer, the mother loves literature, theater, and dance, one grandmother writes poetry, and an uncle conducts a chorale. Were each of these relatives, in whatever ways they devised, to share aspects of their aesthetic loves with the children in the family, the experiences of all concerned would be rich indeed. Oliver Sacks, in his memoir, *Uncle Tungsten*, regales his readers with the lasting effects of a talented cluster of relations on his life, as does Primo Levi in the first chapter of *The Periodic Table*, in which he likens the traces of his wildly idiosyncratic relatives to those of inert, noble, and rare gases.

In a Sculptor's Studio

What happens, a parent occasionally puzzles, when a child is drawn to and gifted in an art for which she herself has no aptitude or knowledge? This happened to my mother, and she managed to invent, I see now looking back, some rather clever solutions. I would claim that many challenging moments for parents and teachers occur under just these sorts of circumstances. A young person's unanticipated inclination manifests itself, and before you know it you find yourself shanghaied and deposited on the shores of a hitherto unexplored wilderness. What you discover right away is that, like Robinson Crusoe, you have to start learning fast. Next, you find a good teacher for the child.

In my mother's case, she was knowledgeable about art history but not about studio art. Noticing from the start that she had a visual child on her hands, one who loved to draw and paint, she made numerous arrangements to enable me to pursue these interests, but the one I want to describe was the most remarkable of all. It inspired me later on as a parent, and it may serve that function for you.

Seeing her small daughter as a somewhat independent-spirited and rebellious creature for whom ordinary classes were not the preferred milieu, she found a way to create a unique "apprenticeship" for me in the atelier of a sculptor. I was eight years old, and as I reflect on this solution now, it seems incredible to me that a serious working artist would have agreed to such a plan. Charlotte Neubauer was the name of the sculptor, as I recall, and how my mother found her I shall never know. Her studio seemed vast to me, with its high ceilings and several rooms. She needed plenty of space because she worked on a grand scale—human figures, mainly, that were larger than life and, of course, nude. Why, I wonder in retrospect, did this fact not perturb my sedate and proper mother? And how did my mother, even granted her persuasive rhetoric and legendary charm, ever manage to convince this artist to agree to have an eight-year-old there every Saturday for months on end? (I cannot remember exactly how long the arrangement lasted.) These sessions were not, after all, formal lessons. No other children were present. Alone with the artist, I worked on my projects while she worked on hers.

What I remember most about these studio hours is the perfect bliss they gave me. Charlie (pronounced "Sharlie") Neubauer was a tall, taciturn figure with wild gray hair; she wore no makeup and dressed in wrinkly, clay-spattered overalls. To me, she represented the complete obverse of my mother, who was petite, always elegantly and immaculately turned out, and loquacious. Unlike my mother, who monitored every breath I took, Charlie, deeply immersed in her own work, left me alone. I sat at a rough wooden table in her dimly lit studio with access to all the clay and all the tools I could possibly desire. It was quiet and cool there, and no one interfered with me. I was allowed and even, as I realize now, *expected*, to become completely absorbed in my work so that, week after week, when my mother would arrive to fetch me, her sudden appearance felt like an electric shock. Her entrance into the studio seemed an intrusion, which I experienced rather like an awakening from a daydream, when you cannot believe time has actually elapsed.

If I encountered a technical problem during the morning or had any sort of question, I felt shy about interrupting Charlie, who was also working. But not having recourse to instant help forced me to become more self-reliant and resourceful. Furthermore, patience proved a reliable solution, for every now and then she would withdraw from her own work and, recalling my presence, wander over to check on me and see what I was up to. She would offer me a technical tip or correct something that had not been sufficiently well built to withstand the kiln. She fired all my good pieces. What was most wonderful about all this was that my mother, having arranged it and set it up, removed herself from it henceforth. Unlike almost everything else in my childhood, she allowed this experience to be exclusively mine. It was a part of *my* life and *not* of hers.

What I learned those Saturdays in the studio went far beyond technical knowledge, although the craftsmanship Charlie taught me has stood me in good stead. I learned firsthand the absorption and passion of being an artist. I discovered that there was at least one woman in the world I could revere who was nothing at all like my own mother. At the same time, I never grew close to Charlie Neubauer. She was not a warm person, and we never talked; she was simply not adept at communicating with words. Her media were space, volume, mass, clay, plaster, and symbolic three-dimensional form, and what she did with these was, to me, grand and imposing. Her bony, eloquently gestural human figures, built on giant armatures in different stages of completion, surrounded me and formed an eerily silent populace that shared the studio with me as I worked. I probably had dreams in which they came to life and moved by their own accord, but I doubt if they ever spoke.

My own clay pieces, small, delicate, and detailed, differed radically from hers. Occasionally I modeled figures that illustrated my children's books, such as Heidi feeding her goat Schwanli or a fairy-tale princess in a conical hat and kirtle, or a figure of Pan playing his double flute, or the horse Black Beauty. Charlie made no effort whatsoever to influence me. I would simply arrive with my mother, who immediately left, settle myself at the wooden table, and begin to work either on something new or on a piece I had begun on a previous Saturday. There were days when Charlie did not even bother to greet me at the door or say good-bye when my mother came for me. Politeness did not count for much with her, as it did for my family; it was simply not an important value. She lived exclusively for her work and was wholly absorbed by it. Like the knight in Keats's poem, she had, over the years, grown thin and wan. For her single-minded intensity and above all for the opportunity she gave me on those timeless Saturdays to live as I could live in no other quadrant of my life, I truly loved her. And although it was most certainly an unrequited love, it never registered as such to me. Even today as I reanimate her fading picture for you in these pages, my awe and gratitude to her are rekindled, along with an undying measure of shy affection.

Parents do, then, find masterful solutions. It takes a bit of sleuthing. You might have to talk with friends, even strangers, and deploy all the information-gathering resources you can muster. The next step might be to take the child to try something out, at which point, in some cases, you could do well to step back and wait. Children let you know when they are satisfied. Parenthetically, while helping a young mother by driving her son one morning to a summer camp he was attending, I glanced into my rearview mirror just in time to catch his face brightening into a smile as we approached the turnoff from the road that led into the camp property. Clearly, he was having a marvelous time there. Parental backstepping, however, should ideally be adjusted to the personality and, of course, to the age of a child, because for some children parental involvement, at least early on, can be a crucial element of success. Although such was not true in my case at age eight, one could cite the achievements, apropos, of the Suzuki method of teaching musical instruments, wherein each child must have a parent willing to take an active part for several years, even when that parent is not musically gifted or trained, and there are many offshoots and modifications of this method of instruction in instrumental music.

A Wish to Dance

What happens when a child initiates an arena of imaginative play that seems to her parents unwholesome or excessive? A fictional case in point may be gleaned from Jane Hamilton's novel *Disobedience*, where we meet a girl called Elvira who is obsessed with the American Civil War and its lore to the extent that she lives and breathes nothing else. We are told she reads everything about it that she can get her hands on, actually sews herself an authentic soldier's uniform of the period, which she proudly wears, asks for a gun for her birthday, learns how to make hardtack and eats it, renames herself by adding a masculine suffix to her given name (Elviron), and, in general, organizes her entire life around the fiction that she *is* a Civil War soldier. She even shaves her head. Her mother protests against all of this highly unfeminine behavior, while her father, a history teacher, defends it on the grounds that, through it, the girl is learning all sorts of transferable skills.

This example is useful because it brings us face-to-face with opposing parental attitudes and conflicts of values that inhere in many such situations. Here is a true-life example of scars left by a conflict between a mother and daughter.

"When I was a girl," my colleague told me, "I longed to be a ballerina. I watched Moira Shearer again and again as she danced in *The Red Shoes*, and I yearned for a life in the ballet. That was my dream. I wanted to twirl and leap and pirouette onstage *en pointe* in ravishing costumes, my hair all coiffed in a perfect chignon. Actually, I was quite a good dancer, but my mother opposed it. She set herself against it with a vengeance, fearing perhaps that professional dancing might be too dangerous in some way for me, or that a career in the ballet might prevent me later on somehow from meeting the right sort of man, or something of the kind; I don't really know. Perhaps she thought it wasn't proper for her daughter." In any case, the result, this woman explained, was that as she approached adolescence, she was forbidden to attend class, and that in consequence she gradually relinquished her cherished dream of performing. Her fantasy of gossamer tutus, sparkling tiaras, stage lights, and soaring music, her memories of practice rooms with their strewn-about leg warmers, resin, and orange slices all faded, but the longing and disappointment, the sting of her mother's refusal, remained throughout her adult years.

Her story elicited my sympathy, for I, too, had longed to be a dancer, and like hers, my mother had opposed me. In my case, however, my mother's power ended with her early death, and in my young adulthood I did manage to perform for several years with a modern dance company, thereby fulfilling my childhood dream. Our low-budget state-supported company, the Potpourri Dancers, was led by a dynamic spirit named Fanya del Borgo. We rehearsed in a ramshackle building in Croton-on-Hudson, New York, and we presented programs of piquant works, some abstract, some suggestively narrative, mainly to young audiences. For me, the rehearsals, costumes, props, and sense of being part of an ensemble and thus contributing to an effect greater than any of its parts furnished a continuous source of pleasure. I loved everything about it, even the cold, drafty practice room that others cursed. For me the entire enterprise was suffused with glamour—a glamour that I suspect now, however, in the light of my colleague's story, must have been enhanced by a sense of the forbidden. I enjoyed even the challenge of learning new choreography, which was always difficult for me, and of teaching my roles to new dancers.

My colleague's story made me realize, once again, not only how powerful parents can be in these matters, for good or ill, but also the evanescence of certain windows of opportunity. A ballerina or a male dancer (or a violinist) needs to start early and to stay with it because the growing body must be enlisted in time. Once developed past a certain point, the flesh, if not the spirit, loses its malleability. I wondered but never quite managed to ask my colleague whether she goes to the ballet at all anymore and enjoys it still, or whether her mother's disapprobation had cast a pall upon the art for her forever.

My thoughts on dilemmas such as this, thoughts that involve not a solution but avenues of approach, may be illustrated by a story that involves religion rather than aesthetics.

Michelle, a Jewish girl, is growing up in a Connecticut town where, from her earliest years, she has had scant contact with children of her own religious and ethnic heritage. Her mother, a highly idealistic but secular person, comes from an assimilated family that has lived in the United States since the late nineteenth century. Active in various civic organizations, she, like her daughter, has many non-Jewish friends. Michelle's father, on the other hand, had attended a cheder as a child and continues to cherish religious feelings. Strongly committed to the local Jewish community in which he plays a respected role, he tells his daughters that, as a small boy, he saw an apparition of light that seemed to him a mystical, spiritual phenomenon. Despite his wish to pass on a Judaic legacy, however, he deplores fanaticism and recoils from what he perceives as the narrow-mindedness of extreme religiosity.

Surrounded in her neighborhood by Christian children of various denominations, Michelle has always been invited to their gatherings. Every year in public school she sings what seem to her to be beautiful Christmas songs, and she attends annual caroling parties that finish with cocoa and marshmallows in front of blazing fireplaces at the gracious homes of her Protestant friends. An avid reader, she encounters literature that refers to the New Testament; she learns its stories. When her mother takes her to art museums, she sees works that include the lives of the Catholic saints as well, figures about whose lives she reads eagerly. Little by little, she begins to fantasize about becoming Christian. She dares not, however, discuss these thoughts with her parents.

Eventually, encouraged by her friends, she develops an elaborate plan for a clandestine baptism that is to take place in the old stone Gothic Trinity Church of lower Manhattan. Two of her closest school friends help her prepare and pledge to go with her. On the appointed day, she dons a white lace dress and, with one Catholic and one Episcopalian friend, travels by train to the church.

Almost immediately, her younger sister, who has overheard the whisperings, divulges the deed to the girls' parents. They are incredulous. They confront Michelle with markedly different reactions. Here is where I want to make my analogy with the realm of the aesthetic. Michelle's mother feels outraged. She acts as though her daughter has personally

betrayed her and treats the incident as though it represents a permanent alteration in Michelle's identity and therefore a repudiation of her
mothering. She is so hurt that she berates the girl with angry tirades.
Michelle's father, on the other hand, is calmer. He talks with his daughter about his disapproval but assures her of his ongoing confidence in
her and in the traditions into which she was born.

"You will return; I'm certain of that," he declares. "This act must
have some special meaning for you at this moment in your life, but
you're very young. I believe that in the future you'll come to see things
differently."

Here we have vastly different parental reactions. Once again, the
mother takes a more fearful, conservative position, while the father
espouses a more liberal and permissive one—an alignment, however,
that is by no means the rule. As in the areas of imaginative play and
acting out fantasies, a parent of either sex who is more experienced,
better informed, and less conflicted in a given area will be the one who
can sustain a calmer attitude and take a farther-reaching perspective. In
this case, Michelle's father, who is more firmly grounded in his own
religious convictions and has already tested them, feels less threatened
by her defection. Her mother, on the other hand, with little knowledge
of her own religious heritage and doubtless many unresolved questions of her own, is understandably more distraught. Again, we might
want to reconsider—in this light—the story of the mother who refused
to let her daughter study ballet. It would be interesting to know whether
that mother had herself studied ballet and what her relation to dance
had been in her own childhood.

Faith in a child's potential to handle whatever it is he or she is experimenting with is founded, I am suggesting, not only on an assessment of
that particular child's strengths and weaknesses but on a parent's *own*
confidence with respect to the area in question. Admittedly, in the examples I have offered here, there are many factors I have set aside in order
not to digress. My point is that parents who have had only rare and
limited experiences in the arts may find it more difficult to refrain from
warning, criticizing, and opposing their children when psychic risks
seem to be involved. On the other hand, parents who have had, every

now and then, the experience of venturing into the realms of the fantastic or, we might say, who have themselves encountered—in her various guises—*la belle dame sans merci* and survived to tell the tale may be better able to withstand these sorts of forays on the part of their offspring. Religion has, needless to say, been used here solely as a metaphor for ventures in the domain of the aesthetic.

Lilliputians, Wolves, and the Deafness of Beethoven

In the previous story, it is significant that Michelle cannot speak openly to either of her parents about her feelings. Clearly her silence stems from a fear of opposition. Children, however, keep secrets from their parents for a variety of reasons, one of which is to maintain and preserve their own psychic boundaries. Consider how many children endow their mothers with a sixth sense—an uncanny ability to know all about them before they know for themselves. Thus, an aura of surveillance may seem to exist even under the most benign circumstances, and many children, as a consequence, feel the need to hold fast to the slippery knowledge that what is inside their heads is in fact private and unknown to others. Rather than saying excitedly "Look at this!" children may at times need to keep their aesthetic experiences to themselves, and this privacy should be respected.

In the following anecdotes, two little girls interweave their cultural and fantasy lives with their everyday reality and do not talk about it with anyone. One of them transposes characters from the pages of her books into her living quarters, thereby making her surroundings all the more exciting and colorful to herself, and an important element of this aesthetic pleasure is that it is solitary and unshared.

Marie-Claire, a six-year-old girl living in France, has been given a beautiful rare children's illustrated vintage edition of *Gulliver's Travels* translated into French. Captivated by its pictures of the Lilliputians, she imagines that under her bed at night a whole world of them exists— a veritable city of little people. When she wakes up in the morning, she knows that she must be very careful where she puts her feet down, otherwise they might catch her! She has also heard the story of Little Red Riding Hood from her grandmother. When she is in her house at night with all the windows and shutters closed, she imagines that wolves are circling the house, and while this fantasy seems frightening and shivery to her, it also gives her a special feeling of safety and coziness in her bed, for she is absolutely certain that by morning all the wolves will have slunk silently away.

Here, in order to taste the delicious pleasure of scaring and rescuing herself, the little girl needs to keep her fantasies a secret. To tell them to adults would be to risk a deflation that could easily destroy that pleasure.

Chloe, an almost-six-year-old with a head of tumbling flaxen curls, is garbed in a hand-stitched pinafore dress and unmatched socks. It is late on a Saturday morning in August, and she has just emerged from a children's concert at Tanglewood with her grandparents, an aunt, and an uncle. They are walking slowly across the lawn after the special event in Ozawa Hall, where they have listened to music by Beethoven, Berlioz, and Liszt. Chloe is being plied with questions by her well-meaning visiting aunt:

"And Chloe dear, how about *you*? Do you play an instrument yet?"

"No," she murmurs in a small voice.

"Do you like to sing, then?"

"No," she whispers, head down. "But . . . sometimes I umm-mm, I *hum*," she offers, trying to be compliant. She attempts to articulate something about the music she makes for herself, music she makes *"inside herself,"* as she puts it, inside her head. Struggling to be clear, she frustrates her aunt with her stammering efforts. The well-intentioned but intrusive lady, striding beside her on the expanse of green, demands impatiently: "But, dear, don't you ever *share* any of that music with anyone else?"

The little girl looks down at the grass now and starts, imperceptibly at first, to move away. Opening up an ever-increasing physical distance between herself and the adults, she says, almost inaudibly, "No . . . it's just very private." And then she runs off.

Settling herself into the grass on a hillock with her face cupped in her hands and her back to her family, she remains alone as her adult relatives walk on, chattering with one another and quickly oblivious of her.

Later, in the car on the way home, Chloe's grandfather, to whom the foregoing events have not gone unobserved, speaks softly and pointedly about Beethoven and his deafness. "Beethoven," he remarks gently, "was able to hear his music in *his* head. In fact, he heard a silent music, available only to himself at first. Many other composers, as well, begin with a silent music that feels very private to them, especially at first when it's just beginning to take form. For some, it may even feel secret, just like Chloe's."

Listening to these wise words, I wondered to myself whether Chloe was listening and whether her grandfather's sensitivity gave her a feeling of being understood or whether his words had simply floated by, beyond her ken, as she withdrew further into her own world, beyond the reach of adult conversation.

Hiding from the Sitter

When I was a child and our parents went out together for the evening, they occasionally left my sister and me to be cared for by a good-hearted crippled girl who walked on crutches and suffered from a speech impediment that caused her to try for what seemed like forever before any words emerged from her mouth. Because she limped and was exceedingly kind, Bonnie could easily be hoodwinked and was therefore our favorite sitter. Her alternate, whose name escapes me, was a formidable individual not to be toyed with. Shrill-voiced, hunch-backed, and wizened, she dressed in black and seemed the incarnation of every witch in my illustrated fairy tales. Her presence filled me with dread. Secretly, I believed she had cast a spell on my parents and forced them to hire her so that she could exercise her magic powers over me. She threatened me with tales of wicked children who had been spooked away through their bedroom windows at night and hideously tortured and who never came back, and she warned me never to breathe a word of these tales to my parents or else the demons would surely come for me.

Whenever my mother told us she was going out, I begged her to let us have Bonnie and trembled speechlessly if she said the other woman was coming. Never did I breathe a word to her of my fears. Wide-eyed, I took the other sitter's warnings to heart, believing her grim invocations of the terrible torments that had befallen the children who had betrayed her. I knew she had privileged access to my innermost soul and could peer into the darkest corners of my mind.

Therefore, sometimes, just after my mother left (she never went off without bidding us good-bye), I would run to my room to hide and be alone. Crawling under my bed with a supply of illustrated books, I remained there as long as possible. Squeezed under my so-called youth bed, I would stretch out, never knowing how long my solitude would last before being interrupted. Inevitably, an irregular tapping of footsteps would warn me that the sitter was approaching. Even when Bonnie was with us, I hid. This practice, I realize more fully now, had a great deal to do with the need I articulated above—namely, the need children have to keep themselves intact and not intruded upon.

One night, engrossed under my bed with a stack of books, I absolutely refused to come out. Poor Bonnie! Her disability made it difficult for her to bend down, but she must have decided finally to extricate me bodily after all her pleas, exhortations, and commands had failed. For a long time I resisted her, fighting, as it were, for my freedom. Finally, she managed to say something that actually frightened me; perhaps she caught hold of me and pulled. In any case, my soft cheek was suddenly ripping along the sharp unfinished edge of the bed's supporting beam, and I emerged into the light screaming, a wound gaping on my face. Shocked speechless, Bonnie herded me somehow into the kitchen, where she tried frantically to wash my face with a dish towel and succeeded only in opening the wound still more. Distraught by my piercing shrieks and by the vast quantity of blood, she applied tincture of iodine to the wound, which stung so agonizingly that I was beside myself. I can still see her fumbling for the wall telephone and trying several numbers before she reached my parents, and then, after what seemed an interminable wait, their arrival, horror-stricken, in all their finery.

Barely stopping to chastise Bonnie for what they took to be her incompetence, they left her behind with my sister, who by that time was wailing inconsolably herself. They rushed me to the hospital, where apparently (I remember nothing of this part) an emergency-room doctor stitched up my cheek while trying to reassure my mother that her daughter would not be disfigured for life. Thus, the need for privacy in childhood can be so strong that it occasionally leads children to protect it even in the face of strenuous opposition and potential harm.

Saying No

Of course, prohibition can, under some circumstances, prove a painful goad to children's imaginative and aesthetic lives. Parents who forbid their children to dance, sing, act, or pursue the visual arts may find, to their dismay, that their strictures prove just the tonic needed by certain rebellious spirits. In Ingmar Bergman's autobiographical film *Fanny and Alexander*, we observe how increasingly sadistic religious regulations give rise in the protagonist to a rich fantasy life that blossoms into a passion for all that has been forbidden to him—all that is exciting, sensuous, dramatic, intense, and that evades the confines of his impoverished daily life. Another illustration of parental limits giving rise to fantasy can be found in the classic picture book *Where the Wild Things Are* by Maurice Sendak, which begins with little Max defying his mother by putting nails into the wall to build himself a sort of hanging tent so as to hide, presumably from her surveillance.

Less drastic than parental negativity, the experiences of absence and loss are often—for children as well as adults—great prompts to fantasy and creativity. After observing the famous bead-and-reel game played by a toddler who was dangling his toy over the edge of his play-pen and then pulling it back while mouthing syllables that sounded like *fort* and *da* ("away" and "there" in German) in the absence of his mother, Freud observed that the very origins of language and of symbolic function may lie in our need to invoke, in their absence, the presence of those whose existence is vital to us.

The "Somebody's-Going-Away" Pain

Five-year-old Peter is the son of a dedicated physician who works exceedingly long hours but who makes special efforts to spend time with him and to develop between them a close rapport. Peter, in addition to being deeply devoted to his father and mother, is attached to grandparents on both sides, and to several aunts and uncles who visit him for brief periods but then vanish unpredictably from his daily life. One morning, as Peter is playing upstairs in his parents' bedroom, his father excuses himself to go to the bathroom. Peter objects: "No, Daddy, you can't do that. You can't go, or I'll get a 'somebody's-going-away' pain!"

Peter's father, rather than just laughing, ridiculing his son, or riding roughshod over this unexpected but inventive protest, asks Peter to explain to him what such a thing would be like. Interestingly, this young son of a doctor has spontaneously dreamt up the notion of a "pain." Getting very excited, Peter suddenly says he has an idea. Marching down two flights of stairs by himself, he fetches paper, crayons, and a pen. Then, while his father goes off to the bathroom, he draws a picture of the "somebody's-going-away" pain.

The image resembles a whirlwind or dust storm with a stick figure of Peter himself in the middle, caught up, as it were, in the tornado of colored lines. After drawing this picture and realizing that his father has not yet reappeared, Peter now pierces the paper all over with pen pricks, thus perforating the image with holes that give it a more aggressive and sinister look.

Here we see a child responding to a momentary feeling of loss with an actively artistic solution that is remarkable principally because it came into being so spontaneously. It was he who initiated the solution. The possibility of doing so, moreover, has been fostered by his dad's *interest* in what he was feeling—an interest that makes worthwhile the child's effort to perform an aesthetic and communicative act. The pen pricks, furthermore, are noteworthy in that they suggest a turning not only of passive into active but of sadness into aggression—a move with which we are all familiar but that occurs, in this homely incident, in a constructive rather than a harmful way.

Peter's choice of drawing as a means of coping with loss and of trying to express what he is feeling could well be encouraged by his parents in the future. I don't know what ensued when his dad reappeared, but I trust he was eager to look at the picture and to listen to whatever Peter wanted to say about it. Also, beyond encouraging Peter to continue to express himself artistically in the future, his parents might now indirectly draw upon this spontaneous gesture when introducing him to the works of other "artists." This child, if he continues along these lines, might, over time, be able to grasp intuitively how, like his own, others' needs and inner states can be transformed into graphic representations.

Thus, the beginnings of an aesthetic education occur—having sprung from a child's own feelings and actions and a parent's sensitive response. It is notable that Peter was able, initially, to articulate something about what he was feeling to his dad—he put into words the pain he thought he would have when his dad vanished briefly. Yet, it was the artistic medium that completed his self-expression. Words were insufficient. The activity of drawing proved essential and physical. In fact, when Peter got his initial brainstorm, he *left* his dad to go get the supplies from another floor of the house, so that, in the process of expressing himself he was also turning passive into active in the sense of momentarily leaving his dad even before his dad left him. Thus, physicality frequently proves a crucial element of the aesthetic—moving, touching, listening, marking, and seeing. It functions to release and to concretize amorphous feelings and to liberate us in a manner first described, perhaps, by Aristotle in his *Poetics*.

A Stepfather's Gift

It is especially gratifying when parents who are neither talented nor trained in music or drawing or theater or dance simply let go of their inhibitions and sing and dance and sketch—however simply—or play the guitar or the piano with their children. Permit me to give one final example here. A stepfather with no formal musical training (he was unable to read music) had, on his travels after college, purchased a simple wooden recorder-like instrument with a sweet tone and taught himself to play a few tunes on it. When his little stepson heard him one day, he begged to try it, too, and soon the man was teaching the child all he knew about the instrument. Within a few months, the little boy, who turned out to be highly gifted musically, had absorbed all his stepfather could teach him. The child's parents conferred at that point and found an outstanding private teacher for him. Eventually, the boy went on to major in oboe and composition at the Juilliard School's Pre-College Division.

An interesting sideline to this story is that the stepfather told me that, once it was clear that the child had surpassed him, it took tremendous effort on his part not to stop playing the recorder with him. His impulse was to bow out. This was because his own father, he explained sadly, had taught him a variety of skills, including tennis and ice-skating, but that, just as soon as his own skill equaled or exceeded that of his father, his father had withdrawn, using as an excuse the fact that his role as a teacher was no longer required. This behavior, the man explained, was extremely painful for him, for it was as though he had been given a no-win choice between doing his best but risking his dad's companionship or holding back his best efforts and faking incompetence in order to keep his dad with him. Because of this childhood suffering on his part, he made a concerted effort to continue playing duets with his stepson even when the boy's prowess far exceeded his own, and he did so right up to the time when the boy himself ceased to show an interest.

My principal motive in recounting this story is to emphasize that, despite his own lack of formal training in music, this stepfather graciously shared with a small child what was pleasurable to him. Eventually, music became for that child a major interest and passion, but no one could have predicted this in advance. The stepfather's gift, I would aver, continues to count as an important early step in the history of that child's musical education, which, I am told, has since progressed under the tutelage of master teachers at prestigious institutions. Parents, in other words, and adults more generally, need not excel at any art form in order to be able to share it with a child. They need only to love it.

Back and Forth

Parents need not serve in a merely *reactive* capacity to their children's aesthetic lives. Identifying familiar objects by their colors, shapes, and textures, pointing out the lacy loveliness of a grove of snow-laden fir trees or the delicacy of a crescent moon, or dancing impetuously to the music one loves not only helps to sensitize children to these aesthetic pleasures; it also lets them know that such percepts and responses are of value and that they matter to us. It is important, too, for us to remain silently in the wings at times and to allow our children the right, as Rilke writes in *Letters to a Young Poet*, "to be solitary the way one was solitary as a child, when the grownups went around involved with things that seemed important and big because they themselves looked so busy and because one comprehended nothing of their doings."

Chapter Three

I Want Music!

Then the music started. . . . For a minute the opening
balanced from one side to the other. Like a walk or
march. Like God strutting in the night. The outside
of her was suddenly froze and only that first part of
the music was hot inside her heart. She could not
even hear what sounded after, but she sat there waiting and froze, with her fists tight.
  —Carson McCullers, *The Heart Is a Lonely Hunter*

What sticks in my mind even more than the performance is the audience: schoolchildren, a thousand or
so of them, hanging wide-eyed and open-mouthed
on every word, inhaling Schiller's sonorous and rhymi-
cally electrifying lines, and in the balcony, where I
was sitting, leaning forward as though wanting to fly
onto the stage themselves.
  —Michael Steinberg, "Notes on *Luisa Miller*"

A Fragment of Memory

The parents of a little girl not much more than two have leased a summer cottage somewhere on a grassy spot near the beach in Shippan
Point, Connecticut. One of their acquaintances is an opera singer, and
while they occupy the cottage, this soprano, whose name floats back as

Niki . . . Niki Galpere . . . enters the room where the child is about to go to sleep one evening and sings to her. The stranger has a full, buxom figure and coils of black hair, and when she opens her mouth, golden sound soars to fill every particle of space in the room, causing the little girl to ache with pleasure and to sense that what she is hearing must be coming from somewhere else. It is a voice unlike any other. She begs her mother to let the soprano sing for her again and again, and when they leave at summer's end, it is this voice that lingers and is missed above all.

Years later, in an opera house, when that child, all grown up, finds herself looking toward the stage at the live human beings standing before her with their mouths open, she feels convinced, just as she was as a child, that the magnificent music she hears is coming from somewhere else, not from mere flesh-and-blood creatures like herself.

I Want Music!

That was long ago. But recently, this very same lady has come visiting at the home of a two-year-old. Asked to take care of him for part of an afternoon, she has gently conveyed him, still groggy with sleep after a delayed afternoon nap, into his high chair and offered him a snack of assorted tidbits. He rubs his eyes, looks at her, and announces: "I want music!"

Surprised, she smiles. She is pleased to note that her young companion already shares her enthusiasm for listening to music while dining. In compliance with his request, she switches on the nearby CD player. The little fellow, however, frowns at "Yellow Submarine," which is the first song to come on, possibly a current favorite of an older sibling.

"NO!" he protests. " 'Thnowy Day!' "

Puzzled, the lady thinks: But *that's* not a song; *The Snowy Day* (she seems to recall) is a picture book by Ezra Jack Keats. Patiently, she asks him to explain more clearly what music he wants; all he can manage, though, is to screw up his face and repeat: " 'Thnowy Day.' "

Her only recourse is to try each disc currently in the family's player and hope the right one pops up. Glowering at his tray, the little boy listens intently to the music. At length, a gentle, masculine voice begins to croon: "Fro-sty the Snow-man . . . ," and now a charmed smile steals over the child's face. He reaches out, with gusto, and then, as if by magic, the raisins and goldfish crackers disappear from his tray. He wants, of course, to hear the song "aGAIN!"

Music matters profoundly in children's lives, and every family has its own way of introducing it at home. Some mothers and dads sing lullabies at bedtime. Some play the guitar or the piano or other instruments. Some families keep the radio on as background or play recordings on their various electronic devices. Some enjoy singing ensemble around the piano or a cappella. A friend who grew up in one of Baltimore's African American neighborhoods tells me that music for him was all about his mom's and his grandmother's singing in the Baptist church they attended regularly when he was small; he is now a passionate guitarist. Music forms an integral part of children's participation in celebrations, holidays, and religious ceremonies, and I know at least one young mother who prepares for long family auto trips by making composite CDs of all her children's favorite music so they can listen, enjoy, and sing along while traveling.

Building with Blocks to Brahms

Television is another medium that can introduce children to music and augment their musical knowledge and experience. The possibilities are legion. One program I know well, *Mister Rogers' Neighborhood,* makes a point of including music at the beginning and end of each show as well as throughout. Fred Rogers, the author-creator and host of this show, himself a composer as well as a puppeteer, sings directly to his audience, and—with a smile and a snap of his fingers—invites them to join in; as the songs are repeated, children actually can and do. Among his programs (which were aired nationwide for nearly half a century, making his the longest-running series on public television), one show provides a stunning example of how music can be introduced and conjoined with other spheres of learning in a cross-modal style exquisitely attuned to the fluid sensibilities of young children.

In this show, Rogers, after greeting his audience (musically), holds up for the camera the first page of the score of Brahms's Symphony no. 2 in D Major, op. 73. Pointing out its features, he goes over the page in detail, explaining how a symphony is "built" up out of notes that seem to be nothing more than funny little black marks on paper and how all the musicians in the orchestra must pay attention to lines written especially for their instruments. To associate the score with the sounds it gives rise to, Rogers takes out a recording of the symphony and plays the opening bars of the first movement. Listening with his child audience (and it is quite clear how much he loves it), he settles himself down on the floor after a few minutes and shows the children some hand-painted wooden blocks. As the symphonic movement continues, he gradually begins to build with these blocks, slowly constructing an edifice to the music. After he has fashioned a simple structure, he stops the music and, momentarily abandoning his blocks, walks over to his studio movie screen, which he calls "Picture Picture." Here he invites the audience to watch a short black-and-white film in which laborers are building a house. We observe the piles of planks, tiles, and tools and watch as men climb to the top of the partially completed structure and pound the subroofing into place; Rogers meanwhile provides a running commentary on these activities.

In this way, without fanfare or overt didacticism, the program offers children a rich experience that extends beyond introducing them to a masterwork of classical music. Rogers exposes them not only to the Brahms symphony but also to the relatedness of music to other worlds—its links with the realms of children's play and adults' work. They are invited to make connections between the notions of "building" a symphony and building a house. Without saying so, he democratizes the experience of so-called high art. He gently deconstructs any hierarchy among occupations, that is to say, among notions that composers are somehow loftier or more admirable than construction workers. He shows that both are engaged in the important tasks of making and creating.

In the same program, Rogers forges yet another profound connection. In the Neighborhood of Make-Believe (a segment of the program to which the audience is magically "transported" by means of a red toy trolley with a tinkling bell), he arranges an imaginative transformation: One of his puppet characters, Lady Elaine Fairchilde, decides to use the pattern of notes from the opening bar of the first movement of this Brahms symphony as a blueprint for building a new make-believe castle for the puppet king, Friday XIII. In conceiving of this transposition, Rogers reveals his gift for grasping how developing psyches intertwine multiple strands of experience. He also suggests to children that a musical score *is* in fact a kind of blueprint or set of directions that must be followed if music is to be the result. In the Neighborhood of Make-Believe (as in dreams), our notions do in fact merge, and so here the notes of the score morph into a blueprint rather than being merely analogous to one.

In ingenious moments such as this, the program, while focusing directly and ostensibly on music, also mirrors children's inner and outer lives by flowing seamlessly through various worlds, establishing correspondences among them and exploring associations. Rogers never loses sight of the fact that what he offers on his show is being received by thousands of children *within* their own private playing and sleeping spaces—a crucial fact that holds for all children's television. To be invited into such hallowed spaces requires respect for their sanctity as havens and for their diversity. A little girl I know, immediately after watching this particular program, retreated to her attic playroom and emerged half an hour later having created an amazing structure out of her own building blocks while singing and humming unselfconsciously to herself the entire time.

Music Beyond the Home

My daughter writes from Taipei to tell me of a pre-music class there in which four-year-old Chinese children are asked to pretend to be stalks and reeds growing taller each day despite the churning winds; they are asked to make believe they are pats of butter taken out of the fridge and toast popping up in a toaster. I reflect how such early music movement classes are often the finest low-key way to augment the musical experiences of young children outside their own homes and families. Such classes, I warrant, seek to do far more than basic skills training, and if they succeed, they function quite wonderfully at enhancing the aesthetic lives of children. They often incorporate eurhythmics, simple instruments, listening exercises, song, movement, dance, and fantasy but may draw on a variety of other original sources, and they can be found in many locations. When they vary in quality, the variations stem, in my view, not so much from differences in the theoretical base of the methods touted as from differences in the native endowment and sensitivies of the teachers who implement them.

Earlier, I identified qualities of co-imagination, empathy, and the capacity to modulate from one pace or mood or type of activity to another; these are valuable, if not essential, abilities. No matter how highly recommended or regarded a school may be, it is best for parents of prospective pupils to visit and to meet the teachers firsthand before enrolling their toddlers. That being said, nearly all of the classes I have attended pass muster. In general, they work exceedingly well to augment and refine children's innate pleasure in sound, movement, and make-believe. I have seen children pretending to *make* popcorn and then to *be* popcorn. I have seen toddlers perform hand motions as if swimming in a pool, turn themselves into jack-in-the-boxes and into various animals, with noises and movements to match. I have observed three- and four-year-olds sit in a circle listening quietly to melodies played on a wooden recorder and then sing accompaniments in "la-la," and I have heard them make music about their favorite foods—chocolate, chips, and cookies—and dance gaily about the room waving scarves of yellow, violet, and green.

First experiences in the arts—formal and informal alike—are best undertaken, whenever possible, by parents and children *together*. The class I am about to describe occurred at the Hoff-Barthelson Music School in Scarsdale, New York. Offered to preschool-age children and their parents, it met once a week for just under an hour. The group consisted of nine three- to four-year-olds with their mothers, plus one gifted and magical teacher named Ruth Alperson. The most extraordinary quality of the class was that it always functioned on many levels simultaneously. While the children themselves were gradually being inducted into the art of sensitive and responsive listening, their mothers were participating in the teaching techniques so that they could grasp, in ever more subtle ways, the fundamentals of sound, rhythm, and musical structure. Alperson afforded a range of opportunities for both mothers and children to relate to one another: first, in familiar pairs (each mother with her own child), and then gradually, as time went on, as part of less familiar groups—groups of just mothers, groups of children, groups of children with teacher instead of mother, and so on. Transitions from belonging to one of these to belonging to another matter tremendously, as we know, when children are taken into the opera house, the concert hall, or the theater, where likewise they must form part of a larger, unfamiliar, and undifferentiated assemblage.

At the beginning of each class, Alperson asks the children to take off their shoes so they can move about freely, and by the second session, all the mothers are spontaneously removing their shoes as well. We are in a spacious room with a wall of windows and a wooden dance floor, quite empty except for chairs around the edges and a grand piano. Nine mothers now occupy chairs in a semicircle. The children sit on the floor in front of their mothers, everyone facing into the circle, the pairs all forming a group around Alperson, who relaxes cross-legged and barefoot in the center with her autoharp and begins to play a song that is repeated from session to session so that, very quickly, the children come to learn it by heart and chime in on their own. Thus, in the initial arrangement of the class, the children are experiencing both closeness and separation vis-à-vis their mothers because, while they are seated right in front of them, their gazes and attention are focused on the teacher. A transfer is occurring from the dyad of mother-child to the wider world. Alperson sings a number of songs at this point, among them various "hello" songs that feature the names of the children and involve them in singing both their own names and the names of their peers. They listen, sing, and listen. Musical experience thus coincides with becoming aware of one another and of themselves as a part of a newly forming community.

Alperson changes activities frequently not only to vary the content she is manifestly teaching but also to respond with alacrity to the children's alternating needs for active and passive, loud and soft, motoric and reflective moments. She stops to address the mothers so as to explain the objective of a particular exercise or to involve them actively with the children. Clearly she wants the mothers to understand her approach and to comprehend her modulations from movement of various kinds to tranquil listening.

She brings in and plays a variety of instruments, including wooden sticks and bells, for and with them. She has them listen to tapes of performances with some of these instruments and occasionally asks them to make corresponding sounds. The children often combine large motor movements with their music. Occasionally they dance with patterned fabrics or diaphanous scarves or march in time with, or in counterpoint to, the music. Low and soothing, her singing voice and manner possess a mesmerizing quality. The aura she creates captivates everyone. When she tells the children to imagine they are in a forest and that their mothers, standing with arms akimbo, are the trees, this seems to become literally so, just as when Max's bedroom is transformed into a forest in Maurice Sendak's *Where the Wild Things Are.* We simply believe it. We are there.

At one point, when the group has been meeting for over a month, she metamorphoses into a Pied Piper leading the toddlers on a tour of exploration so as to discover what they can hear in different parts of the room. She ends up crouched underneath the enormous piano with them as one of the mothers strikes the keys and pushes the pedals. Why did she wait a whole month to do this? Why did she not do it on the first day of class? Because being so young, the children needed time. As strangers to her and to one another, some of them would not have been willing right away to leave their mothers' sides to follow her. Rather than invite a failure, even with only one shy child, she waited until the time was ripe. By one month's time, every child had become acclimated to the class, and all were willing to participate.

One lesson in Alperson's class is paradigmatic. On this day, she requests the mothers to gather without their children on one side of the room so as to form an impromptu ensemble. The mothers are then given, at her prearranged signal, a task: They must simulate a rain shower that is to grow ever stronger until it crescendos in a violent downpour. Welcoming the women's creativity but not relying solely on it, she suggests a few ways to achieve this effect: snapping their fingers, clicking their tongues, or tapping in any way they can devise in order to imitate the rhythmic sounds of falling rain.

Now she gathers the children together and makes a "house" of her arms. She explains that, as it is a beautiful day, they will all go "outside" for a make-believe walk. She asks them to *listen* very carefully. Then she and the children begin to circulate slowly about the room in a group. At her signal, the mothers begin, tentatively and shyly at first, to make rain. Alperson and the children, wandering about the room on their walk, hear the sounds, and the children identify them as rain. Deciding at first that it seems to be only a small shower, they continue on their walk. However, as the storm continues and peaks, the children become anxious, and Alperson runs with them across the floor and gathers them into a shelter—the grand piano. Still exhorting the children to listen, she now signals the mothers to diminish the rain so that, at length, she and the children can go "outside" again and continue their walk in the "sunshine."

The purpose of this exercise is of course to teach the children to listen; on another level, it functions psychologically to enable them to transfer their trust to their teacher. None of the children, by now, run fearfully back to their mommies. For the mothers themselves, the exercise affords an opportunity to collaborate as a team, to lift their inhibitions about making sounds in unorthodox ways, and to realize that, for themselves as a group, in order to coordinate their efforts and function effectively, it is as important to listen attentively to one another as it is for the children to listen to them. This is true, Alperson points out, for every musical ensemble, instrumental or vocal.

Throughout the class Alperson experimented with many techniques to foster this multilevel functioning. Her evident love of experimentation and her willingness to take risks were important factors. Constantly on the alert for the idiosyncrasies of her group and exquisitely sensitive to responses evoked by any exercise she introduced, she seamlessly shifted, for example, ever so slightly from a quieter to a more active mode when a particular exercise seemed to tax the attention span of the children. Her comfort at abandoning one direction when she saw it was not working inspired me as a teacher, and in it I saw her deep and generous commitment to the individual children themselves, to their mothers, and to the music, rather than to any plan she had made for the day's session.

In experiences such as this, aesthetic education works not only to prepare young children for a lifetime of experiences in the arts but to strengthen the bonds between parents and children by providing them with rich, indelible occasions for learning and growing together. Fallout from these classes inevitably settles in the home. One young father who takes his son regularly to a Saturday-morning preschool music class at the Peabody Conservatory in Baltimore, a class in which parents are urged to participate, told me he's had several dreams about the experience; correspondingly, his son derives enormous pleasure from CDs given out by this school to reinforce the music heard in the class, and the little boy has already begun to ask his daddy when he can learn to play the cello and the piano.

Music from What Others Throw Away: Abu the Flutemaker

Beyond classes, what about *other* kinds of extrafamilial musical experiences for young children, ones designed expressly for them? Sometimes, if you are lucky, you simply happen upon them.

Picture a warm, breezy morning in June. You are in downtown Baltimore, an urban milieu characterized by racial, economic, and cultural diversity. A yellow tent has been set up on a grassy plot in Mount Vernon, near the Doric column erected in 1829 to honor George Washington and across from two of the most renowned cultural institutions of the city, the Peabody Conservatory and the Walters Art Museum. A homeless man in a colorful but frayed print shirt reclines on a bench under a tree. Four- and five-year-old children from a nearby inner-city prekindergarten have gathered along with their teachers on the grass around the yellow tent. A few curious adults who were strolling by join them. The children sit quietly side by side on a green tarpaulin set out in front of the tent. One little girl wears many pigtails braided with rainbow-colored ribbons. A diminutive fellow in a peaked cap turned backward sports a purple Ravens T-shirt, while a chubbier fellow sprawling nearby wears an oversized vest emblazoned with a Maryland crab; another child has dark curls that spill wildly over her checkered sundress. All are watching one man. He looks like a wizard. He calls himself Abu.

Abu the Flutemaker is a venerable Baltimore institution, an artist who, for many years, has been creating his own highly unusual musical instruments from objects other people have thrown away. For this performance, he has garbed himself in a woven Berber hat from Benin, West Africa, and a mustard-colored hand-printed robe from Nigeria. About thirty or so bright faces gaze up at him in wonder and anticipation as he smiles broadly and infectiously. A moment of silence ensues when we can hear only the squawking of birds and dull rumble of the city. Then, without comment, Abu begins to beat, steadily and energetically. His practiced hands move up and down on what look like two great columns decorated with blue bands that have been transformed into percussion instruments. Soon he moves over to three even larger columns, over six feet high, so that he has to climb up to reach them. These, he tells the children, are what he calls his *thunder drums.* He made them out of discarded porch columns, he says, and he plays them not with his bare hands but with sticks, and their sounds are deeper and more resonant. Moving dextrously, he covers the improvised stage that he and his assistant have created under the tent, and he shows the children all sorts of amazing instruments. He explains how he fashioned each one out of some kind of scrap material (a horn made from a hollowed-out bedpost from his grandmother's bed, a bass harp that was once a dented metal trash can, a clarinet made from a wooden chair leg, a xylophone from a dresser drawer and broken mirror pieces, kalimbas from empty sardine cans), and he demonstrates how each instrument, played with hands or mouth, can produce an exciting medley of musical sound.

Spellbound, the children watch and listen to this extraordinary man who teaches all of us that nothing need go to waste and that art can spring from the humblest beginnings. He blows, he beats, and sometimes he plays several instruments at once—including whistles and a nose flute and a single-stringed sitar. Then, just when the children can no longer contain themselves because they are so full of the desire to go up onstage with him and try out the instruments themselves, he asks slyly: "How about it? Do I have any drummers around here? Any musicians around here?" In this way, smiling with unconcealed pleasure, he invites all the children to join him. Everyone does. Abu sets the tempo and the children join in, many hammering and tapping on kalimbas made from sardine cans that Abu's assistant hands out to them.

Sitting on the grass listening, I am thrilled by this impromptu ensemble, by its rhythmical, musical, and dramatic force. Passersby stop to listen and to watch. The children keep playing as Abu switches over now to his flute; nobody wants it to end.

Children's Musical Theater

Admittedly, Abu is unique. But what about the multitude of other performance possibilities designed for very young audiences? Suppose you are a parent eager to introduce your child to concerts, musical theater, or opera but you live, let's suppose, in a region where grand opera is inaccessible. One possibility might be to check your local college or university, where, not infrequently, high-quality musical performances are offered for children. Sometimes these are presented by students in training, sometimes by professionals, and often by casts that include both. Normally, they are inexpensive. I imagine you asking: "But how can I tell in advance whether a show will be worthwhile? I don't have time to preview it. Even making time to take my child involves a major commitment." Unfortunately, you can't know beforehand. Risks, however, in the realm of the aesthetic, are worth taking. Try out your local company; give them a chance. Should the worst scenario occur and you find you have taken your child to a tasteless event, make the best of it; nearly every live performance has *something* to admire, even if it is only the ambience, and disappointments can be the spur to fruitful conversation afterward. Children may offer surprisingly astute insights when poorly crafted, incoherent pieces fail to hold their interest. Encouraged to explain, they can often peg just why and how they were bored. This, too, is part of their aesthetic education.

Music as Another Character Onstage

I am sitting between two boys, six and eight years old, in the second row of a spacious new theater at the George Mason University Center for the Arts in Fairfax, Virginia. (When taking children to performances in conventional spaces, do opt for seats as far front as possible, where, by virtue of their proximity to the stage, children can more easily be drawn in physically—perceptually and auditorily.) We are here for the premiere performance of a musical drama called *The Odyssey of Telémaca* by composer David Maddox and playwright Mary Hall Surface. We were attracted by the felicitous name of their venue: the Theater of the First Amendment. Subsequently, I learned that the soundtrack for this fine show won the coveted Parents' Choice Gold Award for 2004. Inspired by Homer's *Odyssey,* the story unfolds not in ancient Greece but in the Sonoran Desert of northern Mexico in 1885, and instead of featuring Telemachus, son of Odysseus, its hero— Omero—is father to a brave young daughter called Telémaca. Furthermore, instead of transforming Omero's men, later on, into swine, the Circe character here, La Llorona (the Weeping Woman)—who derives from Mexican legends and who appears as a magnificent towering puppet on stilts with a great papier-mâché head, clawlike hands, and diaphanous fluttering draperies—enchants Omero's men by turning them into javelinas. Musical numbers, moreover, are sung in Spanish as well as in English. Thus, this work pays homage not only to ancient

Greece but also to the luxuriant imagination of various Latino cultural traditions.

Seated up close, we peer into the orchestra pit and are startled by the musicians. Splendidly garbed in sombreros with brightly colored bands, their shoulders covered by brilliantly decorated handwoven serapes in patterns of orange, yellow, red, and blue, they smile at the children and offer friendly words of greeting. I point out the instruments to the boys and ask them to identify them. We count seven: a percussion ensemble, guitar, violin, bass, accordion, piano, and trumpet. The lights dim, and we settle into our seats.

The overture begins stunningly with a trumpet solo—soulful and melancholy. What a stroke of genius, for the children's attention is caught instantly by the slow tempo of this haunting music, so different from what they are used to hearing: a masterful choice, played in the dark with the curtain closed. The boys listen enraptured. They do *not* lean over to watch the trumpeter, even though he is in full view; it is the sheer beauty of the music itself that arrests them. It engages them so fully that they need no other kind of sensory experience. I am thinking: "We're off to an incredible start."

The curtain rises on a dramatic set, minimal but meticulously crafted—the stark expanse of a desert, a slanting horizon of yellow sand on a gentle diagonal that stretches across the stage with streaks of cloud above. In garments vibrantly colored and typical of Mexican art, a young mother appears stage left. With her baby in her arms, she recounts a legend about a scorpion who lies to a trusting turtle. Please carry me across the water, the scorpion asks, but the turtle refuses because he is afraid. When the scorpion promises, however, not to bite him, the turtle relents. Then, halfway across, the scorpion bites the turtle. When the turtle asks the scorpion why he has done so, since now both of them must drown, the scorpion replies that he could not do otherwise because he is a scorpion. Thus, at the start, the children in the audience are introduced to themes of trust and betrayal, essence and existence, promises made but not kept, and to the inevitability of one's fate.

As to the music! How I wish I could convey its tangy contagious liveliness. Skillfully, the composer matches his tempos and orchestration to the characters' shifting moods and to the changing circumstances of their lives so that close emotional ties unite the music with the story. Bright, bubbly dance numbers alternate with yearning and anguish as distance in space and time grows between family members in the story. Maddox, a composer both whimsical and serious, eclectic but thoroughly original, draws inspiration not only from the mariachi traditions of northern Mexico but from what he calls Tex-Mex and Tex-swing from the southwestern USA as well as from Asian music, polkas, and waltzes. He composes, he told me, always with the story in mind and even thinks of his music as "another character onstage." This is why the band is in costume: They are a part of the same world as the actors and actresses. The goal is to create an integration of visual and aural experience that opens up "the magic we are presenting." For Maddox, hiding from the audience is not an option. He is after revelation. He wants the children in the audience to grasp and absorb whatever makes his music *sound* the way it does, to *wait* for the music to happen, and to feel its presence as a fully dramatic participant in the action as well as the mood. That he achieves this was proved nearly a year after the performance. Visiting in the home of the older of the two boys who had attended with me, I asked him casually whether he still recalled the performance we'd gone to the previous spring called *The Odyssey of Telémaca*. "Oh," he said, smiling, without a moment's hesitation, "you mean the one with the trumpet solo?"

Intermission

The older of these boys was prepared for the show by his grandmother. Wisely believing that it would enrich his experience, she had been reading to him over several weeks from an abridged version of the *Odyssey*. The younger child, on the other hand, came with no clear expectations. During the intermission, it was clear to me that the older boy seemed slightly dismayed. He was enjoying the show, but, he confessed, he felt disappointed because he found the story so different from what he had learned and anticipated. There was a sense of letdown that the younger child had been spared, and this confession interested me because, as I note, his well-meant preparation seemed not only to cause him to feel betrayed but also to prevent him from enjoying the production in its own right rather than feel continual remorse for what it was not, namely, Homer. Still, the preparation gave him something the other child lacked: perspective.

Fascinatingly, by the end of the show, this boy had come around completely. He had made peace with *Telémaca*, had fallen under its spell. And I think that, *because* of his advance preparation and the challenges it presented, he went away, all in all, with an enhanced and extremely rich emotional and intellectual experience. As John Dewey writes, "The [beholder] as well as the artist has to perceive, meet, and overcome problems . . . in order to perceive esthetically, he must remake his past experiences so that they can enter integrally into a new pattern." For this eight-year-old boy, *The Odyssey of Telémaca*, after Homer, had— on account of his prior exposure—offered him puzzles and problems to solve, and while those problems may at first have felt irksome and interfered with his pleasure, they had, by the end, contributed significantly to the depth of his aesthetic encounter.

Keeping Quiet in the Dark

Moving now from choices about which performance to take a child to and from questions about preparation (to which we'll return), let's think about the movement of a small child from her own private world of fantasy and imagination into the domain of shared cultural experience. We can see right away that an initial hurdle comes from the barriers she encounters in the conventions of the theater and the concert hall itself, which she cannot help but experience at first as novel and restrictive. To adults, of course, these conventions seem second nature; we scarcely give them a nod. But what are they? They include the strictly demarcated boundary between the performers and the audience in terms of space and light (the clear separation, in other words, of stage from seating), the imposed silence of the audience, and the expected coalescence of the members of the audience into an undifferentiated, behaviorally passive mass. Everybody in the audience wants to hear the performers onstage, but *nobody*, a child soon learns, wants to hear the voices of his neighbors in the theater. Just to articulate these conventions that we take completely for granted is to realize how, to an active, curious, outspoken three- to seven-year-old, they might seem artificial and oppressive.

It is worth noting that these bounded spaces of cultural performance and the prescribed behaviors associated with them—a darkened house, a lighted stage, and respectful silence—which have become familiar to adults but seem so unnatural at first to children, are a relatively recent phenomenon in theater history.

Consider the custom of a darkened auditorium and a lighted stage. Actually, these related practices did not arise and become standard in European theater until the end of the nineteenth century, when the flamboyant, eccentric, and brilliantly innovative American dancer Loïe Fuller took fin de siècle Paris by storm. To dramatize the effects of her whirling diaphanous garments and limb extensions, Fuller insisted on a darkened theater. Illuminating her performances with mobile magic lanterns and gels and projected images, she began—apparently after befriending Marie Curie—to apply fluorescent chemicals to her fabrics so that darkness offstage became a structural element of her art as well as a foil for her spectacular displays. Before her, however, concert and theatrical halls were always lit so that people could observe one another as well as the action onstage. With the advent, however, of Wagnerian opera, of Loïe Fuller's dance, and of early turn-of-the-century cinema, late-arriving spectators often found themselves escorted to their seats by means of lighted matches. Some of them were at first, as we can imagine, quite perturbed by these new practices. Thus, to know a bit of history may help us to empathize more readily with our children for whom such conventions probably seem, as they once did to the adults who initially encountered them, counterintuitive, bizarre, and even a little bit frightening.

As a brief aside, take the ordinary Euro-American convention of eating meals with spoons, forks, and knives, which seems quite natural to children brought up in this way. The naturalness of such conventions shifts, however, as soon as children notice that some people use chopsticks, for example, or that Europeans handle their utensils somewhat differently from Americans, and that there are many ways to set a table. What I want to suggest at this point is that to put oneself into the psyche of a child, it helps occasionally to pretend to be a traveler in a foreign land or a wanderer in the annals of history.

Spellbound or Squirming? How Long Can a Child Sit Still?

The attention span of young children is limited, and performance length must count as an important factor when we consider the suitability of an artistic event for them. Figure that any child who is able to sit spellbound for an hour or two while being read to would be a good candidate for an adult-length production, provided the event has been well chosen and the child is rested and prepared. Some children, however, simply fidget by nature and quickly grow impatient. While this trait is subject to modification, and while age and context are critical variables, I want to suggest that there are genuine personality differences that affect our ability to concentrate. Given at birth, children's temperamental differences deserve respect.

Even to observe infants less than one year old is to note a wide spectrum in attention span. I remember a little fellow, for example, who at nine months of age was given a large silver orb—one of those shiny spheres children used to make by sticking their tinfoil chewing gum wrappers together. Lying on his back or tummy in the playpen, still too young to crawl, this infant would regard the scintillating object with intense fascination and try awkwardly to manipulate it. Watching him and trying to fathom what was captivating his gaze, his mother thought it might have been the glint of the light on its facets and folds. In any case, the baby was capable of contemplating his orb for hours in blissful contentment and required no other source of stimulation while he was in that state. Later on, this child grew up to display unusual powers of concentration. Other infants of his age, however, might well have contemplated the silver ball for just a few moments and then moved on to other sources of interest. If your child is normally jumpy and skittish, I would, for her sake and yours, wait before expecting her to sit through a full-length opera, concert, ballet, or musical. Works made expressly for children that last for one hour rather than two might be ideal. Still, even as I write these words, I realize that there are some young children who are so precociously drawn to one art form or another that, in its presence, their normal behavior completely shifts. Music, I warrant, is preeminent among those arts.

Seeing It Again on Video

DVDs and videos lend themselves to a high degree of individualized manipulation and thus can provide experiences adapted to the temporal needs of young children. A video can be paused and then continued so that the timing of an experience is controlled to match the requirements of a viewer. Children can stop watching to have a drink, ask a question, or make a trip to the bathroom, and parents who utilize these media do well to take advantage of this perk. At home, also, rather than in a public space, children's responses, inquiries, and possible anxieties can be heard and addressed on the spot without disturbing the aesthetic experiences of strangers. While this is a tremendous boon, it might be best to avail oneself of it reflectively. Our previous training in spectatorship notwithstanding, we might, with respect to these new media, consider altering our habits. When a child wants to stop a video or recording, say, to respond or to repeat something, or when a parent wants to make an interpretation or offer an explanation, the integrity of the work itself can be disrupted. A work of high quality deserves perhaps an initial and a subsequent viewing without breaks.

One option I do *not* recommend is the use of electronic devices as partial preparation for live performances of a given work. This ploy is fraught with all the disadvantages discussed earlier with regard to the setting up of expectations that may be thwarted. All live productions necessarily depart from any electronically reproduced version. The reverse might be preferable: In other words, the use of a video or DVD *after* your child has experienced the live performance and wants to go back for more. Needless to say, the watching of home videos does not prepare children for becoming part of a conventional audience in a public sphere, where personal interchange must be postponed and where the curtain goes up whether one is ready or not. Live theater, as the ancient Greeks developed it and as it has existed cross-culturally for centuries, functions importantly as a richly *communal* affair, an experience that, in fact, actually constitutes communities and reinforces them. Even sitting together with strangers in a darkened movie theater conveys something of this spirit, which is absent during a private viewing.

Children's Questions During the Performance

What about interruptions? At a recent outdoor production of *Hansel and Gretel* by and for children at the Little Red Schoolhouse in the Berkshires, I saw a lady silence her three-year-old granddaughter quite crudely by clapping her hand over the child's mouth. This struck me as a humiliating gesture, almost like muzzling a dog. Other adults respond to children's questions sotto voce during a performance, and still others ignore such questions out of embarrassment or irritation or with the covert expectation that if they are not responded to they will cease. This last approach seems highly infelicitous and very likely to backfire. One mother I observed, however, did something extremely inventive and salubrious. She pointed out to her four-year-old (in the same *Hansel and Gretel* production) that, while the set was being changed and the log cabin in the clearing was being exchanged for the witch's gingerbread house, there would be—for just a few minutes—an intermission and therefore a good time to talk. I would advocate for something of this sort. By answering softly, by whispering a brief reply, you are tacitly reminding your child of the convention of silence while satisfying him (at least partially) and reassuring him that you have heard his question and that you are still with him experiencing the music and/or drama together. In other words, you are instructing and assisting him without jeopardizing the experience of your fellow audience members.

With regard to concentration during the performance, notwithstanding the personality givens mentioned above, there are steps that can be taken to improve a child's attention span. Above all, I would advocate for providing good role models. After all, one of the most reliable motivators of human behavior is imitation. What beloved adults do is, for better or for worse, reiterated by their children. We can, therefore, model good concentration. In addition, we can try to provide experiences of such compelling interest and pleasure that children will want to remain fully present so as not to miss a trick. One of the beauties of opera as an artistic form, in this regard, is its multifaceted appeal, its feast of both vocal and instrumental music, its narrative played out on an often elaborately designed stage by costumed characters who appear and vanish and act and mime and often dance as well as sing with ravishing, painstakingly trained voices.

Concentration during a performance is also improved by preparation and knowledge. Just as you would consult a guidebook before taking a journey to a previously unbeheld corner of the globe or ask a well-traveled friend to give you some pointers before your departure, so it is with children before a musical or indeed any performance. As usual, there are no foolproof recipes, no cookie-cutter solutions. Later on, we will consider *Hansel and Gretel* in this light because this century-old work could well serve as an excellent first grand-opera choice for children and one that most parents *can* in fact prepare them for. Few adults, on the other hand, encountering contemporary works for children, can possibly know what to expect and therefore, even with the best intentions, be able to provide anything but the most rudimentary introduction.

To Texaco with Love

While the finest productions made expressly for children are complete and delightful unto themselves, it is encounters with masterworks in the opera house, the concert hall, and the ballet theater with full orchestra, chorus, and all the accoutrements of these complex and elaborate arts that may be seen as culminating experiences.

How would you feel, for example, about taking your five-, six-, or eight-year-old to Humperdinck's *Hansel and Gretel*? Or to Mozart's *Magic Flute*? Or to Ravel's *L'enfant et les sortilèges*, or Bizet's *Carmen*? How about Prokofiev's *Peter and the Wolf*, or Tchaikovsky's ballets *The Nutcracker* or *Swan Lake*? Although these later works are not operas, much about them is, from the viewpoint of a child, similar. Grand opera, however, because of its formal conventions, sometimes proves a difficult art form for young children, but it is one that, once one has been captivated by it, may easily grow into a lifelong passion.

For decades in the United States, countless children from coast to coast were introduced to opera by listening to the radio. For more than half a century, Texaco sponsored live Saturday-afternoon broadcasts of performances at the Metropolitan Opera House in New York City. One colleague of mine, a senior professor of history who grew up in Indiana, said that as a boy he would stretch out on the living room couch to listen to these programs. After a while, he began to look forward to the *entr'acte* quizzes and interviews, with their sophisticated repartee among divas, critics, and guests. Even though he failed to make complete sense of what was being talked about and certainly had an insufficient frame of reference for the arcane musical references being bandied about, he nevertheless got "hooked as a kid." Years before he ever witnessed a live production, he considered himself an opera buff. When he *did* see his first staged opera, he realized that he had previously visualized every character, scene, and action in his mind. With flecks of gray dappling his hair, he is now an aficionado.

Telling Aida from Amneris

Visualization sometimes turns out to be a problem for young children when they are taken to an opera for the first time. The problem can be illustrated by my own earliest experience of Verdi's *Aida* at the Metropolitan Opera House when I was just under nine. In part because *Aida* was my first opera, I have a special affection for it. Yet, when I recall that day, my chagrin and disappointment are easy to revive. How betrayed I felt by the production in spite of its pageantry and glamour. Having been told the story in advance, I had created a mental image of each character. I had envisioned the enslaved Aida as a lovely and delicate heroine; whereas her rival, Amneris, had taken the form of a woman of unsurpassed ugliness. When the curtains parted to reveal Amneris, my expectations were so thwarted that I became instantly confused and lost track of the plot. The role of the malevolent Egyptian princess who abuses her royal powers to steal away Aida's beloved Radames was played by a svelte, gorgeously costumed, raven-haired mezzo, whereas my darling Aida, the Ethiopian princess, notwithstanding her heavenly voice, lumbered clumsily about the stage, her formless body lost in folds of heavy drapery. I could not orient myself for a while because it was so difficult for me to comprehend the casting choices, which had been based, of course, not on appearance but on voice. As an opera neophyte, I did not understand that the range and quality of the singers' *voices* are what matter, not what they look like. I just wanted the two singers to be reversed! Nothing else in the production (not even all the colorfully attired live animals onstage) compensated me for this perceived treachery. I remember trying to talk to my father about it afterward, but he, a true opera lover, turned perfidious as well. Chuckling at my misery, my childish naïveté, and my literalism, he simply told me to use my imagination at the opera and not be so concrete. I had been burned, though, and it took the promise of Humperdinck's *Hansel and Gretel* to lure me back to the Met the following season.

Grand Opera: *Hansel and Gretel*

Hansel and Gretel is in many ways an ideal first opera for children. Its music is melodic and accessible, its protagonists are children, its plot is a well-known fairy tale. Furthermore, on a practical note, because of its long-standing tradition of being performed in winter at holiday time (a tradition that goes back, incidentally, to its premiere in Weimar on December 23, 1893, under the baton of Richard Strauss), it is an opera frequently performed in the United States and Europe today and one that can therefore actually be heard and seen live by a multitude of children.

Let's pretend that you have already purchased your tickets and are ready to prepare your child for the performance. How to begin? I would say to start not with the music, even though, of course, this is paramount, but with a story. Start with *your* story. In my case, that would be not the tale of the libretto per se but the story of my own first experience with *Hansel and Gretel* when I was a child. Why? Because this genre of narrative provides a tantalizing starting point in the arts; children get enormous pleasure from hearing about the childhoods of their parents, grandparents, aunts, uncles, and teachers. Rarely do they listen passively to such tales. And since, of course, your own experience was inevitably different from what the child's will be, you can take this occasion to explain how the conception of a musical work and its mise-en-scène change from era to era and from one production and performance to another. The essence—that is to say, the *music*, however—remains. What matters is that, with your childhood story, you are conveying your remembered pleasure and establishing an important thread of continuity between your life and your child's in terms of the specific work of art.

The Gingerbread Witch and *The Magic Mountain*

With *Hansel and Gretel*, I would revisit the fairy tale. What about staging a cooperative retelling or reenacting, as in a playlet, with different voices of family members taking the parts? Because in Humperdinck's opera, the words are sung rather than spoken, you might experiment with this for fun. Singing words rather than saying them always seems strange even to first-time operagoers well past childhood; therefore, playing with this mode in advance can help it seem less alien when it is encountered onstage. It is also worthwhile to explain to children that fairy tales are not "one-ofs," as Maria Tatar puts it in her *Classic Fairy Tales,* but that they exist, rather, in many versions, since for generations they were not written down but transmitted by storytellers whose memories were imprecise and who often put their own spin on their tales. To do this might be to forestall reactions like the one of the little boy at *The Odyssey of Telémaca,* for the Humperdinck-Wette libretto can be seen as just another variant. For a child, knowledge of this may help to prepare her for the moments when an event she has expected to take place in the story is not in fact occurring onstage, whereas events never mentioned in the well-known versions of the fairy tale with which she is familiar take place instead. A thoughtful adult, however, might *not* want to reveal in advance just what these alterations are. I would simply say: Be on the lookout. Good preparation entails not giving everything away.

In fact, the version set by Humperdinck differs from the now-classic version by the brothers Grimm in several details. The brother and sister, for instance, are punished in the opera not because their stepmother has an intrinsically nasty and selfish personality but because they, particularly Hansel, have failed to perform their household duties in her absence. Instead of working, they play, and Gretel persuades Hansel to dance with her to one of the most famous melodies in the opera. It is hardly necessary, however, to tell this in advance. Every child will discover it for herself. At the end, however, the operatic version differs dramatically from that of the brothers Grimm with respect to the witch's death. In the Humperdinck, her demise releases a spell, which she had cast on dozens of children who nibbled, over time, at her house. These children, whom she previously transformed into gingerbread, are now, as Hansel and Gretel tap them one by one to the music, released from the immobilized state in which she had entrapped them. As they come alive, they sing and rejoice. Hansel and Gretel thus end the story as triumphant liberators not only of themselves but also of a community of bewitched children, and in a supremely satisfying moment for the child in all of us, the baked witch herself returns to the stage, emerging from the oven in the form of a witch-shaped cake, a metamorphosis that is inscribed also in the music. The curtain falls on a finale that celebrates solidarity, community, freedom, and the reuniting of parents with their children.

So much for the plot. After all, "music," as Joseph Kerman puts it in *Opera as Drama*, "is the essential artistic medium in opera, the medium that bears the ultimate responsibility for articulating drama." With *Hansel and Gretel*, I would focus in advance on just three numbers: the children's duet from act 1, "Brother, Come Dance with Me"; Gretel's song "A Little Man Stands in the Wood" from the opening of act 2; and the prayer "Now I Lay Me Down to Sleep," from the end of act 2. Each of these exquisite melodies is easy to learn and can be played on the piano or rehearsed electronically. Repetition helps so that the music becomes familiar enough for the children to sing or hum along. In our house, my sister and I would dance to the duet, performing in sequence the motions of tapping with our feet, clapping with our hands, nodding with our heads, and clicking with our fingers (which was always the hardest part). One wants to assure that, by the time of the performance, each of these numbers will be recognizable and welcomed with delight.

What if the opera is sung in German with or without titles? This is not a problem. Even when opera is sung in English, colorful orchestration often overwhelms the vocalists so that, unless one knows a libretto by heart, one never grasps all the words. What matters is being able to follow the story without getting lost, feeling sufficiently familiar with what is going on so that one can relax and take in all the wondrous effects that the operatic genre provides.

For me, as a little girl, and I am sure for many children, the most magical moment in *Hansel and Gretel* comes when the brother and sister fall asleep in the woods, and the covey of protecting angels appears to keep them safe throughout the night. In the Metropolitan Opera version, these angels, played by children, wore stiff golden robes and halos and seemed to float in a serene procession across the sky to celestial music that appeared to descend from heaven itself. I wonder how many other children's dreams have been visited, like mine, by these gracefully moving angels who continue to glide and sway across the horizon of the mind in pastel visions of serenity.

Scored for high voices, *Hansel and Gretel* requires that women— a soprano and a mezzo—sing the roles of Hansel and the Sandman. This gender bending may, for some children, seem distracting, and therefore it might be advisable to address it in advance. How lengthy an explanation to offer is moot and depends on the sensibilities of your child. What can be stressed is the overriding importance of *imagination* (although, as we saw earlier, my father's conversation with me about *Aida* failed to achieve the desired result. That was, however, after the fact.)

Historically, of course, from classical antiquity through the Shakespearean age, men have played female roles, and in certain forms of Chinese opera, only men perform, whereas in others the reverse is true; in still other traditions, only the voice type matters: Japanese Kabuki actors are exclusively male. Audiences, in all of these situations, cope. Here we have the reverse, and some children will scarcely notice the actual genders of the performers, absorbed as they are in the magical world onstage. Others will not be happy when Hansel appears as a woman dressed up as a boy. A first-rate production, however, and the glorious music itself, should evoke the willing suspension of disbelief, so that, by the time the sister and brother realize they are lost in the forest in act 2, even the most skeptical in the audience find themselves bewitched. The orchestration, in truly Wagnerian terms at this point, conveys an almost palpable sense of anxiety, dread, and foreboding.

Playing the music of the opera in advance in its entirety, showing a videotape of a previous production, or, indeed, spending too much time in detailed preparation would not, in my view, be wise. Spontaneity and surprise are of the essence. Wonder (as Bettelheim wrote) counts more than the best-laid groundwork. This is why preparation for aesthetic experience must not give too much away. A moment from my own childhood returns by way of example. Nestled in a cavernous armchair in my family's living room, I have been absorbed for hours reading and have not heard my mother call me. She enters the room quietly, looks down at me, and asks me gently what I'm reading. When I tell her it is *The Magic Mountain* by Thomas Mann, she is silent for a moment and then gives an audible sigh: "Oh, how I envy you!" she exclaims.

Glancing up in wonder, I ask her why.

"Because," she returns, "I would give anything to have the experience of reading that book again for the first time!"

This—the unique encounter with a work of art for the first time—is precisely what we do not want to kill with our preparations. That incomparable thrill. The joy and wonder of a child's amazement. And all of this is true not only for *Hansel and Gretel* but for *The Magic Flute, Die Fledermaus, The Music Man, Into the Woods, Oklahoma!, Peter and the Wolf, The Nutcracker, Swan Lake, Sleeping Beauty, Coppélia,* and a host of other masterworks.

"Please, Can We Go Again Tomorrow?" (Follow-up)

What comes afterward? Are there any follow-up activities that might be valuable? This is a topic dear to my heart and one all too often neglected. I am passionately in favor of follow-up. Far too many children today are yanked without respite from one peak experience to another and afforded no chance to process what they have just heard, seen, and felt.

Immediately after the performance, I would opt for an unprogrammed hour: just free time. Worst would be plunging from one stimulating activity directly into another (opera performance, friend's birthday party, family gathering), wresting the child away and distracting him immediately from all the new perceptions he has just had. Earlier, we spoke of the importance of modulating, as from one key to another, and that is of the essence here. Ideally, one wants to create for a child a psychic and physical space in which to linger for a while in the mood created by the opera. I would bite my tongue to avoid asking questions such as "Did you *like* it?" or "What part did you like *best*?" and so forth. Experiencing a great work of art can be, like running a race, heady, and require time afterward to wind down and recuperate. John Dewey, often cited in these pages, is excellent on this point. An aesthetic experience must be fully undergone and savored and be allowed to move toward its own consummation and closure, he teaches. By ensuring some quiet time afterward, parents can do much to make each aesthetic experience more meaningful for their children.

Perhaps the next day, I would encourage a child to follow up on the performance. Most children need no prompting. Spontaneously, they will hum, sing, dance, draw, dress up, and ask to hear the music. Listening to the music again and again now feels quite different, as children will actually tell you, because they can associate it with scenes and events and characters. Some parents and children sit at the piano and play favorite melodies, or a young child might want to compose music of his own, or even make up his own opera. He might want to describe his experience to a friend, or write about it to a faraway grandparent, aunt, or uncle, or make some drawings of it, or act it out, or dance it, or imagine what could be done with a completely different fairy tale or story. It doesn't matter what. I know a little girl who, after being taken to *The Mikado* at the New York City Opera, came home and spontaneously produced a whole set of pencil drawings of the characters: Yum Yum, Nanki Poo, Katisha, and the others. At her mother's suggestion, they photocopied her pictures and sent them off to Beverly Sills, who was then the company's artistic director. Sills replied with a charming note and an autographed photo, which the little girl cherished and displayed for many years in her bedroom. What matters is that there *be* follow-up. For many children, especially when parents cooperate, that follow-up can go on for weeks. A child may pretend for a long time to be a character in the opera, designate others as such, and call for repeated enactments of the story. Very young children employ puppets, dolls, and stuffed animals and beg to hear the music again and again. Whatever they do, cherish it. For when this follow-up occurs, it means that a work of art is being internalized and becoming a part of what I have elsewhere called the *museum of the mind.*

Swan Lake with Closed Eyes

But suppose your child does not like the opera or, as in my case with *Aida,* has problems with certain aspects of the performance. Under such circumstances, I would strongly advocate for respecting the disaffection and encouraging her to articulate whatever it was that bothered or disappointed her. As was pointed out earlier when I mentioned Kant and the antinomy of taste, it never works to try to convince someone to like a work of art. That would be tantamount to trying to persuade someone to fall in love. Philosophers writing on aesthetics (think of Kant, Hume, and their intellectual descendants) have tried for centuries to resolve this problem of taste, namely, that whereas people are absolutely convinced by their own aesthetic preferences and cannot be persuaded to alter them by reasonable arguments, it seems at the same time intuitive to suppose that there are in fact standards of taste that should be able to be agreed to by all reasonable minds. Yet, such is not apparently the case. Children have a right to their preferences. Fortunately, however, we are able to count on the fact that their naïve tastes gradually undergo modification and development. This occurs principally, however, through pleasurable exposure to superior examples of the art in question. Persuasion is never the best route.

A little boy I know was taken to an enchanting production of *Swan Lake* by the American Ballet Theater. He had the good fortune to have a front-row seat in one of the preferred boxes at the Metropolitan Opera House in New York. Musically gifted, this child had been introduced to Tchaikovsky by his grandfather and had fallen in love with the composer. To his mother's chagrin, he spent the bulk of the performance with his eyes closed, just leaning back listening rapturously to the glorious music. Very upset at first, his mother felt she had wasted his ticket and that he had missed the essential element of the experience since the ballet is, obviously, a spectacle, a *visual* art. As she studied his face, however, she could see that he was blissfully contented. Later on, when they discussed it, he explained to her how much the music meant to him, how great it felt to him just to be there and to hear it played live by the orchestra, how all the dancing onstage had simply felt distracting to him and was spoiling his concentration on the music. At length, his mother relaxed; she had learned a lesson herself. For ultimately, what matters is that the experience be a positive one and one the child is eager to repeat.

Here is another anecdote to illustrate this point. One morning I went with a group of eight-year-olds to an exhibit of contemporary art at the Neuberger Museum in Purchase, New York. After the children had been toured around and shown the art in the galleries—principally sculpture, installation works, and paintings—they were taken to a room in the education wing, given paper and pencils, and asked to draw from memory any object that had particularly engaged them. One little girl ran up to me and asked me whether they could draw *anything* in the whole museum that interested them. I said yes. When I looked over the drawings later, I saw to my amazement that this child had rendered a piano. Where had this been? I wondered. Then I remembered: Apparently, a musical event had been scheduled to take place in the galleries on the afternoon of our visit, and a piano had been installed there in advance. As we walked by it on our tour, I barely noticed it. But the little girl had.

This child (a piano student, as I later learned) had taken less interest in the visual art than in that familiar instrument, which caught her eye right away and to which she felt instantly drawn. It was this object that transformed the unknown museum into an appealing, friendly space for her. Her piano image, while crude, was fully recognizable and drawn with as much painstaking effort as the pictures made by other children who represented works of art in the collection. To have criticized her would have been hurtful and might well, I think, have left her with negative feelings about her trip to the museum—a place to which, ideally, we would wish her to return. Capitalizing, then, on all positive aspects of a child's experience is key.

As I was leaving a recent performance of *Hansel and Gretel,* my eyes lit on two particularly demure little girls who, in a trancelike state, squeezed by the crowd, were being propelled toward the doors of the opera house. Close behind them, I was just able to catch the following exchange:

"Oh!" one said with a sigh. "For my birthday, I want to *have* an opera."

"Can I be in it?" asked the other.

The magic had clearly worked.

Chapter Four

What Is Too Scary?

Would a bird build its nest if it did not have its instinct for confidence in the world?
— Gaston Bachelard, *The Poetics of Space*

A person who has never been afraid has no imagination.
— Robert Henri, *The Art Spirit*

What is too scary for children? What is too disturbing? A *New York Times* article reports increasing instances of violence and profanity in movies rated acceptable for children. Concerned researchers at Harvard's School of Public Health conclude that physicians should discuss media consumption with parents of young children. Should we be concerned?

Some cultural experiences may be frightening or confusing to children, and these two reactions are closely related, because when we do not understand something it can seem dangerous to us. For reasons having to do with the variables of culture, temperament, gender, age, and circumstance, children differ greatly in their capacity to tolerate being afraid and in the objects of their fear. An image or story one child finds frightening at age three may prove to be less so for the same child at age six when, say, a foregrounded psychological issue she had been struggling with has been laid to rest and she is on firmer footing both emotionally and cognitively speaking. By contrast, some cultural experiences that prove disturbing to older children and adults may not be so to young children, whose frame of reference is simply too narrow for them to grasp the inherent danger. We see this clearly in wartime reports concerning children, which provide illustrations of situations in which adults are more frightened than children. Not only is their circle of awareness narrower, their comprehension of future consequences is correspondingly more limited.

A Pandora's Box of Fears

In general, we might anticipate that children who are securely attached, who feel sure of their parents' love and affection, and who are not overprotected might prove less vulnerable than others to scenes of aggression, abandonment, and loss. But this would be a mistake, because gender and personality traits and all the other variables play their roles. To me, the fact that reactions are not predictable is part of what makes the work challenging. In one family, three children all turn out to have different fears and different rates of change and growth. One cringes at the appearance of the wicked stepmother in *Snow White*; another is genuinely unthreatened by her; a third finds her funny. We can speculate as to the causes of these differences and try to respond accordingly, but the limits of our comprehension teach us that we must try to remain ready to welcome the unexpected, especially when it is a question of the psyches of young children, who are changing before our eyes.

Typical sources of fear for most children include a spectrum of representations that reflect, in diverse forms, feelings of disempowerment vis-à-vis their inner and outer worlds. Darkness, for example, can be frightening because, without light, our loved ones are no longer present to help us contain our anxieties. Vision, our major source of knowledge and power, disappears in the dark. Without light, we lose our bearings in the external world. Images of open jaws and teeth bring anxiety to young children who are still struggling with impulses around sucking, swallowing, biting, drinking, eating, and being eaten. Large animals, threatening monsters and ogres, dragons and dinosaurs, all remind children of their smallness and physical frailty. Raging fires and floods can seem analogous to exciting bodily impulses gone out of control. Weapons (especially firearms) and sudden loud noises (such as explosions) disrupt the equilibrium of the relaxed body. Suspenseful scenes of hunt and chase are terrifying if you feel you are, or could be, the quarry. Images of unleashed fury and its aftermath unsettle children whose own anger is poorly channeled and in danger of erupting as well as children who suffer the unbridled rage of others and children who live in families where anger is an unacceptable emotion.

Masks hide people's faces and make you unsure of recognizing the people you know, so that what you previously held to be true is suddenly called into question. Falling from a great height is another primitive fear, as are eyes that seem to survey and follow you. One young city girl, vacationing with her family in a cabin of knotty pine, became so terrified of the knotholes (perhaps because they seemed like eyes watching her, although she could not articulate the reason for her fear) that, in desperation to pacify her so that she could sleep at night, her mother came up with the scheme of covering them all with Band-Aids.

Dinosaurs in the San Bernardino Hills

Reactions to frightening cultural experiences are not easy to gauge—in advance, during, or afterward. Sometimes a child who seems to be doing fine during a movie, play, or story suffers a severe delayed reaction. Here is an example.

At a weekend-long wedding in the San Bernardino hills of California, a young couple has arrived with their three-year-old adopted son. The boy's father suggests we take the little fellow for a walk in the hills. Beforehand, this father mentioned that just a few days earlier they had seen the movie *Jurassic Park.* I was speechless. Even director Steven Spielberg had been quoted in the press as saying he would not allow his own young children to see the film. Nonchalantly, I asked the father how his little boy had reacted during the screening and was told that he had done fine. No bad reactions at all.

"But what about the scene in which the dinosaur devours the lawyer while he's sitting on the toilet? I asked.

"Oh, that was fine," I was told.

"Okay," I said. "But how about the scene where the dinosaurs break into the kitchen, of all places, and try to hunt the children down there?"

Again, I was assured there had been no problem.

It's a beautiful day, and we start up the hill with the little boy between us holding each of us by the hand. Suddenly I feel his small fingers grip mine tightly. "Are there any dinosaurs around here?" he asks.

"No, no," we assure him.

A few paces later, he repeats the question. "Are you *sure*, Daddy?" he asks.

Throughout the weekend, this little guy continues to be on first alert, looking out for dinosaurs. Obsessed by images of them, he lives in terror that they will materialize at any moment. This appears to be, then, a delayed reaction unanticipated by his first-time parents. Their tendency to pooh-pooh his clamoring and to brush off his anxious questions is no doubt intended to help him achieve what they take to be a desirable tough-guy stance, but to me he doesn't seem ready to adopt such an attitude. His imagination is working furiously, and another approach might be to go along with it: Draw some dinosaurs with him, let him name them. Try to enlist the fantasy and work with it rather than push it away.

Age and gender, as noted, are obviously factors here, but personality and temperament matter just as much, and the usual stereotypes prove unhelpful or even detrimental. We all know feisty little girls and timorous boys, and we all know children who suddenly turn fearful and others who overcome their skittishness. A parent's comfort level with his or her own aggressive feelings and with representations of violence and suspense is probably the single most significant variable—after innate disposition—in determining any child's response to frightening cultural experiences.

What Maisie Knew

Three-and-a-half-year-old Maisie was playing in her father's study in Seattle one day when, fatefully, she pulled a picture book off the shelf. It was not, however, a book for children. It was Art Spiegelman's *Maus,* a memoir in comic-book form of the trials of the author-artist's father as a Polish Jew during World War II. Fascinated by its images, Maisie began looking through it and demanded to be told what it was about. Her father, Andy, could at that point have refused by saying simply, "No, this is a book for grown-ups." Instead, he chose to peruse it with her and to explain aspects of it, commencing with the first episode, where little Arty complains to his survivor father, Vladek, that his friends were teasing him when his roller skate came loose and that they called him a "rotten egg." As Maisie and her dad worked their way along in the book, the little girl noticed and pointed out numerous details, including the fact that, as she put it, the moon is "broken." The moon, in point of fact, is represented repeatedly as fractured by an enormous black swastika.

As they progressed, the book frightened Maisie more and more until at last her father stopped reading it to her, but still her fear did not abate. She refused to go into her father's study anymore, saying, as she put it, that the *Maus* book might attack her. At length, in despair, Andy asked her what *she* thought they ought to do about the problem (a ploy in the vein of the wise jester's tactic with Princess Lenore in James Thurber's wonderful picture book *Many Moons*). Maisie immediately came up with a suggestion: Why not write a letter to Art Spiegelman to ask *him* what to do? Obediently, Andy sat down at the computer and faithfully transcribed her words. Several months later a package arrived from New York addressed to Maisie. It included a letter from Art Spiegelman exhorting Maisie not to fear the *Maus* book and some of his other works made especially for children. He told her that he himself is a daddy.

A year later, at about four and a half, Maisie visited me with her parents. Riffling through my piles of old *New Yorkers*, she suddenly appeared with one and announced: "Look! It's an Art Spiegelman."

Indeed, it was one of his *New Yorker* covers. Thus, her father's choice not to deflect her initial interest in *Maus*, while causing some serious anxiety, had also led to a complex chain of experiences that catapulted the little girl into a process of creative problem solving and learning. Clearly, she had learned in many ways from those experiences, and who can tell how this early exposure to *Maus* will recur in her life and work? The inspired moment in parenting clearly came when Andy gave the problem over to *her* for solution. By doing this, he extracted her from her previous state of helplessness and invited her to take the initiative regarding her anxiety. Importantly, he didn't stop there but followed through by implementing her ingenious proposal.

Adults' and Children's Fears May Differ

Adverse reactions to depictions of violence may be found not only among children who have witnessed violence firsthand and who have suffered as victims of physical assault but also among children who have been carefully shielded from such scenes. Yet negative reactions are often complicated by the ambivalence of intense fascination, as in the case of the art historian mentioned earlier who, as a child, loved to scare himself by gazing at Gustave Doré's illustrations of scenes from Dante's *Inferno.*

At the Walters Art Museum in Baltimore, a mother and her small son are emerging from the second-story elevator to confront a large painted triptych featuring a harrowing Crucifixion surrounded by scenes from the Passion of Christ in which Jesus is being tortured. "Look!" exclaims the mother. "There's Jesus. Hello, Jesus!"

The little boy stares at the wall and, pointing his finger, looks up questioningly at his mother for a moment and declares: "Bad men, Mommy! Look, those people are crying!"

Quickly pulling him back from the disturbing image, his mother replies nervously, "Yes, yes, dear, but remember how Jesus came back, didn't he? He is up in heaven now with all the angels. Come, let's look at some happier things." Without another glance at the painting, she hurries him briskly out of the gallery.

Interestingly, whereas the child's focus had gone directly to the tormentors, the perpetrators of the aggression, his mother's response was exclusively on the victim's survival. Her focus seemed to bypass the aggression; she said nothing about it. How can we understand this? Surely, cultural factors play a key role, for, whatever else the picture might have meant to the little boy, he certainly seemed to relate to it as a set of scenes in which a hero is being mistreated by "bad guys" and getting the worst of it. What his mother seemed to be trying to do was to protect him by reminding him that in this story the hero, the "good guy," will eventually prevail and be saved.

On another level, however, it seemed to me as I watched the brief dramatic interchange between child and painting, child and parent, parent and painting, and parent and child, that, whereas the little boy was upset by the violence, he was also willing to look straight at it and to speak about it and question it. He was fascinated by it. His mother, on the other hand, apparently could not bear it and could not bear the thought that her son might be upset by it. As in the anecdote about *Bambi* and the pregnant mother of a toddler, this mother, likewise, left the gallery precipitously, it seemed to me, not only for her child's sake but also for her own. To me, this leaving for her own sake has nothing intrinsically wrong with it, but, as in the previous example, it necessarily limits—at least for that moment—the aesthetic experience of her son. It leaves him with a host of unformulated and unasked questions: Aren't we supposed to look at this? Why aren't we supposed to look at it? If we aren't supposed to look at it, then why is it here in the museum? Are some things in the museum okay to look at and others not? Pulled away, the little boy disappeared without a backward glance, but his mother's hasty withdrawal might not have expunged the painting from his mind.

If parents can, it is helpful and instructive to be open and honest about their own reactions and feelings in a situation like this. Perhaps, in the next gallery, out of sight of the image, this mother might have told her son that she found those Crucifixion and Passion scenes unusually brutal and hard to look at. She really didn't want to stay in the same room with them. Perhaps she could have asked him how *he* felt about them and whether the tormentors had frightened him, too. This sort of dialogue can certainly go on after leaving the gallery.

To rush away when a child is enthralled, however, and to cut off dialogue about a work of art, especially in a museum, where the principal agenda is to look, gives an odd message and a hard one for children to grasp. If we think back to the series of Henry Moore sculptures, we realize that in this case, by contrast, the child was pointing out something to his mother, but she was refusing to look. Of course, her refusal to stay in the room with those images was also a testament to the power of art and its sway over us, its ability to open us up to ourselves so suddenly that we have, sometimes, to shut down fast in return. This particular example, moreover, was complicated by the fact that the image in question is a religious icon transported from its original place in a sanctuary to a secular location where it still carries for some of its viewers the aura of its first contextualization. What we can say for sure is that our reactions at moments like this one are not lost on our children. And I can hear the gentle voice of Mrs. Ramsay repeating to herself: "Children don't forget, children don't forget."

Thieves Are Stealing That Baby

Here now is an example of how perception and incomprehension mingled with imagination can cause anxiety in a small child. A woman and her husband have arrived at Orly Airport in Paris with their four-year-old granddaughter after a week in the south of France visiting relatives. When the grandfather goes off to retrieve their baggage, the woman remains behind with the little girl to wait for the child's father, who has promised to pick them up but who is now late. As they stand waiting for both father and grandfather, the little girl suddenly clutches her grandmother's hand and points to a nearby escalator where two Muslim women in black burkas, their faces completely hidden, are silently ascending. One carries a tiny baby.

"Look, Mamou," the little girl cries out fearfully, "the thieves are stealing that baby!"

Patiently, her grandmother hushes her and explains calmly about the special clothes worn by some women of this religious persuasion. She reassures her granddaughter that no evil deed is being perpetrated. Meanwhile, the father arrives from Versailles followed by the grandfather with their luggage, and all appears to be right again with the world.

Several months later, however, the same couple again takes their granddaughter to the south of France, this time for *réveillon*, the New Year's Eve celebration. Back in Orly, once again the grandfather disappears to fetch the bags while grandmother and granddaughter wait for the child's father. On this occasion, he is not late, but moments after he arrives, he disappears in order to make some pressing business calls on his mobile phone. The little girl stands in the crowd, with her grandmother, and then suddenly she spies him and cries out, "Look, Mamou! There is Papa!"

"Good," comes the answer. "Go and run over to him."

But the little girl refuses to budge. Glued to her grandmother's hand, she shakes her head: "No, Mamou, I cannot. I'm afraid they will steal me away."

What has contributed to the strength and persistence of this child's fantasy? Was it the dark color of the costumes and what appeared to her to have been hoods and masks? Did these features of the women's garb evoke images of miscreants she might have seen in picture books, or on videos or television? In all likelihood, she didn't know the gender of the women and mistook them for men. Furthermore, since she is in fact the "baby" of her own family (she has an older sister), was she identifying with the helplessness and vulnerability of the baby on the escalator? Airports, moreover, often feel to adults as well as children like alien spaces filled with indifferent or hostile strangers. Finally, on both occasions, her grandfather, a burly, imposing former rugby player who is very fond of her, was momentarily absent. This fact suggests that her fear of being stolen away may represent, on a very primitive level, an anxiety over abandonment.

The psychological transformation from fears of being left to fears of being stolen works rather like this: If you can attribute the cause of your separation from loved ones to the badness of someone *else*, you can preserve the inner images of your own loved ones as good. Hence, a child who fears being stolen away wants not to see her own loved ones as the cause of separation. In both instances, this child was separated from her parents for a week. In addition, her father, when he came to the airport to fetch her, came late (the first time) and did not remain with her (the second time). This might have precipitated some anxiety. What we can glean from the story is a heightened awareness of the connection between *incomprehension* and the *apprehension of danger*. We can also remark the occasional failures of even kindly and helpful adult explanations (on the part of the girl's well-meaning grandmother) and the positive value—lest undue tension build—of being on time when you greet a young child from whom you have been separated. It is important, however, to realize that even a frightening fantasy such as this may coexist with a child's pleasant and happy experiences—in this case, having a good holiday and wanting to go off on other occasions.

Might the situation have been handled differently? If the Muslim women had been close by, the grandmother might have taken her little girl over to them and greeted them so that she could see them clearly, make contact with them, and hear their voices. Under the circumstances, however, this wouldn't have been practical. Another approach might involve questioning the child. *Why* was she so afraid? *Why* did she think these women were robbers? Did she understand that one of the women was undoubtedly the baby's mother? Why did they look to her like "bad men," and where had she seen such images in the past? By helping her to trace her imaginative notion back to some of its roots in her cultural life (they look like the robbers in such-and-such a story), she could perhaps allow the alarming material to come closer to the surface rather than to fester, which, as it turned out, was the failed result of the well-meant rational explanation. Asking questions can sometimes help children who are distressed or confused. And so, importantly, can waiting to hear their answers.

We also see in this anecdote the potency of visual images and their power to slide from the surface of the movie or television screen or picture book or magazine page into the daily lives of young children, where they become reattached, sometimes highly inappropriately, to new objects. Apropos of this phenomenon, here is an example drawn from the daily life of a little girl in Germany.

Teletubbies and Neo-Nazis

Clara, an almost-five-year-old girl in Hannover, Germany, had been watching *Teletubbies*, a British television program populated with animated spherical plastic infantlike characters with high-pitched voices. One day, a news broadcast came on the TV screen and reported some recent violent incidents involving the neo-Nazis in Germany. Clara was confused and asked her mother about it. All she knew about such things was that the Nazis had been responsible for her grandfather's war injury. Her mother, Berbeli, explained to her that the neo-Nazis are not peaceful people and that they want everyone who doesn't look like "us" (both mother and daughter are blond) to go away, to leave Germany, and for that reason alone. Clara reflected on this and asked her mother whether her black-haired friend whose mommy comes from Thailand would be among those persecuted by the neo-Nazis. After mulling it over further, she had another idea: "Mutti," she reasoned, "I'm against those neo-Nazis because they will also send away the Teletubbies, who are not from here but from England and who don't look like us either. That isn't right what the neo-Nazis are doing."

Her mother, a professor of German literature, was startled by this connection and amazed at the ingenious way in which the little girl had used the elements of her own cultural life to infuse meaning into an adult moral and political issue.

Scary in the Middle

I know a four-year-old girl named Josie whose parents are quite protective although not overly so. Once when I was about to read her a fairy tale, Josie told me she didn't want to hear it because she had been warned it would be too scary. Only momentarily nonplussed, I comfortably agreed with her by saying that indeed this *was* a scary story but that being scared can sometimes be okay. It can sometimes even be fun. Being scary, I told her, can make a story exciting and interesting. After all, feeling just a little bit worried about how things will turn out in the end makes you want to stick around to *hear* the end. She took that in and nodded sagely at me. Then she informed me that her daddy had told her the same thing. He had said, she reported, that most stories are scary only in the *middle* and that, if you can just wait long enough, things do generally come out all right in the end. With that, we went on to read the story of Beauty and the Beast, which she loved.

Adult interventions, however, do not always prove so successful.

Bodily Integrity and Band-Aids for Whales

Sometimes it can be helpful to correlate a child's fears with the developmental stage he is in. Still, this sort of caveat can be overstressed. Fears overlap, and while some abate, many never wholly disappear. Bodily integrity, for example, is an ongoing issue that can arise dramatically for some children around the time of toilet training, when it seems to them that a part of their bodies is actually being separated from them and relinquished to the flushing waters with an accompaniment of loud noise. Concern for the intactness of the body, moreover, may, in both boys and girls, appear dramatically when they notice the anatomical difference between the sexes. (Remember the two little boys whose anxieties about possible missing body parts were both expressed and masked by appeals to the garments that conceal them.)

A delightful picture book that graphically depicts this genre of anxiety, *Burt Dow, Deep Water Man* by Robert McCloskey, portrays a school of enormous thrashing whales who all demand (and are given) red-and-white candy-striped Band-Aids for their tails even though they have no wounds. Band-Aids are beloved by small children as a tangible sign of the need to keep their bodies intact and to be protected from their coming apart.

Later in these pages I will say a few words about "mirroring" and make the point that beneath our fantasies of wholeness lurk fears of fragmentation and corporeal disintegration, fears that do not vanish with childhood. Adult horror films depend on them. In these films, we find not only severed body parts but also images of human bodies turned inside out (another childhood fantasy), with all their ooze and gore and gooey shapelessness revealed. Likewise, we might recall the uncanny scene at the end of Euripides' *Bacchae,* when the young king Pentheus in drag, lured by Dionysus to spy on the frenzied maenads in the forest, falls out of a tree in which he has perched and is ripped apart, torn limb from limb, by his own mother, Agave, who cannot recognize him and who, in her altered state, imagines him a lion. Early apprehensions about our bodies, captured in vivid images such as these from ancient times up until the present, while waxing and waning around life-cycle stages and events, remain with us. A sensitive parent, knowing her child, may therefore choose to limit that child's exposure to cultural experiences that give priority to a current or a pending issue of concern. (Recall the pregnant mother who didn't wish her little boy to watch *Bambi.*) Contrarily, when time and strength are at a premium, parents may choose exactly the opposite tack and seek out cultural experiences that are highly pertinent to their child's chief concerns as a way of providing him with a safe arena in which to explore and work through the anxieties of the hour.

The World's Bad News

What is the proper response about frightening events that occur in the world and are then represented in the various media to which children today have increasing access? Here we move out to the margins of the aesthetic, but we are, where children are concerned, squarely within the realm of the imagination. Should we bring "the world's bad news," as *Lilith* magazine put it in a 2002 feature article, to children? And if so, how? The *Lilith* editors meant their question to be taken in political terms, but we should consider it more broadly.

Since the tragic events of September 11, 2001, in New York and Washington, D.C., and other more recent disasters worldwide, this question has remained a matter for public debate in the United States as well as a private concern for individual parents. Opinion seems divided between two poles, with a spectrum of views in between. On one end are those who believe children must be shielded from potentially disturbing representations. On the other are those who say children should not be overly guarded and that representations should not be censored for the young. Some people argue that we cannot shield children even if we want to, for children grasp—in some form—more than we adults give them credit for. (Recall Clara and the neo-Nazis.) Still, even if we were to agree with this point of view, many questions remain open. What are the best ways of giving children access to unpleasant truths and helping them sort out the tangled ethical issues that accompany the world's bad news without bewildering them, frightening them unnecessarily, and without inadvertently biasing our own accounts in accord with prevailing ideologies?

We might ask ourselves what we make of differences between the representation of frightening events in real life, past or present, and the depiction of frightening events in the life of the imagination. How separable are these realms? As our first reactions to the radio, television, and photographic coverage of the events of September 11 made us realize, reality and fantasy have now become so confounded by advances in technology that, in an uncanny way, these very advances have returned us to modes of apprehension a bit like shamanism, where elements of dream, fantasy, and waking life seem entwined. If such overlapping strands are difficult for adults to disentangle, imagine the magnitude of the task for growing children who, only gradually and haltingly, must learn to separate their inner from their outer worlds—their hearts' desires from the actualities of daily existence.

The Red Motorcycle

Here is an example of children's inability to separate these realms and an illustration *pari passu* of the grip of the imagination on young children and their "verbal prestidigitation," as Bachelard puts it when he asks quite seriously "why actions of the imagination [should] not be as real as those of perception." It is a story told to me by the mother of a four-year-old girl living in Rhode Island. This mother belonged to a cooperative nursery school car pool in which there was a little boy named Tommy. For several weeks, each time it was this mother's turn to drive, she noticed that Tommy, shortly after settling into his seat, would begin to expatiate on the details of his father's red motorcycle. The two other children in the car, both little girls, sat very quietly as he regaled them with effusive descriptions of the motorcycle—its shiny polished surfaces, its loud whirring noise (which he imitated), its enormous size, its astonishing speed. These descriptions continued until one day the little boy became ill and was unable to go to school. His mother phoned my friend to explain the situation, and my friend remarked in passing: "You know, Tommy goes crazy over his dad's motorcycle. He talks about it all the time in the car. It must be great for your husband to share this with him."

There was a hushed silence on the other end of the line. "But," Tommy's mother finally said, "my husband doesn't have a motorcycle. We've never had a motorcycle."

Both mothers were astonished.

Here we have the persuasive conflation of wish and actuality in the mind of a four-year-old. And we need to be wary of being too censorious about this behavior or of labeling it as *lying*. I would focus, rather, on the richness of Tommy's imagination, the wealth of detail in his elaborate descriptions, and, above all, on the enormously persuasive power of his desire. The story, when I first heard it, made me think of the dramatic dexterity of those *rhapsodes,* those actors and tellers of tales in Plato's *Ion* whose hair stood on end and whose eyes would fill with tears as they regaled their spellbound listeners. Harmless and colorful, Tommy's imaginary red motorcycle gave pleasure both to the teller and to his car-pool mates on their daily rides to school. What the story illuminates for our purposes in this context about children's fears is the driving force of wishes in childhood and their ability to override reality. This feature deserves important consideration in any full discussion of how we bring "the world's bad news" to children or withhold any news, facts, or adult explanations from them.

Lying to Children

Atrocities are occurring every day. Driving in my car with a five-year-old boy the other day, searching for my classical music station on the radio, I inadvertently tuned in to what sounded like a call-in show on which some newsworthy act of barbarism was being discussed. Before I could switch stations, the child heard something that made him ask me a terrifying question, "Is it true that people are killing their own children?"

Cringing, I murmured something inconclusive and then told him that he must have misheard. He was silent. Mozart's music began to fill the car as I sat there aware that the child had in all probability *not* misheard. Young people, after all, who are scarcely more than children themselves, egged on by adults, are taking their own and others' lives in suicide bombings, for example. I drove along in a frozen state knowing full well that we *are* killing our children and knowing that I had misled my young passenger. I had, effectively, lied to him. Wasn't I, too, like that mother in the Walters Art Museum, protecting myself?

Yet maybe children have needs that trump their right to know the kind of truths I had withheld. Maybe our first priorities in terms of what we give children should be safety, trust, and hope. Children *do* distinguish good from bad, right from wrong, after all, and they do it much more harshly than we adults feel comfortable doing. They are, as we know, taking their first steps on the long, steep, serpentine trail of moral development. So, they divide things up in absolute terms. As adults, we have come to understand that these categories need to be modified, but we cannot make this knowledge available to children. They must learn it for themselves. Once the categories are in place, and children are exposed gradually to representations of the world's ills, they may grow increasingly capable, little by little, of seeing the gray areas. Yet again, they may not. We all know adults who never achieve this level of moral development and who remain trapped in bifurcated moral worlds. Adults who cease their mental traveling. How can we bring up children who will want to move beyond inflexibility, beyond places where others are judged as being "for us" or "against us," "insiders" or "out"? Maybe we can best achieve this by *not* bringing the real world in too quickly but instead by encouraging imaginative play that leads both to and beyond the acquisition of categories. This would be my guess.

In the film *The Sweet Hereafter,* directed by Atom Egoyan, a little boy listens intently as his teenaged sitter reads to him from a Kate Greenaway–illustrated *Pied Piper of Hamelin.* Clearly disturbed by the story, the child interrupts to pose a question. If the piper really knew enough magic, he reasons, to get the rats to follow him out of the village of Hamelin, then why couldn't he use his magic to make the villagers pay him? Why did he have to take all their children away? The sitter thinks silently for a minute and says she doesn't know. Then, the boy concludes immediately, that piper must have been *bad.* No, declares the girl firmly, the piper was not bad. Why not? asks the boy. Because, she explains, the villagers had gone back on their word to him. Effectively, they had lied. They had refused to pay him. "He was," she declares quietly, drawing on her own experience of life, "very angry."

In this brief interchange, we can see two different stages of moral development. For a young child, bad behavior belongs irredeemably to bad people. For an adolescent, however, emotions such as anger and the experience of being a victim of injustice are recognized as motivators for bad behavior. For the babysitter, in other words, but not for the younger child, judgments about actions can be separated from judgments about people.

Good Guys and Bad Guys

Children make stark contrasts. They distinguish "good guys" from "bad guys." In addition, they conceive the world in terms of hierarchies. Parents often, as mentioned earlier, reinforce this tendency. A child already described, for example, repeatedly pressed me to reveal my favorite color in spite of the fact that I would always respond by explaining patiently that I enjoy all the colors and cannot name any special favorite. Finally, the questioning simply switched to my favorite ice cream flavor; thus, the template was imposed on an alternative category. Hierarchy matters to young children because it mirrors their experiences of power and lack of power within the family structure as well as their perception of the relative sizes of bodies and objects. A little girl I observed recently, for example, got very angry when she was offered child-sized table utensils rather than the regular ones being given to everyone else. Likewise, she insisted on being given adult-sized portions of food.

Good guy/bad guy scenarios are repetitively enacted by children of both sexes in the widest variety of forms—from games about cops and robbers and superheroes to games about vegetarian versus carnivorous dinosaurs (as we will see in the next chapter) and fairy godmothers versus wicked witches. By distinguishing such categories, children learn at the same time to identify and internalize a host of other basic categories that seem to adults just as potentially blurry and context-dependent as the ethical ones: male/female, dirty/clean, day/night, person/thing, edible/inedible. Before the ground begins to shift, these categories must be in place, and children, in the most imaginative ways, play out their need to feel confident about them. They work (through their play) at establishing a stable ongoing network of connections between their own and others' feelings, ideas, and wishes, on the one hand, and words, acts, images, objects, and symbols on the other.

Confronted prematurely with more complex and layered adult modes of understanding, children cannot readily assimilate them. Listening to us, they, in their wish to comprehend, often invent ingenious alternative meanings. Occasionally, their misapprehensions lead—as we have seen—to fear. Or to behaviors that mask fear, as we have also seen. Instead of learning to make the subtle distinctions they are not ready for, they experience the world as unpredictable, surreal, chaotic, and untrustworthy. James Thurber has written wisely and wittily of this surrealism of childhood, especially with regard to his troubles with idioms and metaphors.

Only gradually can children proceed from the simple and concrete to the general and the complex. Philosopher Thomas Nagel wrote a marvelous essay, "What Is It Like to Be a Bat?," in which he traces the problematics of decentering oneself sufficiently to be able to see the world from an entirely different point of view. Consider how a child's dawning awareness of his own immediate past (yesterday's holiday parade, train ride, picnic, or grandparents' visit) leads to a growing sense of history on a grander scale. Autobiography morphs into history. As children play and grow, their self-centered stories of "me" expand into broader accounts that include an increasing number of "not-me" stories and merge with cultural chronicles that exceed the life span and geographic range of any individual. This process matters profoundly because when the capacity for historical memory is in place, it forms the ground of personal identity, of an ongoing, meaningful sense of self, not only psychologically but also ethically and aesthetically. It forms the basis of individual choice and responsibility. Thus, in children's earliest play and in their storytelling, questioning, and picturing, we can trace the deepest roots of conscience.

Bambi

Not long ago, I was asked by the BBC to speak on a radio program about the death of Bambi's mother, and the request caused me to revisit this Walt Disney film, which had terrified me so in my own childhood. I would like at this point to take *Bambi* as a kind of test case for exploring some of the problems concerning the bringing of bad news to children and children's fears and their imaginative responses to fears in the realm of cultural experience. *Bambi* is, of course, a fiction, an animated movie based on the novel by Felix Salten. It can, however, be fruitfully studied to demonstrate a range of choices that arise when abandonment, death, and natural disaster are presented to young children.

Originally released during the World War II years, *Bambi* has by now passed its sixtieth birthday. An exquisitely crafted work of art and one that conveys important messages to children, particularly messages concerning human beings' thoughtless despoliation of the environment, *Bambi* is, for many children, an extremely frightening film. Several young parents have told me they were so upset by it in their youth that they will not allow their own children to see it. Although I cannot tell exactly how old I was when my parents took me, the experience disturbed me enough so that I grew up saying with vehemence, whenever it was mentioned, "I HATE *Bambi.*" My memory was so negative, in fact, that for a long time I, too, vowed to keep my own children from it. Needless to say, however, they each in time did see it.

What I recall as most upsetting to me as a child was the intoxicating forest fire that blazes across the screen with its swirling tongues of orange and gold and the helpless animals fleeing panic-stricken for their lives. I am not alone. Other adults, queried in informal interviews, cite it; but many say that it was the death of Bambi's mother that frightened them most. For me, in retrospect, this was a minor event. I will, however, venture an interpretation of the disparity between their experience and mine. Those adults who do not remember the death of Bambi's mother invariably *do* recall the forest fire. Some have said they can still see the animals escaping in advance of the flames. My belief is that this vivid memory screens the earlier one, the shooting of Bambi's mother, in precisely the way Freud describes in "Screen Memories," an essay he wrote in 1899. An event, he explains, that is too unbearable to be admitted into consciousness is screened or masked, so to speak, by another event (which may have occurred either before it or after it) that is connected with it by sharing some of its features yet that is not so unbearable that it must be kept out of awareness. Meanwhile, the more profoundly disturbing event is repressed. Thus, the emotions attached to the repressed event can be fully experienced but without any awareness of what is causing them to be so powerful. In my own case, having lost my mother to a premature death some years after seeing the film, I virtually forgot (repressed) the death of Bambi's mother, while the fire with all its vivid drama took its place in my mind. For others, analogous dynamics may come into play for other idiosyncratic reasons. Thus, our minds play their wily and fascinating tricks on us, always eluding our hopes for conclusive understanding.

Actually, what intrigues me is that most of the adults I have interviewed do not remember the death of Bambi's mother per se but simply the *fact* that Bambi's mother dies in the film and that they were very disturbed by this as children. One woman, a research librarian, could recall nothing about the death of the mother except the fact that Bambi was suddenly all alone and that she as a small girl felt similarly alone and terribly sad. Not one adult who had seen the film as a child but had never seen it again could say anything concrete about the death scene or give me the slightest detail concerning it. Each person would say merely that the mother's death had occurred and that it was horrible. Of course, one reason this interests me so much is that the audience never does see Bambi's mother die, and the word *death* is never mentioned.

The Story of *Bambi*

The film begins with exquisite images of the forest in springtime (images originally painted on glass panels and then photographed by overlapping the panels in order to create an illusion of depth) and a voice-over singing "Love is a song that never ends." This sentiment, placed at the opening of the film, conveys a positive message that, no matter what happens, we can count on goodness, nurturance, and everlasting renewal. Clearly, this is the prevailing theme of *Bambi*. Here is a quick run-through of the story.

A fawn is born one spring in the forest. Throughout the spring and summer, he romps and plays under his mother's protective eye. Named by his mother, Bambi learns haltingly to walk and talk and leap. He makes friends with Thumper the rabbit and Flower the skunk and cavorts bashfully with a little doe named Faline. He encounters rain, thunder, and lightning, and learns that the open meadow holds an unknown danger. One day, on the meadow, he is separated from his mother, and shots ring out. Everyone begins to run. He does not understand and is given only the now-famous answer: "Man was in the forest" (which, we must remember, is all the child watching *Bambi* hears as well). Autumn leaves fall. Winter comes, and in a charming scene, Thumper teaches Bambi to skate on a frozen lake. With the first blades of new grass, Bambi and his mother return to the meadow. Suddenly she tells him to run and not look back. Again shots ring out. Bambi reaches the woods and looks for his mother. Fresh snow has begun to fall. He cannot find her. Calling and sobbing, he looks up and sees his father, the stag, Prince of the Forest, who says simply, "Your mother can't be with you anymore. Come, my son."

We are now forty-five minutes into the seventy-five-minute film. Without time for a single breath, we are plunged into spring. Birds chirp gaily; the screen fills with green, blue, yellow, and pink. The owl complains that everyone is falling in love. Bambi reappears on-screen with antlers. He rediscovers Faline and battles another stag for the right to be with her. They are now a couple. Bambi's father returns to warn him that man has reentered the forest, this time in greater numbers. Everyone must flee deep into the forest. Bambi, however, cannot find Faline. Separated, they call helplessly to each other, as Bambi called earlier for his mother. Hunters' bloodthirsty dogs arrive to chase and attack Faline. Bambi, in the nick of time, comes to her rescue by distracting the dogs but is shot as he leaps to escape them. His father returns and forces him to get up despite his wound. They flee together.

By now the hunters' campfire, left untended, has begun to rage out of control, and the entire screen has erupted into swirling flames. Fleeing animals appear in silhouette against the burning falling trees and fiery sky. The tempo and volume of the music keep pace with the rampaging fire and terrified stampeding animals.

At last, there is calm. Faline has survived, and to the melody "Love is a song that never ends," she is reunited with Bambi. Spring returns to the forest, and in a scene that recalls the opening of the film, Faline becomes the mother of newborn twin fawns. The final shot is of Bambi proudly posing on a cliff in the distance. As the new Prince of the Forest, he both imitates and replaces his father; thus, the cycle of renewal and hope that was promised in the opening song has been completed.

The Aesthetics of *Bambi*

What I would like to emphasize first is the aesthetic refinement of *Bambi*. It is a genuine work of art; nothing was spared in its making. Every detail of its conception, design, dramatic structure, color scheme, drawing quality, characterizations, and soundtrack is carefully thought out and lovingly executed. Appropriately vis-à-vis young children who are just becoming aware of the seasons and faithful to the life cycle as it unfolds in the animal kingdom, the action is entirely structured around the four seasons. Moreover, in a subtle analogy with the "unities" of classical French drama in which the narrative must occur within twenty-four hours of one day and in the same location, the carefully crafted action here occurs within the space of exactly the calendar year.

The first actual scene that occurs after the establishing shots of the forest cannot help but bring to mind for many viewers—even if only subliminally, which is, of course, the way the best filmic symbols always work—a classic Nativity scene. A little prince is born, and all the animals come to pay homage to him. He lies on the ground next to his mother, and from the beginning of his life, he possesses a circle of loving friends, a fact that remains important later when he is forced to experience his mother's untimely death. From the very beginning of the story, Bambi and his mother constitute a primal dyad. Bambi's father, on the other hand, missing from the Nativity scene, is shown at first only from a great distance. A regal stag with enormous antlers, he poses majestically on a high ridge or precipice. Bambi's mother, on the other hand, lies low to the ground, close to her little son. The parental roles are thus sharply differentiated; and if we might historicize for just a moment, they genuinely reflect the realities of American family life in the 1940s, when the United States had entered World War II and many fathers were in fact distant and, for the most part, out of sight of their young children. Sadly, for many reasons, this situation obtains in many contemporary families as well.

Before his mother's death, there is, in fact, only one moment when Bambi's father comes near him. Pacing loftily and receiving homage from all the other deer, the great stag glances down for barely a moment at Bambi, then passes silently on. Awed by his presence, the little fawn exclaims: "Mother, he stopped and looked at me," to which his mother replies, "Yes, I know. Everyone respects him, for of all the deer in the forest not one has lived half so long. He is very brave and wise. That is why he is known as the Great Prince of the Forest." That the father makes minimal contact with his son at this stage of his life warrants no comment, but the fact that he has lived so long possesses dramatic irony in light of what is to come.

Small children are, of course, expected to identify with the title character, and the Disney filmmakers spared no effort to achieve this goal. The animators observed young children and animals at play, studied photographs and films of them, and attempted with astonishing success to recapitulate toddlers' poses, antics, and expressions in those they gave to the young deer. Bambi stares at the world upside down from between his legs, looks wide-eyed with surprise at the world around him, hangs his head bashfully, wobbles unsteadily, tumbles clumsily. He is vulnerable, curious, and occasionally petulant. How could any child in the audience resist identifying with him?

Bambi's Mother

Bambi's mother has been endowed with saintliness. Virtually flawless as a parent, she treats her son with infinite tenderness and patience while always gently prodding him toward more mature and adaptive behavior. Thus, for example, when he initially tries to stand up and falls, she gently encourages him to try again. When he asks her why he has never seen the other deer in the forest, she simply replies, "You will." With this answer, she satisfies him. Instead of offering him an explanation of why something he desires has not so far happened, she recognizes the wish implicit in his question and reassures him that it will be granted. She does not behave, in other words, like some parents, who frustrate and bewilder children by trying to answer the question they are manifestly asking but who fail to intuit and respond to the unasked question that underlies it.

Bambi's mother is a model for responding to a child on the deepest level of need. This is, in part, what makes her loss, when it comes, so very painful. When Bambi wants to go the meadow later on, she tells him that he has to be big enough first; he has to be ready. She does not, in other words, simply say no, rather she gives him the pleasure of feeling that there is much to look forward to. She explains that he must never rush out onto the meadow, where he will be unprotected, and asks him to stay in the shelter of the trees while she goes out alone to test the environment and make sure it is safe. She therefore accepts the risk to her own life in order to safeguard her child. "Wait here," she says softly. "I'll go out first. If it's safe, I'll call you." Earlier in these pages, I described a series of sculptures by Henry Moore and cited this sensitively portrayed behavior on the part of Bambi's mother.

When Bambi meets Faline for the first time on the meadow when the two mothers and their fawns are present, he is terribly shy, but his mother does not accept his antisocial behavior. Gently but firmly, she urges him to say hello to Faline, and soon the two are romping gleefully together. At each point, Bambi's mother instinctively knows exactly what she must do to support and exhort her child. At another point, when winter is upon them and snow covers the ground, cold winds blow, and the deer are suffering, she struggles to pluck the last remaining leaves off low-lying branches to feed him, and Bambi complains to her, "Winter sure is long."

She does not at this point berate him for complaining or merely affirm his perceptions. What she says is: "It *seems* long, but it won't last forever."

Bambi continues, "I'm awful hungry, Mother," to which she tenderly assents, "I know."

Thus, she calmly shows him that she has a far-reaching perspective on these matters and can assure him that conditions will change for the better. She doesn't need to say, "Be patient," because she has given him the means to discover patience for himself, and she models it for him. Unlike an overly preemptive mother who rides roughshod over her child's natural pace or a laissez-faire parent who sets no standards and defines no goals, Bambi's mother steers an ideal course of kindness, tact, guidance, concern, and confidence. Perhaps it is inevitable that such a saintly creature be sacrificed. Young children watching the film, while unable, obviously, to articulate what I have just been describing, fall nonetheless under the spell of this benign mother and her nurturing presence.

In general, however, *Bambi* purveys a stereotypic vision of gender. The female role is strictly limited to producing and raising offspring until they are ready for independence. After this, since Bambi's mother has no further part to play, she is dispensable and, in this case, simply dies. On the other hand, the larger, stronger father, equipped with the weapon of antlers—his means of self-defense—can fight for his territory, fight for his right to procreate, and thus play an ongoing role in the drama, for he possesses the wherewithal to survive as long as he can.

Apropos, it is startling but perfectly consistent that, almost immediately after Bambi's mother dies, the little deer himself rather surprisingly appears on-screen with his first antlers. He also uses them right away to fight. These new antlers of Bambi's can be seen as a substitute, both symbolic and actual, for the protection his mother had heretofore afforded him. Likewise, it is noteworthy that immediately after his mother's death, Bambi reencounters the little doe Faline with whom he had played in his mother's presence the previous summer when they were "children." In terms of these animal characters, the film presents a rather perfect oedipal fantasy: the young boy's dead mother being instantaneously replaced by a beautiful girl who becomes her substitute. Bambi, newly equipped with his antlers, battles another stag for the right to be with Faline and, identifying in this way with his father, he wins her and couples with her. His unmourned mother, successfully replaced, has been completely forgotten. She is never mentioned after her death. Faline, however, when she meets Bambi again, asks in a voice eerily reminiscent of Bambi's mother, "Don't you remember me?" What is uncanny here is that there *is* someone who is not being remembered.

The Mother Must Die

Why do mothers have to die? Think of the sudden death of the little elephant's mother in *The Story of Babar* by Jean de Brunhoff. Think of all the dead mothers (and substitute stepmothers) that haunt and inhabit the pages of fairy tales. Perhaps there is a developmental imperative at play here—an enactment of the necessity for each child to relinquish that first cozy intimacy in order to gain a hard-won independence. Perhaps this turn from mother to father must, on some terms, take place, however various the forms of its outward manifestations turn out to be. Even the genders might be and have been questioned without disturbing the basic paradigm. Some psychoanalysts would argue that, in other words, the paradise of mother-child closeness so gloriously celebrated by centuries of Madonna paintings in Christian art (and evoked in the first scene of *Bambi*) needs to be lost and cannot survive for more than a short while in any individual life because children need to move on. Not always, however (as in *Bambi*), because of wanton violence, not always (as in *Bambi*) without mourning or grief, not always (as in *Bambi*) without longing, regret, or sweet memories to which one can return.

The death scene is worth examining in detail because, as we've noted, it is a scene that everyone both remembers and forgets. I know one little boy who was so deeply troubled and confused by it that he could not enjoy the rest of the movie. I am sure he was not alone.

Winter has come to the forest, and the deer are cold and hungry. Bambi's mother, spying some new blades of spring grass under the snow, decides to take her little son out of the forest for a romp in the meadow. Once out there, however, she suddenly becomes tense and alert. We have no clue as to why. We hear and see nothing. Then she whispers anxiously to Bambi, "Quick, quick—the thicket . . . Run . . . Faster, Bambi. Don't look back . . . keep running. Keep running." As they run, we hear the sound of shots, but we see no indication of their source; a child who had never heard such sounds before would have no way of telling what they are. We never see any hunters. *We never see Bambi's mother die.*

What we do see is Bambi, exhausted, reaching the thicket safely and exclaiming: "We made it! We made it, Mother." We watch him as he looks around for her. Again, the snow begins to fall. "Mother?" Bambi calls. And then again—seven or eight times—and, for what seems an eternity, we stay with him and inhabit his breaking heart as he calls and searches, and the snow swirls over him in ever-thicker masses, blinding him, and his fading voice becomes a sob. The scene seems to last forever. Actually, it takes only a couple of minutes. But the children watching are as bereft and frightened as Bambi. They, too, feel abandoned and lost.

Immediately thereafter, with no further explanation and no utterance of the word *death*, we are transported into a jubilant springtime scene where a voice trills: "Let's sing a gay little spring song . . . Let's get together and sing." The loss has been canceled and erased.

Granted the death of the mother, which we have already addressed, however inconclusively, *Bambi* causes us to ask ourselves *how* the experience of death should be presented to young children. There are many choices. Should it (as it is distinctly *not* in *Bambi*) be shown graphically, literally, as it is in so many contemporary vehicles, with all the explicit horror that may entail? Aristotle, in his *Poetics*, argues against this brutal approach and suggests that death *not* be shown visually in drama but instead be narrated verbally so that each member of the audience can imagine it in whatever way she chooses. *Bambi*, however, does not even make it clear that a death has occurred.

Issues of separation and abandonment, rather than actual death, seem to be foregrounded here—first in the summer meadow scene when pre-figuring shots ring out—and later just before the fire when Bambi loses Faline. This may, in fact be an appropriate choice of emphasis, for the irrevocability of death is, in any case, exceedingly hard for young children to grasp. They often try in the most imaginative and ingeni-ous ways to recover beloved relatives, friends, and animals while at the same time acknowledging verbally that they are dead. My German col-league tells me that Clara, her then three-year-old daughter, was deeply attached to her grandfather who lived around the corner and who died very suddenly. When the family explained to the little girl that her grandfather had died and gone to heaven, she accepted this answer with equanimity and was quite calm until a few months had gone by when, one day, she announced firmly to her mother:

"It's enough time, Mutti. Now I want Grandfather to come back from heaven and play with me again."

No Time to Mourn

How do we best represent death to children? How do we represent the unrepresentable? How important is it to speak the word *death*? How important is it, for children who view *Bambi*, to understand that, off camera, so to speak, there are human beings called hunters with weapons called guns who are trying to kill the deer, and that Bambi's mother is a bigger target than her little son, and that she cannot run fast enough to escape? Would a rational understanding such as this help? Even if it solved some of the confusion felt by the little boy mentioned earlier, would it allay his anxiety or quell his profound sense of loss? Would we want, in any case, to do that? What, ideally, would we like children to feel when confronted by the representations of the death of a character they have come to love? Without in any way valorizing the choices made by the Disney team vis-à-vis this death scene, I want to take it as a site from which to raise questions about alternatives.

Death, in every age and in every culture, has remained a mystery subject to magical, mythical, and supernatural treatments. How do we explain to a child what we as adults do not ourselves understand and have such difficulty accepting? To explain, furthermore, may serve to rob a child of her chance to create explanations, to elaborate fantasies. Should we be more aware, perhaps, of foreclosing the "unreality of reality"? For me, as problematic as this death scene is, then, and despite and because of my own repression of it for so many years, I see it also as brilliant. Why? Because it places the viewer directly into Bambi's position. Like the little deer, we have seen nothing. We have understood nothing. We, too, are cold, blind, lost, and we are given no external perspective as spectators. We are drawn fully into the drama. There is nowhere else to go.

For me, what is intensely troubling about the film is what happens immediately afterward. Not, in fact, *what* happens per se but that it happens so fast. We (and Bambi) are given no time. No time to cry. No time to miss and remember her. No time to grieve. No time to mourn. No time to assimilate this trauma, to process what has transpired. If I could do so, I would simply divide the film into two parts and stop it for several minutes of silence just after the death scene. To make a break. To give everyone—children and adults—a chance to take in the loss before moving on. Animal life and human life may differ here. In a recent television documentary, I saw a mother zebra with her new colt amble down to a river in which crocodiles were camouflaged as logs. Unsuspecting, the mother began to swim across the river, her little one following close behind. Suddenly, a crocodile's huge jaws snapped open and the baby zebra instantly disappeared. The mother hesitated, her gait slowed, and one could read into this moment all the poignancy of human feeling as she clambered heavily up onto the riverbank and disappeared into the underbrush, childless. With us human beings, life cannot go on without a period of assimilation and recovery. We need to mourn, and we do not, we *cannot*, replace one human being with another. This is a lesson worth teaching and worth emphasizing for children, but it is the lesson starkly missing from *Bambi*.

The film, therefore, can serve as a teaching tool, if you will. By having made its choices, it can compel us to weigh and originate alternatives. It can help us to reconsider human needs for mourning and for psychic healing before integration, acceptance, and reflective representation can occur. It can help us ponder the extended periods of time that may have to elapse before events that cause mental and physical anguish can be dealt with in transformative ways. It may let us see why, by contrast, when traumatic events are introduced too quickly into the cultural field, the results are so often banal or vulgar. Such too-rapid efforts might be analogized to the crude *acting out* of mental patients during manic episodes. We might reflect on the work of major artists. Recall that a full decade elapsed after the Napoleonic atrocities in Spain before Goya was capable of painting his *Executions of the Third of May, 1808*, a searing indictment of war. With time—with necessary time—comes a measure of tranquillity (one hopes) and renewed capacity to create something new out of past tragedy. Yet with time also come lapses of memory, distortions, and revisions. Truth, by the time it becomes art, has irrevocably changed.

By default, *Bambi* reminds us, moreover, of the human need not only to remember the past but also to pass it on to future generations. Here the thought leads back into the realm of the political, in which *Lilith* posed its "bad news" question. Before turning back in that direction, however, I want to describe a contrasting presentation of death to children, a presentation via television in which loss is openly acknowledged.

Pentagon, Fish, and Trolley

Have you ever noticed how children's attention is drawn by details? So much meaning comes through the fine points. For example, knowing how hard it is for small children to tie their shoelaces, Fred Rogers ties his own at the beginning of every half-hour episode of *Mister Rogers' Neighborhood*. Without fanfare, he has the camera zoom in. Likewise, knowing how children tend to overlook their daily responsibilities to pets, he sprinkles fish food into an aquarium on the set each day and smiles as the fish nibble on their meal.

In one program, Rogers notices that one of the fish in his aquarium has died. Instead of avoiding this potentially distressing incident, however, he seizes upon it as an occasion for introducing a complex medley of related experiences to children. He enters his studio in a tie and black jacket singing his welcome song. The picture screen reads "HI," which he also speaks aloud so as to offer a cross-modal prereading lesson, and then, to the watching child, he adds: "I thought about you this weekend." As is so often the case in genuinely aesthetic work, the levels of meaning and their interconnections blend subtly and emerge only gradually over time. Later on in the show, we will come to see that the purpose of this apparently innocuous sentence is to comfort children with the notion that one can go on existing in another's mind even during absence. On this day, Rogers holds up a pentagon made of wood, and he asks what it looks like and then pauses. Pointing out that it has just as many sides as the fingers of a human hand, he asks his child spectator to hold up her hand as he grasps the pentagon with his own five fingers. Then he requests her to repeat the new word aloud with him, as he pronounces it distinctly once again, and then the children are asked to count their fingers. In this initial segment, then, the manifest focus is on cognition.

Rogers moves over now to his picture screen, "Picture Picture," and asks it to show—please—a movie starting with the title "FISH." This printed word will matter, as we shall see. To buoyant piano accompaniment, we watch as several intricately patterned fish appear gliding through the water of an aquarium on-screen, and Rogers points out how graceful they are. Seamlessly, he moves over to his own aquarium, where, he tells us soberly as he looks in, there seems to be something unusual. The camera brings us nearer, and he asks: "Do you see a dead fish?" Knowing that *death* is a notion that can be confusing and poorly grasped, he offers a simple definition. While the camera zooms in on a slender gray fish lying on its side at the bottom, Rogers observes that the animal is neither breathing nor moving. Removing it with a net but keeping it in a small amount of water, he refuses to give up on it immediately. First, we must try to rescue and save. Sometimes, he remarks hopefully, if you put a very sick fish in water with salt, it revives. Soft music plays as he attempts to preserve the tiny animal's life. We are taken in close. The water ripples so as to make the fish seem to move, but Rogers uses this illusion to make an important distinction between being able to move by yourself, which you can do only when you are alive, and moving because of something else. The fish is no bigger than Rogers's thumb. He allows a silence to occur. Then, at length, he says, "We had better bury it."

Wrapping the fish in a paper towel, he goes out to the backyard, camera following, and finds a spot in the grass. There he digs a hole, places the fish in, and covers it up with earth. Then, sitting quietly on the grass with the trowel in his hand, he tells the children a story about his own childhood. Seeing him there, beside the new grave, we perceive the way he is connecting threads, just as Dewey advocated in *Art as Experience*, holding on to the past and carrying it along. Rogers reminisces about a dog called Mitzi whom he loved very much but who eventually grew old and then, one day, died. "I was very sad," he says gently. "We were good pals."

He remembers crying and that, when his grandmother heard him, she came over and put her arms around him. "My dad said we'd have to bury Mitzi, but I didn't want to." He thought he could keep her and *pretend* she was still alive. "But my dad said that her body was dead and we'd have to bury her. And we did."

Back now in the studio, Rogers holds up a toy dog like the one his aunt and uncle gave him after Mitzi died. He shows how he played with it by making it lie down and then pop right up. He does this several times without interpretation. He has already spoken a lot about movement.

"Would you like to see a picture of Mitzi?" he asks, then presents a black-and-white photo of a scruffy, nondescript-looking terrier: "Even now, I remember Mitzi's prickly fur and curly tail."

Each loss reminds us of others, and even a four-year-old has a past. Apropos of that, the mother of two children recently told me that she overheard her six-year-old son say to his older sister: "Remember when we were little?" Rogers segues into song, and using the music to make a transition between moods, he calls the red trolley so as to make a corresponding shift into the Neighborhood of Make-Believe.

Before that, however, he does something extremely interesting: He explains just how the trolley works. He shows the children that its wheels must remain on their tracks in order for electricity to give it power to progress. At first, we do not grasp the reason for this lesson, but later we will see that Rogers, with his multilayered consciousness, will take the occasion of the fish's death to teach important differences between the world of living creatures and that of nonliving machines.

As we enter the realm of make-believe, we find a miniature castle and two human characters, Lady Aberlin and Bob Dog, the latter of whom is practicing his tricks. When Bob Dog attempts to show off his tricks to the trolley, however, the little red vehicle fails to respond with its usual tinkling sound. It remains silent and inert. Bob Dog asks worriedly: "Is the trolley *dead*?" A doctor puppet character is sent for to examine it and inquires whether the power has gone off, since a trolley works by electricity. Another puppet, the queen, now appears and explains to everyone that the trolley is *not* dead because "Trolleys are machines. They aren't alive; so they can't die." The trolley, they discover, has merely slipped off its track and become momentarily detached from its source of energy. That's all. Once put back, it can travel and ring its bell again. Unlike the little gray fish, machines are responsive to a quick fix.

When the trolley returns to the studio on its track, Rogers pushes its button to make it move rapidly back and forth several times. With a twinkle in his eye, he asks his audience:

"Did you like that? I thought you would."

After all that has gone before, the sight of the trolley moving again cannot help but give children a special sense of pleasure and relief.

Rogers walks over to the aquarium to feed his other fish, and we hear the delicate piano notes that serve to remind us of the little fish that died earlier. He picks up the wooden pentagon and muses: Why not put this on the fish's grave? Neighbor Bob Trow (the alter ego of Bob Dog) stops by, thus connecting the worlds of make-believe and "reality," and the two men use hammer and nails to fashion a grave marker out of the wooden plaque. They draw a picture of the fish on the marker and print the letters for the word FISH, exactly as it had been written earlier in the program. Going outside into the backyard, they kneel down in the grass to put the marker in place.

Rogers returns alone to the studio. In the final moments of the half hour, he sits facing the audience with the toy dog in his lap and quietly sings a song called "Some Things I Don't Understand." The words convey a child's puzzlement, confusion, and disappointment over aspects of life that seem to make no sense. He asks his audience whether they ask a lot of "why" questions. He did when he was little, he adds, and still does. To expand the theme beyond the subject of actual death, he asks whether they have ever felt sad about losing anything special. But, then too, on the other hand, he points out, children sometimes feel like jumping around, just like Bob Dog. Modulating into a different key, Rogers puts his jacket back on, changes his shoes, and snaps his fingers. As he shifts to his singing voice and familiar good-bye song, we experience a sense of solace and the restoration of good feelings. Leaving the set, however, he pronounces words that have turned heavy with significance: "I was glad you were with me today."

A five-year-old who viewed this program with me sat spellbound, not moving a muscle. Just as an etching plate absorbs the sensitive impressions of an artist's gravure needle, this child's face and body language recorded all the gradations of mood the program drew forth. For the program was not only about the death of a pet. It was also about remembering what you love even when it's gone. It was about trying to save something or someone before giving up on it; about defining living creatures as being able to "move" on their own rather than being manipulated from the outside. It was about the acceptance of finality and about letting people know how you feel so they can comfort you. About how moments in the present recall moments in the past and how playing with a toy can help. About the idea that there are no final answers but only questions that need to be asked over and over again. Above all, it was, unlike *Bambi*, about the importance of sharing sadness and going through it together.

Telling the Truth to Children

A former Stanford student of mine told me that during her junior year abroad in Central America, she spent an afternoon in El Salvador visiting the gardens of Jesuit priests at the university there. She learned that in the late 1980s six priests along with their housekeeper and a child were brutally murdered for speaking out against the oppressive military regime then in power. The fragmented bodies of those priests, who had been grotesquely gunned down, had been photographed, and my student saw these photographs along with jars of their blood and scraps of their clothing that had been exhibited to document the atrocity. Her horror increased when she was informed that most of the soldiers who committed these crimes against humanity were trained in her own country, at Fort Benning, Georgia, in the United States. She was outraged. She felt personally betrayed by the fact that she had never been told about her country's participation in such barbarism. A little girl of nine when the events occurred, she had learned nothing about them either then or in the intervening years. Now, as a young adult, she wondered why we erase the truth when we speak to children. She began to question whether there might be any good ways at all to tell them the world's bad news.

Her story led me to wonder whether we should, then, let children know that the United States of America, in addition to aiding other countries generously, has been directly and indirectly responsible for wars and for coups d'état all over the world that have brought untold suffering to innocent people. Or should we continue to keep this information hidden from them? And if so, for how long? What about religion? Every major world religion has been responsible for hostilities toward outsiders and guilty of aggression, however subtle, toward members of its own. Should we present these facts to children, and if so, how?

Hope, Wonder, and Dappled Things

A full answer to the question and to our own broader question about what is too scary would involve not simply avoiding overprotection by distorting history and shielding children from unpleasant realities but also avoiding a cynical disregard for their birthright to hope. They have the right to trust, to believe in goodness, and to feel safe in the world. If we keep in mind notions of empathy and modulation as we interact with individual children and if we pay careful heed to their questions and interpretations, we will be better equipped to adapt our explanations to their step-by-step development. Bad news should, ideally, be communicated to children in a manner best suited to what they are up to hearing, seeing, and comprehending at a given point—a call that, as we know (remember the well-meaning parents who took their son to see *Jurassic Park*), is far from easy.

As parents and concerned adults, our most significant and rewarding task vis-à-vis children concerns, perhaps, just the opposite of relaying the world's bad news. Rather than apprise them of evil and disaster—which they'll learn about in any case—I would think it best to confront such ills when necessary (as I failed to do in the car that day with the five-year-old) but at the same time to defy it. What I mean by defiance is not denial but rather a shift of emphasis over to a deep and abiding reverence for life and to the leavening and curative properties of humor. In other words, in the interests of "reality," we must try not to squelch children's inborn lust for life or crush their insatiable curiosity, their inclination to trust strangers, their habit of dawdling while they notice every detail, their wonder about life in all its forms and incarnations, their posing of interminable rounds of questions, and their way of both pretending and believing that wishes can come true.

What matters most is not informing children that groups of people hate one another, make war on one another, behave violently toward one another, and betray one another's trust. Children know this. They feel it. They observe it in countless forms: at home and on the street, in their cultural lives, in their peer groups, even in the world of animals. To affirm the message of life's goodness, we can offer them—as a part of our ongoing interactions with them—a treasure trove of cultural experience, of books and plays and songs and pictures that celebrate the variegated nature of life, its multiplicity and diversity. Think of Gerard Manley Hopkins's poem "Pied Beauty," where he writes:

> Glory be to God for dappled things—
> For skies of couple-colour as a brindled cow . . .
> All things counter, original, spare, strange;
>   Whatever is fickle, freckled (who knows how?)

By laughing with them, by holding them in our arms, by taking their hands in ours, by hearing what they have to tell us, we teach them to affirm life. And then, when the bad news comes—which it inevitably does—we may be able to help them best by sharing some of the sorrows with them and by not hiding our feelings so that, in knowing our hearts, they can be less fearful of their own. With Bachelard, we must teach them to say: "I will be an inhabitant of the world, in spite of the world."

Chapter Five

Children's Rooms,
Sites of Refuge, and Being Lost

The way it appears to my child's eye, it is not a building, but is quite dissolved and distributed inside me:
here one room, there another, and here a bit of corridor which, however, does not connect the two rooms,
but is conserved in me in fragmentary form. Thus the
whole thing is scattered about inside me . . .
                            —Rainer Maria Rilke,
              The Notebooks of Malte Laurids Brigge

Lost in desart wild
Is your little child.
              —William Blake, "The Little Girl Lost"

Spaces, as we like to think, can be inner or outer, but for children the
gates swing back and forth. When Pablo Neruda remembered his
childhood, he wrote about the rain: "Threads of rain fell, like long nee-
dles of glass snapping off on the roofs or coming up against the windows in transparent waves."

Why would children's *rooms* matter? Because, like stage sets, artists'
studios, professional offices, scientific laboratories, and scholars' studies, they are the setting for significant learning, dreaming, working, and
playing. They are also, of course, places of refuge, sites of interiority
and solitude, where a child can be alone in a space redolent of himself.
Telescoping developmental stages as we have done all along in these

pages rather than taking them one by one, let's explore some of the reasons why the room assigned to a particular child and everything in it may come to matter in all sorts of ways to that child, to carry symbolic meaning of permanent significance frequently remembered in years to come, and why therefore that room and its contents—also the aesthetic qualities of a child's surroundings more generally—merit our care and consideration.

My long-standing interest in this topic reemerged while I was helping, several years ago, to curate a traveling exhibition of selected objects from the Sigmund Freud antiquities collection from the Freud Museum in London. How could such an experience have stimulated my thinking about the subtle and far-reaching effects of childhood living and play spaces?

A Thickly Textured Stage Set

By the end of his life, Sigmund Freud had amassed a vast art collection—more than two thousand ancient art objects (statuettes, plaques, vases, receptacles, and the like), which were gathered in his consulting room in Vienna and, to his immense relief, saved from confiscation by the Nazis and brought to London when he was forced to flee his home in 1938. Sixty-seven of these objects—principally statuettes and busts but also vessels, reliefs, and reliquaries from Greece, Rome, Egypt, and China—were brought to the United States a half century later and placed on display in museums from coast to coast for more than two years. While preoccupied with them and busy interpreting them for their potential viewers, I found myself reflecting not only on their particularity as objects chosen by the founder of psychoanalysis but also on the significance, more generally, of the possessions and décor that surround each of us as we live, play, work, and grow from our earliest years into adulthood.

In Freud's case, the antiquities collection was housed in his consulting room so that, as he listened to his patients and penned theories that were to alter self-understanding in the twentieth century, these ancient objects encircled him. They shared his physical and psychical space. He worked, as it were, under their gaze. Intimately present to him visually and close enough for him to touch, the carved and limned figurines of his collection formed, in the company of books and pictures, a thickly textured stage set against which his patients' narratives and dialogues could be played out. Perceiving deep undercurrents that seemed to flow between these artifacts and Freud's metaphoric choices as they appear in his writings, I found myself reflecting on similar processes that occur in all of us—processes frequently unnoticed, processes that silently link our fantasies with our surroundings.

Apropos, French author Didier Anzieu made an interesting point about Freud's so-called Rome dreams (reported in *The Interpretation of Dreams*). He noticed that they occurred just after Freud had begun to collect antiquities. Anzieu traces the imagery of the Rome dreams directly to Freud's nascent antiquities collection and in so doing offers an interpretation of Freud's creativity that sheds light not only on how he was "worked on," we might say, by the objects that surrounded him but also on the way in which all of us are impacted by our aesthetic surroundings. In the case of children, we can be sure that the effects are even more pronounced, magnified by the sensitivity of youthful perceptual apparati and by the dearth of previously existing schemata.

Visualizing Freud at his writing desk (as in the famous etching by Max Pollack of 1914), Anzieu speculates that he was able to segue directly from seeing to writing. By reflecting simultaneously on the statuary and on the graphic imagery in Freud's Rome dreams, Anzieu postulates a powerful connection between *vision* and *verbalization*. He speculates that Freud was able to translate what he saw or grasped intuitively into written language—that he was able to leap *"from the body to the code"*—as he puts it. This formulation may have more general relevance. Envisaging Freud surrounded by his carefully chosen art collection and attempting to fathom its impact on him as he listened and wrote suggests a model for the impact of inhabited spaces and material objects as they affect the minds of all of us and particularly the minds of growing children. From Anzieu's interpretation of Freud's leap from body to code to the influence of young children's rooms on their mental growth seems less like a leap than a tiptoe.

Living Spaces and the Beginnings of the Self

How does such influence take place? One way to start is to make use of certain notions of incipient memory (as described by L. S. Vygotsky), in particular, the ideas of *recognition* and *evocative memory* as formulated by Selma Fraiberg and by Daniel Stern. These notions may help us understand what happens in a child's inner world in relation to the external spaces filled with objects that he or she inhabits. *Recognition memory* occurs in the presence of an object (you confront an object and say: "Yes, I know this thing"). *Evocative memory* occurs in the absence of an object (you are away from something but can recall it). In the earliest stages of development, young children respond to whatever is immediately present and connect it with their recent experiences of it. Increasingly, they are able to recall an object or person even after it has disappeared (and to signal that they can recall it even when it is no longer in view). To give an example from my own current life, I know that when former students appear on campus pathways or write to me from afar, I almost invariably remember them; whereas, if somebody were to ask me to come up with a list of all my former students, I would find it impossible to do so. What binds these two forms of memory is that both, even recognition or evocative memory, require a trigger of some sort. Vygotsky argues that in the latter case, the trigger may be a culturally constructed sign with the most tenuous metaphoric or metonymic connections to its referent, but clearly it is recognition memory that is principally stimulated by a child's room and its contents. Becoming familiar with the objects in one's vicinity, experiencing their ongoing presence over time, manipulating them, learning to identify them—all of this stimulates the function of memory.

Furthermore, when we reflect on the premise that continuity of experience is fundamental to the creation of an ongoing sense of self, we can see that it is the milieu with which we are surrounded day by day that forms, to a degree, our earliest intimations of who we are. Dwelling within a particularly designed and constructed space, inventing and rediscovering it, a child invents and discovers herself.

Metaphoric Mirrors and Imagined Wholeness

For the newborn baby, first sensations are acute but disjointed. Unequipped to sort them out and unable to attribute them reliably to either an outside or an inside source, infants live in a universe in which boundaries have yet to be discovered. Remember William James's "booming, buzzing confusion" and Freud's "oceanic" sensation. Painful cramps in the baby's tummy, for example, and the piercing shrieks of a siren are equivalent in that they simply feel bad; they hurt. Gradually, however, as children are handled, fed, sung to, and spoken to, a sense of boundedness and integrity develops, along with an ability to discriminate. Some theorists have used the metaphor of "mirroring" to describe this process. Little by little, what is occurring internally is differentiated from what is taking place outside the body. What is seen, touched, heard, smelt, and tasted are all gradually distinguished from one another; what is thought and dreamt is distinguished from phenomena external to the self. The loving gazes, speech, and attention of nurturing adults provide a refuge from fragmentation, an integrating mirror, as it were, which can never, however—like a looking glass itself—be completely accurate. A child's growing sense of cohesiveness, in other words, is never total.

Despite the most sensitive parenting, a residue of unrepresented, unprocessed psychic matter persists, belying our façades of integrity. Built up from the outside by the mirroring activities of others and by the unique sociocultural matrix into which every child is born, an illusion of wholeness can overlap but never fully match a child's inner drives and potentials. Hence, for everyone, child and adult, the possibility of a lapse into fragmentation continues to lurk beneath the surface of our more or less fragile constructs of wholeness. (This was mentioned earlier under the rubric of bodily integrity and the fears concerning it.) Those who are sick, those who have suffered trauma of any kind, those who are mentally ill, those under the influence of narcotic substances and/or deprived of them, and certain unusually creative individuals may dwell precariously on the edge of this divide, but most of us manage much of the time to avoid it.

To grasp the notion in concrete terms, think of how you feel when you pass a mirror and glance into it. For most people, the reflection is mildly reassuring. It confirms our expectations. The image seems to reaffirm not only that we still exist but that we still are who we think we are. We are not prone to reminding ourselves, under such circumstances, that what we actually see in the mirror is but a distorted image (reversed and reduced), incomplete, and a synecdoche—a deceptive fraction, in other words—of our actual bodies and selves. The wholeness we experience seems quite real.

A child's surroundings are but an extension of that mirror. Yet they are rarely taken to be so. What I am proposing here is that it is not enough to consider the role of children's early caretakers in the creation of self; we must add the surrounding aesthetic accoutrements, especially the sleeping and playing quarters—with their décor, openness (or lack thereof) to the outside world, their toys and animals, dolls, music (or lack thereof), and books, and so on. The notion of a "mirroring function" (as theorized by Jacques Lacan) should be expanded beyond the looking glass and taken both concretely and metaphorically to include a child's extended yet intimate nonhuman environment. As she gazes, crawls, toddles about, as she manipulates shapes, weights, and textures, learns to name them and to miss them when she cannot find them, as she employs them in her fantasy, play, and dreams, she is growing into the person she will become.

Think for a moment about whether and how many times in your life you have dreamt of your childhood home. It lives on within you, distorted no doubt—as in the lines by Rilke that form the epigraph to this chapter—yet remains a fundamental building block of the personality you have constructed. Recognition memory and mirroring are thus powerful notions that help us to intuit the formative impact of children's rooms on their future development.

We may gain further insight into the depths of feeling associated with children's rooms and the objects they possess by returning briefly to Freud's art collection. His enthusiasm for each newly acquired objet d'art was such that he formed the habit of bringing his newest, most recently purchased object to the dining room table and putting it near his plate so he could contemplate it while eating dinner. Then he would carefully return the object to its place in his consulting room, where it would remain permanently on display. I find this practice remarkable and highly suggestive. It reminds me of children's wishes not to be parted from their new toys or birthday presents, and the association with eating seems especially primitive and sensual. How frequently do parents warn their children that toys must not be placed on the dining room table?

The Family Romance

Freud's passionate attachment to his antiquities collection and to the ambience of his Viennese study at Berggasse 19 (which he replicated as soon as possible upon his arrival in London at Maresfield Gardens) probably had its roots in many complex agendas including the enactment of a kind of *family romance*. I wish to take a moment to explain this notion, for it has an important bearing on the topic of children's rooms. Freud, who was born Jewish, did not collect Judaica. He encircled himself with the relics of classical Greek, Roman, ancient Egyptian, and Asian civilizations. By surrounding himself with remnants of those other, more "noble" cultures—as he and his epoch held them to be—he reinvented for himself visually, as it were, a whole new lineage, an alternative ancestry. However, it is not Freud's practice I want to examine here but rather the general notion of the family romance itself.

The term, invented by Freud, denotes a prevalent fantasy in childhood: the notion that the people with whom a child lives and who call themselves "mother" and "father" are not in fact that child's *real* parents. Children invent stories that entail their being mistakenly identified, kidnapped, lost at birth (think of *Peter Pan*), or clandestinely adopted. Children may secretly pretend that they are, in reality, the offspring of far more exalted and exotic parents than would appear to be the case. Normally, this family romance occurs when children, on the brink of increasing independence, experience strong needs to disengage from the emotional climate of the nuclear family and move beyond it while remaining within it. Formerly idealized parents are seen at this point as possessing failings heretofore unnoticed. Thus, the so-called family romance confers on the child a brand-new set of imaginary parents and ancestors who are embraced and elaborated partly in order to justify a devaluation of the existing ones. Of course, as Freud points out, the child's real parents are also in fact clandestinely honored in this fantasy, since it is *their* finest qualities that are bestowed upon the new, make-believe parental figures.

Starting at about age eight or nine, in many cases, these fantasies come into play. One little girl from a Boston family fervently hoped, almost believed, and told her bunkmates at summer camp in northern New England that her parents were not her parents because she had been adopted at birth and was actually the daughter of Native Americans. She persuaded the other children and herself—by halves, I suspect—that she belonged to one of the western nations (specifically, the Blackfoot), and she renamed herself (an important element of the fantasy) Moonbeam, no doubt because this seemed distant, mysterious, and exotic. With her long hair combed into two braids and with her prowess at archery as well as her fleetness in running, she managed to convince her bunkmates that she was in fact an Indian princess. Gullibly and admiringly, they corroborated her fantasy.

The phenomenon of family romance is remarkably useful as a concept for interpreting themes and details of individual children's rooms and living spaces. It enables us to consider them as milieus both productive of and reflective of such reveries. Moreover, if we choose to take the notion of family romance a step further, we can use it to explore the fantasies of parents with regard to their expectations for their children, since in fact it is they, more often than the children themselves, who make many of the actual aesthetic choices concerning children's rooms—the selection of colors, décor, furniture, fixtures, and ornaments, as well as toys. And not only just early on. What do these choices say about parents' aspirations for their children? About their constructions of gender? And of class? About their desires to assimilate, if they are immigrants or members of a racial or religious minority, or about their wishes to preserve their heritage by means of the material culture carried with them from their lands of origin? Parental aesthetic choices often entail covert expectations and ideologies that are never explicitly articulated. How do children's inner lives and future aesthetic choices reflect these early environments—whether by following through on them or by rebelling strenuously against them?

A Roomful of Cats

To offer an example of bedroom décor serving as the locus for the expression of a child's inner life rather than that of her parents, I would like to cite the case of ten-year-old Delphine, a little girl who lives in a gracious house in the Parisian suburb of Saint-Remy-l'Honoré, near Versailles. As is typical of many children's rooms I have observed in France, this one was, on the afternoon I saw it (I had requested Delphine's mother *not* to straighten it up before my visit), impeccably clean, neat, and simply furnished. Bed, dresser, desk, chair, and bookshelves were unremarkable. What struck me as extraordinary was the feline motif that dominated and overshadowed every other reference in the room. Cats were everywhere. Delphine's mother even opened a large box on the floor of the little girl's closet and showed me a collection of cat figurines not yet shelved—two hundred of them—and the walls were covered with posters and photographs of cats and colored pictures of cats rendered by Delphine herself. A cleverly constructed cat mobile swayed from the ceiling. It was impossible to look in any direction without encountering either a two- or three-dimensional representation of a cat.

When I asked Delphine's mother about the motif, she told me a fascinating story. Her present husband, she explained to me, was not Delphine's father. Back when she and Delphine and her birth father had all lived together, there had been a fourth "family member," a beloved doggy called Fannie to whom the little girl was greatly attached. After the parents' divorce and the child's separation from her father, Fannie had come with the mother and daughter to their new apartment, which they lived in for a couple of years before the mother's remarriage to her current husband. One year after the breakup, however, Fannie had died, a devastating blow to Delphine, who, as we can imagine, must have felt Fannie to be a tangible link with her past, a symbol of the first years of her life when she had lived with both of her biological parents. Realizing how distraught the child was, her mother offered to buy her a replacement puppy. The little girl bitterly refused. A few years later, however, she asked her mother for a cat. Ever since then, her mother told me, Delphine had been passionately and inordinately devoted to cats.

After hearing this story, I was able to perceive the room as a vehicle for the child's expression of inner yearnings and fantasies. For Delphine, the décor of her bedroom possesses rich symbolic significance. I noticed no pictures of her father on display, or of herself as a small girl with her mother and father together, and no images of the beloved Fannie. However, the ubiquitous cats served as a testament both to all that was so painfully lost and at the same time to the child's fervent desire to begin anew and to reattach to objects that have connections with but are different from the lost originals. In this vignette, we can catch a glimpse of the links between overt aesthetic choices and more hidden inner themes.

Reinventing Oneself Through Fantasy and Material Culture

Turning once again to Sigmund Freud and his art collection, there was ample cause for a concealed agenda where he was concerned. Without digressing too far, I want to suggest very cursorily that his aesthetic choices probably satisfied wishes to create harmony among many discordant aspects of his life. As a nonobservant, professionally discriminated against, and eventually exiled Austrian Jew, Freud, who had rejected the religion of his own ancestors (certainly in terms of ritual and practice; he refused, for example, to observe the Sabbath, although his bride was the daughter of a rabbi), very likely was trying to claim—through his antiquities collection—a kind of alternative heritage composed of all the avatars of ancient learning most honored by the dominant culture of his time. In this he was not alone.

Similarly, we can use the notion of family romance to think about the ways in which minority, immigrant, and second-generation children growing up in the United States in our media-driven culture must learn to cope with the discrepant realities in their young lives. These children's rooms and their object choices—their toys, books, clothes, pictures, and knickknacks—all reflect corresponding efforts to deny and repudiate as well as to discover, salvage, and reinvent alternate self-images. Picture a small dark-skinned girl playing with a blue-eyed doll, or a brown-haired, olive-complexioned child drawing pictures of golden-haired princesses with tiny retroussé noses, images that do not resemble her but that *do* resemble the illustrations in her fairy-tale books, her videos, and the dolls on her shelf and that thus seem to her the epitome of beauty and innocence. Apropos, this facile association of blond hair with purity and refinement and of dark hair with vulgarity and seductiveness seems to have continued apparently unabated into the present century. We need not invoke Toni Morrison's *The Bluest Eye* to find these prejudices, for they persist, to the shame of those who perpetuate them, in all sorts of cultural products, and they are, sad to say, alive and well.

Remembering Your Childhood Room

What, then, are the roles played by the physical objects that surround each of us as we live, work, and dream? Try to remember your own childhood room. Did you have the same one until you left home for college, or did you, with your family, relocate several times? Even so, is there a special space you can still see in your mind's eye? Do you recall its colors or the way the light came through the window? Did you trace raindrops with your fingers on the pane? Can you still picture the shape and size of the room, the texture of your quilt or blanket, the comfort of your bed, a favorite doll or teddy bear, a picture on the wall? Can you remember the scene you beheld when you looked outdoors?

My sister especially treasures her memory of the smell and snap of freshly starched linens that she recalls being stretched tautly over her bed when she was a little girl. Another woman speaks of being forced to share her bedroom throughout childhood with an aged grandmother. She recalls the welter of ambivalent feelings—her sorrow, confusion, relief, and subsequent guilt—when that grandmother eventually died, abandoning the room entirely to her. She remembers assuaging her guilt by preserving everything as it had been when the grandmother was alive and waiting a long time before rearranging things to suit herself. A philosophy professor told me how much she loathed the insipid pink walls her mother had chosen for her girlhood bedroom and how she prayed year after year to be delivered from them. What she yearned for were bolder, more strident hues and the right to arrange the space she lived in according to her own lights.

The Secret Meanings of a Room

Part of the reason I remember my room so well is that at a certain point my mother actually *did* let me make decisions about how it was decorated. Left to my own rebellious devices, I probably would have opted for blank walls on which I could paint murals. Just once, as an extremely young child, I had tried to do that when my parents were out. Caught by the babysitter in flagrante delicto and severely punished, I subsequently nursed a long-thwarted desire to fill up walls with bright colors and forms. Nevertheless, years later, as a young mother, I unreflectively perpetuated my own upbringing by instructing my children that the proper word for a "crayon" was an "only-on-paper." Even so, there were one or two walls of my adult home that completely vanished under a collage of childish tempera and crayoned imagery. Still later, the early deprivation continued to affect me: Fascinated by the phenomenon of wild-style New York City subway-car graffiti, I drove around the streets of the Bronx with a camera photographing graffitied trains and walls and ended up writing a passionate essay about them. Thus, the negative aesthetics—the not being allowed to do something in childhood (as with the little girl whose mother was afraid to let her study ballet too seriously)—can sometimes prove just as generative as being encouraged to do so. The philosopher who hated pink, parenthetically, is now spending her spare time redecorating a late-nineteenth-century mansion in Silicon Valley.

As for me, knowing my mother, I agreed to wallpaper. Although willing to entertain my preferences, my mother could not at the same time refrain from imposing on me her traditional, highly refined, art-history-informed taste. Yet despite, or perhaps because of, the limitations she set, my childhood bedroom continues to be one of those spaces to which I return in dreams and mentally reinhabit. Mostly, my time in that room was spent propped in bed reading, drawing, or writing, and listening occasionally (but only when I was ill) to the radio. It is from this perspective that the room appears to me now: from a twin bed (the one I slept on) with its mate placed parallel but closer to the door. To find me, you would pass through a short curving corridor that branched from a central hallway on the second floor of a Tudor-style stone-and-stucco house with leaded windows and a slate roof. The little corridor would lead you into an ample room carpeted in green with a double exposure and walls covered by yellow roses climbing up white trellises. Because of the passageway, my room set me apart from the rest of my family. The domain I inhabited seemed slightly hidden and a bit remote from all the other upstairs rooms. A person coming in, because of this private corridor, would be unable to see me right away, and I would hear only a gradual crescendo of footsteps. Ever since then, the sound of footsteps approaching has filled me with a slight frisson. This may be because the footsteps I heard most often were those of my mother in her high-heeled shoes. My heart would beat faster as the clicking grew louder, and I waited with trepidation for the appearance of that formidable presence which was about to disrupt my solitude. Like many mothers, mine was both adored and dreaded.

I never explained it to my mother, for fear she would pronounce it ridiculous, but my greatest wish was for a bedroom that would remind me of the out-of-doors. I simply asked her for a green carpet and varnished wood furniture that (I secretly hoped) would call to mind grass and trees. When she insisted on wallpaper, I settled for a pattern that depicted the flower of my birth month—the rose—in climbing, tumbling, and sensuous profusion over trellises overgrown with thick tiers of leafy foliage. The roses I chose were, not insignificantly, yellow, and replete with thorns. My mother persuaded me one day to accompany her to a fine-furniture store in the city. After gazing in boredom at dozens of desks, each one uglier than the next and all crammed into an alien, dimly lit space, I finally spied one I knew I could fall in love with and managed to cajole her into letting me have it although she pronounced it impractical. It was a fragile rolltop desk of knotty pine with a delicate chair to match. Afterward, she proved right: I never used it. My desk was merely symbolic. It stood across the room from my bed and contained secret treasures locked up in a narrow upright drawer secured by means of a trefoil bronze key. In this drawer, I carefully managed to sequester precious objects and writings but then promptly forgot about them, thereby initiating a lifelong cycle of hiding, losing, and finding. As for the activities normally associated with desks, I did those on my bed or occasionally on the floor.

A tiny private bathroom was attached diagonally to my room. Its one narrow, highly placed window looked like those found in illustrations of fairy-tale castles, and the bathroom was strictly mine, not shared with my sister. Somehow, this miniature bathroom, the winding entrance corridor, and the room's multipaneled leaded windows all seemed to lend my room an aura of fantasy. What I still see most clearly, though—beyond the yellow-petaled roses (which for years seemed to smell faintly of sweet wallpaper paste) and the greensward carpet and the chestnut wood—are *books*. Books scattered on my "other" bed, obscuring the coverlet. Books scattered carelessly. Books scattered tenderly. Books from school, books from the library, books from friends, books given as birthday presents. Books whose jackets and titles and pages transported me to other sites while my body remained in that room. As Bachelard writes, "Is there one among us who has not spent romantic moments in the tower of a book he has read?"

And today, as I envision those heaps of childhood books with all their glorious temptations, I recall the words of the Czech writer Bohumil Hrabal: "When I read I don't really read; I pop a beautiful sentence into my mouth and suck it like a fruit drop, or I sip it like a liqueur until the thought dissolves in me like alcohol, infusing brain and heart and coursing on through the veins to the root of each blood vessel."

An Aesthetics of Mess

In keeping with the customs and circumstances of her own youth, my mother hired a woman to arrive punctually each morning and perform a series of housekeeping tasks. Small-boned and taciturn, her straightened black hair pulled back and pinned into a bun at the nape of her neck, Marion was with us for a number of years. Each afternoon when I returned from school, she could be found sipping tea on the upholstered scarlet window seat of the dining alcove. Occasionally, she would break her long silences to regale me with cautionary tales about spoiled children in other houses where she had worked. My favorite story involved a wealthy family with a pair of daughters about the same ages as my sister and me. These girls, according to Marion, simply tore off their clothes (I always imagined the most theatrical gestures) and flung them heedlessly to the floor so that, as the days of the week rolled by, mounds of wrinkled sweaters, skirts, soiled blouses, underwear, and fetid socks arose in their rooms. The girls blithely ignored these malodorous mountains. Counting on the premise that they would eventually reform their ways, their mother instructed Marion not to pick anything up. So it went. In my imagination, these heaps of divested clothes mounted ever higher until at last they reached the ceiling and the poor neglectful girls were bereft of anything at all to wear—they simply had to go naked. This story, with my own secret ending, gave me great pleasure. I loved to hear it retold, and there might have been more than a twinge of envy in my demand for it. Ah, to have had the freedom to make a mess of one's room and to dwell in it sans interference, sans reproach, and *sans vêtements!*

A charming picture book entitled *Small Pig* by Arnold Lobel, ostensibly addressed to young children (but, like all fine works in this genre, addressed actually to both children and adults), can be taken as a cautionary tale for parents. Its title character, a sensuous and lovable little piglet, lives on a rural farm and loves to wallow in the mud after every rainstorm. The farmer's wife, however, with maddeningly familiar housewifely efficiency, appears to spoil the piglet's pleasure by using her noisy vacuum cleaner to absorb all the muddy moisture that accumulates in the yard. She does this once too often, and the piglet, feeling disgruntled and oppressed, runs away from home. After several misadventures, he gets stuck in a square of wet concrete, which he gleefully mistakes for mud. Pried loose after much ado by the fire department, he is eventually returned to the farm, and the farmer's wife, thrilled to have him safely back, promises never to vacuum his muddy playground again.

Parents, at all stages of their children's lives, struggle mightily with messes, and it might even prove useful to consider the notion of an *aesthetics of mess.* While the relative proportions of order to chaos and cleanliness to grime differ from family to family and from one cultural milieu to another, most children adore the latter, and it seems important to allow them to experience it from time to time, especially in the sanctity of their own private spaces.

As for my room, immaculately clean and neat, except for the books on my "other" bed, it sometimes felt alien to me. I think that, without being able to articulate it as such, I craved the right to mess it up. My being prohibited from doing so rendered the room somehow not wholly mine. The spirit of my mother—like the queen in *Snow White*—hovered. That image jibes also with my fear of approaching footsteps, for as you may remember, when the queen's mirror displeased her, she

of whatever they are able to find. Brooks uses armchairs, sheets, blankets, and colorful quilts as well as sticks and stones to construct—both indoors and outdoors—her tents, huts, and cavelike structures. In addition to making these cozy but also eerie and uncanny enclosures, she photographs them and has exhibited her photographs. Sometimes, she says, she climbs inside the structures and spends time there just to sense the changes they induce in her perception of her body and her consciousness. Anxiety, she says, plays an important role in her work—stemming from memories of visceral feelings of embarrassment, shame, curiosity about the forbidden, and fears of being discovered by grownups. She also questions people she meets about their own deep-rooted connections to such places in their pasts. In 1999 she initiated a collaborative interactive drawing project, still ongoing as of this writing, in which she asks volunteers to put down on paper whatever they remember of their own childhood experiences of this kind.

Brooks's term for what children do when they build their refuges is *primary architecture*, and this notion dovetails nicely with the theme we are considering here because, seeking privacy and autonomy, children sometimes produce such structures in their own rooms or, contrarily, they go elsewhere because the kind of refuge they are seeking cannot always be found in their designated room at home.

What about you? Did you ever build a fort, an igloo, or a tree house? A tabernacle of old sheets thrown over a card table? Perhaps a friend sequestered herself in your hideaway with you and you whispered furtively together. Possibly you took with you an imaginary companion. Or a pet, or a favorite toy. Maybe you even spoke in a secret language, because, as Bachelard says, "Words—I often imagine this—are little houses, each with its cellar and garret." The neurologist Oliver Sacks, in his memoir, *Uncle Tungsten*, tells of crawling happily into a triangular space under the stairs of his parents' London house where the Passover dishes were kept hidden all year when they were not in use and writes: "I felt snug here, in my secret hideaway—no one besides me was small enough to fit in."

The Found Refuge

Many children also find rather than make their alternative spaces. The shady spot under a special tree, perhaps, or a perch in its branches. As for me, I developed a habit, for a brief time in elementary school, of "running away." When interrogated and punished, I was unable to explain myself. Some of my departures were caused by fear of a certain gym teacher who seemed a surly tyrant to me, as, with a black megaphone fastened prosthetically, as it were, to his mouth, he dominated the school playing field, ranting in a voice that blended in my imagination with the guttural harangues of ogres (as in "Fee-fi-fo-fum"). Anything I could do to avoid him was desirable. A new pupil in sixth grade, the year when bodies are growing at noticably different rates, I was small, physically immature, and ashamed to be scrutinized by others in my regulation gym suit, mortified to be chosen last for every sports team, humiliated above all by being bellowed at. Thus, a pattern developed.

On gym-class days, I would descend to the breakfast room for my obligatory oatmeal and cod-liver oil and then dash away to school. But occasionally, instead of going to school, I would double back. Gingerly and furtively I would climb down into one of those leaf-filled wells that surround the basement windows of old houses like ours. Fortunately, our housekeeper had the habit of leaving one window slightly ajar to air out the laundry she had hung to dry, and reaching with my small fingers, I was just able to unlatch the bar and squeeze myself through. Tiptoeing to the tiny bathroom on that underground floor, I silently slipped the bolt and locked myself in. It was cold enough down there for me to keep my coat on. Before curling into a ball between the toilet bowl and the sink, I would pull the cord to turn on the one faint lightbulb overhead, take a book from my school bag, then settle down to read. The hours sped by as I disappeared into historic times and spaces. It was not until years later, when reading about the Renaissance scholar Erasmus in the pages of Bachelard, that I realized such secret disappearances are not unique. Erasmus eventually found himself "a nook in his fine house in which he could put his little body with safety [and confined] himself to one room until he could breathe the parched air that was necessary to him."

My mother thought me too young for a wristwatch, and so my anxiety that the housekeeper would stumble upon me and divulge my hiding place was trumped by a more urgent fear—namely, that lost in a book, I might fail to reappear at lunchtime. How would I know when to stop reading and retrace my steps, when to climb out of the window, double back, and pretend to come home from school? Eventually, I was found out and severely chastised. "Dire consequences," my father warned, are the fruits of misbehavior.

Milady Beheaded in the Attic

Another scene of clandestine activity took place that same year in a nearby turreted house belonging to my friend Mary Lennon. The trapdoor leading to her family's attic was hidden in Mary's bedroom, and she and her siblings were in possession of massive stacks of comic books, including the so-called Classic Comics, which I had been forbidden to read. Whereas other children spent their weekly allowances on these treasures, my sister and I were not permitted to do so. Mary, however, a loyal comrade, vowed to protect me even if it meant evading the truth on my behalf. Joyfully and shamefully, I would run weekdays after school to her parents' imposing house, where she and I, our hair done similarly in neatly matching braids, would smile conspiratorily as the oaken door swung heavily behind us. Once upstairs in her bedroom, we would try as silently as possible to release the folding staircase that led up into the dark attic. Equipped with flashlights and laden with our comic-book treasures, we ascended as lightly as possible, tiptoeing after each other. How delicious it was to be there amidst the dank odors and eerie shadows we cast! Never will I forget my terror when Milady, in the Classic Comics version of Dumas's *Three Musketeers*, was about to be beheaded. Her kneeling form in silhouette and that of her hooded executioner still haunt my dreams, for, like her, I felt myself to be culpable, wicked, and engaged in wrongdoing.

Under the Table

What child has never found sanctuary in a closet or a bathroom or behind the living room draperies or under a table? Mélanie, the mother of two young daughters, grew up on a farm in Belgium with her grandparents. She says she, too, had the habit of running away, in her case to a spot under the massive dining room table over which her grandmother always hung a heavy tablecloth that fell to the floor. There she would go with her supply of dolls, simple toys, and picture books and play alone until she was obliged by the command *"À table!"* to reappear for dinner. She hid not because she was profoundly unhappy but rather because she felt a need to escape from all the demands that the grownups were making on her and from their perpetual surveillance as well as from the other children in the house. She felt, she said, the need to find a nook where she could be completely at ease—a refuge where she could play and pretend to be anything she wanted, free of scrutiny.

A Girl's Room as the History of Her Childhood

All children need at times to escape from their parents and from everyone else. But not everyone has an artist for a father. In Kassel, I met a sculptor who told me about the bedroom of his eldest daughter, now a teenager, who also described it to me before I saw it for myself. Fanciful paintings made over the years by her father and other members of her family ever since her earliest childhood cover the walls of Deborah's room. She was born, she explained to me, shortly after her parents' divorce and has lived all her life with her mother in a town not far from the city of Kassel. What makes her bedroom so extraordinary is that, because of the paintings, its walls tell a history of her life in images. Over the years, Deborah and her mother have maintained warm ties with her father and with what Deborah calls "the other part" of his family—his second wife and two other daughters in Kassel. Her room symbolizes these continuing bonds among a group of people who, under other circumstances, might easily have drifted apart or allowed their connections to break.

The first paintings in her room were by her mother, made when Deborah was just a baby, and consist of a sun, two puffy clouds, an apple tree, and a meadow strewn with flowers. Deborah says that no one knows the exact date of these images but that, in her memory, they have always been there. Her father, her sister Grete, and she made the later paintings. She told me that when she was ill and could not go to school, her mother, a nurse, was sometimes unable to stay at home to take care of her, and so her father would come over, and as she lay in bed, she would tell him what she wanted him to paint on the walls. Gradually, animals and other images appeared: rabbits, crocodiles, ducks, birds, human faces, flowers, and butterflies. Sometimes, she says, she and her sister would "help" their artist father. He might paint a bird, and then she would contribute the plumes. She remembers that when he painted a railway station, she and her sister added the windows and entrance. Train tracks zigzag whimsically across the door lintels and ceiling.

Although Deborah is nineteen years old now and all the furnishings in her room have changed since her earliest childhood, she says she will never repaint or cover the walls. Despite the fact that they are primarily redolent of childhood, she is deeply attached to them. Comparing them to a book in which she is able to "read" her life, she says that, just as she would never destroy a book of any kind, she would not, by the same token, efface these walls, and she fervently hopes they can be preserved forever.

Recall the musically *untutored* stepfather who shared his love of music by means of simple tunes on the recorder; here we see how a professional artist found a way to share his prowess with his daughter and to do so within *her* private space and under her direction, thereby co-creating with her a lasting monument to the special nature of their unique family. Most parents are not artists, and many would not be comfortable with the notion of painting on bedroom walls, but this story, I believe, has rich symbolic and inspirational value. It speaks to the dual messages often given by children with respect to their rooms: "Please come see my room!" versus "P-r-i-v-a-t-e—KEEP OUT." Deborah's room, I can say now that I have seen it and spent time in it myself, radiates an unmistakable aura of privacy, even of sanctity, but it also stands, at the same time, as a powerful testament to her membership in an ongoing community. Thus, in both subtle and quite deliberate ways, as we have seen, parents can identify with children's needs to create their special spaces—spaces unique, intimate, and highly individualized but that remind them that, even when they are most alone, they are never absolutely alone.

Preparing for a Life of Visual Pleasures

Children's rooms, then, should perhaps best be seen as collaborative works-in-progress. Recently, I observed a young couple cooperate one weekend to hang pictures on the freshly painted walls of their four-month-old son's room. Up to this point little Michael had been sleeping in a cradle in their bedroom, but he was growing too large for that, and they had decided to take the step of transferring him into a room of his own, a transition that is always emotional as well as spatial. It was deeply moving for me to watch as they carefully considered where to hang each image they had selected, how high to place it, and how each picture would appear not only from the point of view of an adult entering the room but to the little fellow himself as he lay or played in his crib. They hung a brightly colored mobile with tiny clowns and a Picasso reproduction of a large clown, a richly vibrant Guatemalan weaving, a delicately framed birth certificate illustrated with Noah's ark animals and lettered in calligraphy. Two Japanese paper cutouts came next, followed by an appliquéd folk art piece representing fruits and vegetables. The room sprang to life. With tenderness and care, these parents were, it seemed to me, creating for their baby a site of aesthetic learning and exploration, the beginning of a lifetime of visual pleasures.

Looking Out the Window

As you think back, did your room feel capacious or cramped? Were you lucky enough to have a designated space that felt cozy and "just right"? This question evokes another children's story, that of Goldilocks and the Three Bears, which taps directly into the way children feel about spaces and objects and how they have to be neither too big nor too small, too soft nor too hard, too hot nor too cold. My own room felt big to me as I sat in my bed and looked around. It was also cold and drafty in winter. A corner room, it looked out over our garden, where my father had planted flowers, bushes, and some vegetables, to my delight. It makes me sad to think of that garden, because my father loved it so, and, although he tried to interest me in it and entice me to work with him there on weekends, my nose was permanently buried in a book. No one in my family joined him in the garden. Just for a couple of summers when I was very small, and we were living in an apartment building with garden plots out back, did I toddle after him, and the smell and texture of the earth linger still in my memory. There, like so many children, I dug my proverbial holes "to China," squealed at the wiggly shiny brown earthworms, marveled at parades of ants, and sprinkled freshly planted seedlings with my heavy tin watering can. Later, when we lived in the Tudor house in Larchmont, my father would sally forth in his soft leather jacket and mustard-colored gardening gloves. From the height of my bedroom, I could look down and watch his back bent over as he weeded and pruned beneath my castle window. I can still hear him whistling happily to himself, content in his solitude.

Being Alone

Solitude. Do you remember your feelings when you were alone in your room? How vividly mine return: that millstone of unrest, which submerged me—the shame-laden pleasure of being all by myself with books and colors and drawing pads. My mother's ideal was sociability, and she labored to convince me that, contrary to my instincts, no one is ever voluntarily alone. Being too much alone, she taught, is a sign of cowardice, a pusillanimous capitulation to states of morbidity. The seeping fear she engendered in me was that to enjoy my solitude—even for a few hours—might be to bring it upon myself forever. When I was alone in my room, lost in a daydream or a book, such worries rarely abated. Yet Bachelard writes movingly of the pleasures of refuge and about the seeker "of refuges [who] dreams of a hut, of a nest, or of nooks and corners in which he would like to hide away, like an animal in its hole." Some children, I am sure, are fortunate enough to experience such pleasures without remorse, and the aesthetic value of these secret spaces along with the freedom tasted in them cannot be underestimated. "Alone," as Bachelard continues, "we are at the origin of all real action that we are not 'obliged' to perform." It is only when we are alone that we can encounter certain of our dreams. "Love your solitude," writes Rilke in his *Letters to a Young Poet*. "The necessary thing is after all but this: solitude, great inner solitude. Going-into-oneself for hours meeting no one—this one must be able to attain."

Where Are You? Where Am I?

Solitude *can*, however, mean abandonment, loss of place, loss of self, and a corresponding sense of terror. While considering Walt Disney's *Bambi*, we saw that one of the most compelling dramas in childhood is being lost or imagining that one is lost. Children, moreover, sometimes think they are lost or feel lost when in fact they are not; conversely, they may actually *be* lost without being aware that they are. What matters in these cases, as with other forms of psychic pain, is the subjective experience. Memories of being lost often endure for a lifetime. William Blake's *Songs of Innocence* and *Songs of Experience* include several poems about children lost and found. In his searing novel, *Call It Sleep*, about an immigrant boy growing up in the slums of New York's Lower East Side during the early twentieth century, Henry Roth creates an unforgettable scene when the boy is lost and, through vision blurred by tears, he watches the unfamiliar streets begin "stealthily to wheel. He could feel them turning under his feet, though never a house changed place— backward to forward, side by side—a sly inexorable carousel."

Olivier, a Frenchman in his thirties, informs me that he still dreams of the time he was lost as a little boy. His parents had taken him with them into a curtain shop in Paris, and he was hiding happily among the draperies when suddenly he realized he was alone. He vividly recalls his terror and the tears that streamed down his mother's face when they were reunited and she embraced him, as well as his father's irritation and stern reproof.

Another Frenchman tells me that he remembers being lost as a child. When he was growing up, he and his parents used to make an annual pilgrimage to his grandparents' estate in the south of France, near Perpignan. His grandfather, on one fine morning, took him into the orchard to pick peaches. Almost immediately a neighbor accosted the old man, and soon the two were gesticulating wildly, drawn into a heated discussion. The child, ignored by his grandfather, tried to capture the interest of a lively little dog that had accompanied the neighbor. Indifferent to his blandishments, the dog trotted off; hopefully, the boy followed it. Time passed, and all of a sudden he realized he had no idea where he was. The nearby trees loomed taller than they ought to have been and far too dark; unlike the friendly trees of the orchard, they seemed bizarre and menacing. With a shock he realized he was lost and had no clue how to find his way back to his grandfather. Sobbing, he stumbled along, following the dog as it rambled nose to the earth. He recalls talking to the animal and tearfully imploring it to lead him back to his grandfather. At length, it did so. The elderly gentleman, still immersed in conversation with the neighbor, looked down at the tear-stricken face of his little grandson and roared mightily: "Idiot! You were never lost! The dog—being a dog—knew its way home all along."

Nevertheless, those moments of fear in the orchard were real, and the ring of his grandfather's scornful voice remains in my friend's memory decades later. Interestingly, before telling me this story, he framed it by repeating in a self-deprecatory manner (thereby unwittingly replaying his grandfather's mockery of him) that, although what he was about to tell me was *apparently* a story about being lost, he had in fact probably *not* been lost. Still, the experience survives as his most powerful memory of being so, and it represents his paradigm association to this theme. In it, we see another instance of a child's mixing of what we later come to separate out as subjective and objective experience.

Reflecting on this not-atypical tale, we can see, beyond its depiction of the fear that comes from sensing one does not know one's way back and may never be able to get back, the almost grotesque asymmetry between a child's and an adult's perspective. Emphasizing this gap, I want to propose that just as a not-lost child may feel radically abandoned, so, likewise, a lost child's actual experience may differ markedly from his or her "reality" as assessed by adults external to it. In making this point, I do not intend to mystify children's experiences but merely to emphasize how important it is to remember, to watch, and to listen.

It is striking how frequently children's stories of being lost feature the uncomprehending, unsympathetic attitude of adults. Rather than being greeted with expressions of unadulterated gratitude, relief, and joy, recovered children meet frequently with a barrage of resentment. Why should this be so? In addition to irritation over the inconvenience caused, anger may be a result of adult guilt in such situations—guilt that flips over easily into the more tolerable emotion of self-righteous rage. For some adults, it may be hard to identify consciously with children's terrors at being lost, a difficulty that comes, I suspect, from the fact that this dreaded state (abandonment) is one that many of us work hard, throughout our lifetimes, to avoid. For exiled adults, for instance, the way home may be forever barred because the once-known past has simply vanished. Unlike most lost children, who continue to hope, exiled persons may experience a hopelessness that precludes even an imaginary return, a hopelessness that works psychologically to rebuff all desire for return and that fosters, in some instances, a protective denial that may spill over into a crippling constraint on feelings more generally and lead in extreme cases to apathy and to failures of empathy.

"Peekaboo," or Taking Control of Being Lost

In the earliest years of life, children play the game of peekaboo or hide-and-seek, as it is called later on, with its many variations, first passive and then active. Why? Children all over the world engage in ritualized forms of these dramas of separation and loss, I warrant, in order (along the lines of Freud's findings vis-à-vis the *fort-da* game mentioned earlier) to try to master their daily experiences of appearance and disappearance and to prepare themselves for their occurrence in the future. Surprisingly, however, in a review article by child psychologists that tabulates variations on the game as observed in a sample of children ranging in age from seven to seventeen months ("Peekaboo and the Learning of Rule Structures," by Jerome S. Bruner et al.), the authors eschew this interpretation. "It is hard," they write, "to imagine *any function* for peekaboo aside from practice in the learning of rules in converting 'gut play' into play with conventions" (my italics). This statement is followed by a demurral that another possible function for the game might be the exploration of boundaries between the "real" and the "make-believe." Respectfully, I must ask: What *about* that so-called gut play? We cannot ignore it and shunt it aside. Surely, what gives peekaboo its emotional resonance, its power, its delight, and its permanence in the repertory of childhood games is precisely its connection with the most deeply rooted "gut" fear of all, namely, abandonment.

This meaning, in fact, is not lost even on the Hollywood creators of a popular recent animated film for children, *Ice Age*, written by Michael Berg, Michael J. Wilson, and Peter Ackerman, which contains four incidents of the peekaboo game, played to great effect by a small child and his animal friends, including a saber-toothed tiger, Diego, who had initially wanted to destroy the child but who grows increasingly responsive to his innocent trust and eventually comes to love him.

Even the child psychologists who do not make this interpretation relate a telling example from their own survey. One little boy, apparently, is unable to play the peekaboo game with his mother. They consider his failure "instructive," as they put it, but they do not see it as a failure in negotiating the boundaries between one human being and another, nor as a failure to prepare safely in play for separations in the future, as I do. They attribute the failure in his case to his mother's practice of starting the game without getting his full attention, to her taking control of the game, and to her foreclosing the child's role, therefore, as initiator. He, consequently, never becomes an agent in the game, and the game disappears from his (and their joint) repertoire. The authors do not mention any anxiety on the part of the mother, nor do they characterize her behavior in emotional terms at all. In my experience, however, mothers who manifest this kind of impatience often reveal a latent anxiety (over boundaries), which is passed on to their children, who, as in this case, withdraw. The authors, though, make an analogy between this failed game of peekaboo and problems in the acquisition of language (also a mother-child negotiation). They refer to mothers who too quickly step in to correct their children's utterances, thereby causing their children to drop the lexical items interfered with. What the authors prioritize here, therefore, is loss of cognitive function—rules and grammar. What matters far more to me, however, are the *emotional* lacunae that may result: in other words, the child's ensuing incapacity not only to understand the rules, linguistic or otherwise, but even to access the feelings that precipitate these cultural elaborations.

The infant game of peekaboo is soon followed, in a variety of forms, by the drama of hide-and-seek with its complex mixture of relinquishing versus anticipating. Normally, small children do not want to be lost. Even Hansel and Gretel, despite the deprivations and machinations of their wicked stepmother, manage on every occasion possible to leave a trail behind in order to find their way home. On the other hand, with what delight do they exclaim when they spy the witch's gingerbread house with its frosted roof and candy-cane trim! And remember Dorothy's mixed reactions when, after having been tossed about by the cyclone, she arrives in the colorful, magical Land of Oz? My point is that, notwithstanding their fears of the unknown and their deep longings for home, even for a home that may no longer feel safe, children possess strong adaptive capacities that enable them to welcome the new. In childhood, hope and desire are so infused with curiosity that reason and adversity—even in the wake of extreme forms of trauma—cannot always trample them.

For lost children, then, the hope of return tends to persevere in the form of pulsating dreams and wishes—witness the final scene of *Hansel and Gretel*. All the children (see my earlier discussion of the last scene of the Humperdinck opera) *do* eventually go home, but in the meantime, present adventures preempt full attention. There are some children, however, who withdraw into passive states—into postures characteristic of bereavement. It is extremely significant that in the film *Bambi*, before the scenes of death and bereavement are over, the little deer's father returns and offers himself as a substitute for the lost mother. The salutary paternal presence at this moment is not only physically but also psychologically necessary for the transition that follows—to the previously described scene of springtime merriment—which, however, as I have protested, comes far too quickly and without preparation.

Losing a Child

To lose one's child is to feel instantly helpless and, in a very real sense, lost as well. It may rekindle the panic of an all-but-forgotten moment when one was abandoned oneself as well as all the other anxieties called forth by present circumstances and manifest dangers and by a sense of failed responsibility. From a deep psychological perspective, an important loss, no matter how it actually happens, counts on a very primitive level as a desertion, just as a death, however irrationally and unconsciously, counts as a murder. (If you doubt these notions, try to encourage a physician who deals with dying patients to talk freely with you; he may tell you he has been accused and vilified by relatives of deceased patients and subjected to their unjustified accusations, rage, and blame.)

In part, such primitive recriminations occur because of our human tendency to attribute personal agency as a cause even in situations where it clearly is not. Just as ancient peoples populated the heavens and the rivers and the trees with deities who possessed given names and, often, human forms, so we moderns are more comfortable somehow to blame bad news on somebody or on several somebodies than to attribute its cause to fate, chance, or luck. Perhaps we do this to preserve the illusion that, as human beings, we retain the power to control events or at least understand them. In any case, it is not only, as Blake says, that "mercy hath a human heart and pity a human face" but that we try also to give evil a human face. Philosopher Susan Neiman demonstrates in a recent book how difficult it is, philosophically and psychologically, to avoid humanizing and/or rationalizing both man-made and natural disasters. When anything goes wrong, we feel that *someone* must be at fault. Therefore, if a child is lost, *someone* must be to blame. If it is not the parents, then it must be the child herself. Hence, the projection of rage. We saw a similar phenomenon at play earlier in the anecdote about the little French girl who, separated from her parents, thought that strangers were stealing a baby in Orly Airport.

From their earliest moments, in order to feel safe, children must endow their parents, the beings on whom their lives depend, with puissance. Omnipotence implies, however, the capacity to destroy as well as to protect. From a young child's point of view, nothing happens at all without the agency of her parents. If she is lost, it is they who have lost her, but it is also they who can find her. And these currents run so deep and last so long that parents of a lost child, reacting childishly themselves, may attribute that false agency in turn to their child. Greeting her not with embraces but with explosions of anger, they may behave as though she were not the victim but the perpetrator of her own disappearance, as if she willed it. Beset with remorse at their own corresponding failure to protect her, they reject their unwanted feelings of shame and punish the returning child, who must then suffer doubly and at the same time learn an unfortunate lesson about how to cope with such emergencies in the future.

Snow Flurries in New England and a Forest of Legs

Mixtures of fantasy and reality, familiarity and discomfort, alternating feelings of identification and disjunction, believing that one is here and not here—all these may characterize moments of make-believe and play in children's lives and also moments when children feel they are lost.

Rachel, a New Yorker of seven, is traveling one winter by car with her family to a new destination in Canada's Laurentian Mountains at the beginning of their annual ski vacation. As they pass through northern New England, snow begins to fall and the landscape darkens. Rachel's older brother, a precocious teenager and a self-proclaimed expert with mazes and maps, informs their father that he has discovered a shortcut, a faster route than the one proposed by the ski lodge to which they are heading. Reluctantly, Rachel's father veers off the highway onto a smaller road while the weather conditions steadily worsen. As the small road divides and branches and the storm continues, it becomes increasingly evident that none of the country roads in the area is marked in any way. The family is lost.

Rachel peers out her window. Dark woods surround her, populated, in her fervid imagination, by wild bears and other ferocious beasts. Her mother, seated in the front of the car, suggests they stop at the next dwelling they approach to ask their way, but Rachel's older sister objects vehemently: "No!" she protests. "I won't get out of the car. All the people around here have guns."

Huddling and shivering in the backseat, Rachel remains silent. With each passing moment, she grows more frightened. Enveloped by the whirling snow and howling winds and by the disputatious words of her anxious family, she feels utterly lost. What matters most is not *where* she is in terms of any map but the psychic pain of feeling alone and unprotected, even though, in actuality, her family is all around her.

As for me, what I remember goes something like this: My mother has taken me shopping. I am small, perhaps about four. Mother, elegant and efficient, stands at the counter of a glass display case, and I, at my eye level, am looking through the pane admiring a splendid array of colorful objects the details of which I can no longer recall. I know simply that I am safe and happy, enjoying the sparkling sight, as my mother talks animatedly with a saleswoman. Suddenly I look up, and she is no longer there. In a mounting panic, I walk around the whole store searching for her. Growing more and more afraid, I realize that she is gone. She has left me. I watch as strangers enter and others depart through the doorway of the shop. She will be next. She will come back and rescue me. "Find me, Mommy!" I plead. But she never comes. It is up to me. I must find her. Slipping through the doorway, I'm out now on the concrete sidewalk of a busy street. Grown-ups pass me by. I'm too small to scan their faces; I can see only their legs. This is my strongest memory: searching for my mother amidst a forest of legs— legs clad in boots and pants and stockings and high-heeled shoes. Which way shall I turn? I walk and cry at the same time, alone in that thicket of moving limbs.

How my mother found me, I do not know, but the moment we were reunited, she became furious. Uncharacteristically raising her voice, she chastised me in public. Weak with joy, I could only collapse, relieved beyond words to be with her once more and humiliated to have lost her. The moving cavalcade of enormous legs that surrounded me and the waves of panic I endured that day have remained with me ever since.

Chapter Six

Treasures

There was a child went forth every day,
And the first object he looked upon,
That object he became . . .
                    —Walt Whitman, *Leaves of Grass*

Every beloved object is the center of a garden of
paradise.
                    —Bohumil Hrabal, *Too Loud a Solitude*

Tom was literally rolling in wealth. He had, besides
the things before mentioned, twelve marbles, part of a
jews-harp, a piece of blue bottle glass to look through,
a spool cannon, a key that wouldn't unlock anything,
a fragment of chalk, a glass stopper of a decanter, a
tin soldier, a couple of tadpoles, six firecrackers, a
kitten with only one eye, a brass doorknob, a dog
collar—but no dog—the handle of a knife, four pieces
of orange peel, and a dilapidated old window sash.
                    —Mark Twain, *The Adventures of Tom Sawyer*

Raggedy, Rubber, and Rag Dolls

Have you ever noticed how a toddler who comes to greet you is nearly
always holding or dragging something? That designated object may

in time be set aside in favor of another, and yet again another, and another, but most children cannot do without treasures. Chosen objects are zealously guarded, preserved, hidden, and, if lost or damaged, may wreak devastation because so much has been invested in them. Were you able to hold on to any of yours?

A smudge-faced Raggedy Ann smiles wistfully at me. Why, as I gaze at her, does she seem redolent of pluck and whimsy mingled with the expectable nostalgia? Her worn cotton face, grime gray with age, still boasts its archetypal black button eyes. Faded wisps of wool hair, nominally vermillion, poke every which way around her painted face, but plenty of stuffing has gone. Zigzagging across her wrinkly lozenge-shaped arms and striped legs are irregular slants of red, white, and black—the earnest stitches of the child who tried repeatedly to mend her. Lifting up her dress, a patchwork shift borrowed from a less favored doll, reveals her pantalettes and the telltale heart imprinted on her chest: I LOVE YOU. Her legs dangle and flop when you lift her. How frail and weightless she has become after all these years. What was there about her that made her my favorite?

A lady writes to me from Paris. Growing up in the south of France—in the Midi—Dominique had two best dolls, and all of her earliest ones, she assures me, were made, like mine, of cloth. Her great first love was a nameless rag doll, which disappeared one day, and even now the grief remains with her, for she never learned what became of it. Of all her dolls, this one, in the worst condition, was the one she fancied. She thinks her mother might have tossed it out one day because it was so ugly, or given it away to the Gypsies who came begging for old clothes. Later on Dominique received other dolls, especially at Christmastime: elegant celluloid creatures in charming outfits with elaborate coiffures. They arrived in beribboned boxes, but they never interested her. She was forever warned to be careful with them so as not to spoil their finery; their arms and legs might so easily become dislocated.

One Christmas, however, in the late 1950s, an extraordinary doll appeared. It was one of the first Bella dolls made of a rubbery vinyl, and it turned out to be a dream come true. Absolutely unbreakable, Dominique says. She could drop it, throw it, scold it, spank it, bathe it, feed it, comb and brush its hair, and, in fact, play with it as roughly or as gently as she chose. All her other dolls were relegated to the shelf, and this one, also nameless like the first, became her second love. Her parents paid no attention to it whatsoever, and their disregard accounted in part for her strong attachment to it. Nobody cared what she did with it; it was hers and only hers.

Like my Raggedy, this second special doll of Dominique's exists today buried under scarves inside her Parisian armoire. Its once-blond hair has dulled, its rubber skin has gone dark and sticky in spots; its fingers are partly eaten away, and as she takes it out and holds it at arm's length to examine it, she finds it very small. But, oh, how large it was to her then, she exclaims, how grand and important and beloved.

It is not easy to tell what factors make a particular object special to a child, but what matters is that some objects *do* become important and that, when they do, we adults must try to valorize their importance while at the same time not interfere too much with the attachment. Many authors have cited D. W. Winnicott's celebrated identification of what he called the *transitional object* or the first *not-me* possession. Winnicott taught that an infant's favored blanket or soft toy animal is both found and made, or, we might say, both given and chosen, in that the baby selects it from among whatever objects have been made available and imbues it with a significance far beyond its obvious external qualities. Probably you can recall some frayed, unwashed coverlet you dreaded to lose in the supermarket or a matted-fur teddy bear with missing limbs that was slightly embarrassing to take along but that couldn't be left behind. Winnicott stresses the point that we adults must not challenge children's attachments to these privileged objects for the same reason I offered earlier with regard to the little girl who was spinning at the Guggenheim—we do not want to inhibit the further elaboration of their imagination and their play.

The Riddle of the Hobbyhorse

Sometimes objects matter to children just because of what can be done to them and with them. This was the way Dominique interpreted her attraction to the rubber dolly, and it is exactly the way E. H. Gombrich understands a young child's relationship with a hobbyhorse. The hobbyhorse, he points out, need not *look* at all like a real horse. Likewise, he explains, a kitten chases a ball of yarn—not, in other words, because the ball looks anything like a mouse, but because the kitten can *do* to the ball what it might well do to a live mouse. Any stick or pole, therefore, that a child can ride becomes ipso facto a hobbyhorse, and it is the riding, not the appearance, that proves the decisive factor.

Here we may pause to wonder about the relationship between such early treasures and children's subsequent investment in the realm of the arts and in objects of greater cultural significance. Winnicott, in an essay called "The Location of Cultural Experience," argues that such initial objects can actually be seen as embryonic forms of works of art themselves and a child's play as the *anlage* of theater. I wonder, however, whether such elisions might prove too facile. Skeptically, I remain unconvinced that we can trace an unbroken line from children's dolls and treasures or indeed their towers of blocks or scribbles to later works of art that communicate across the gaps between one human consciousness and another. The tenuous links are there, but many intervening steps are missing. I would profess that it is in these very steps, in the elaboration of early experiences and in their refinement, in each child's cherishing and embellishing of the first objects, that cultural experience has its true beginnings. As Freud observed with regard to other people's daydreams, we really don't much care about them unless and until they are elaborated into narratives that can engage us on many levels and hold us. Every child begins with preferences, feelings, and loves. Only, however, when these are developed and expanded upon so that they flower in interesting, unprecedented ways do they attain value for strangers. The role of the adult in this elaborative process remains unclear, for as we have noted, to countenance children's imaginative play and to provide it room and air and to engage with it seems optimal, yet paradoxically, the reverse sometimes proves catalytic. Children who are thwarted surprise us occasionally by drawing on inner wellsprings of passion that drive them to create.

"Don't Move Anything! It Isn't Finished"

To elaborate with objects can often mean to use them in ways for which they were not intended; recall the little boy who transformed his mother's egg slicer into a musical instrument. I know a little girl whose wooden and cardboard puzzle pictures could not be completed by visiting children because they were always missing parts. The reason was clear: This girl had no interest whatever in solving puzzles—instead, she took their brightest and most intriguingly shaped pieces and made believe that they were magical morsels of food for her stuffed animals and dolls.

Seven-year-old Adam has been hard at work in the playroom for over an hour. I come down the stairs to take a look, and a wonderful sight greets my eyes: a wildly fanciful architectural contraption has arisen and transformed the space. It consists of two mahogany leather-topped stools with a folding chair placed between them, all three pieces connected by a red-and-white-striped jump rope that is suspended and held in place by a stack of picture books. An upended wicker basket is surmounted by a strategically placed rattan bull in fuchsia, aqua, and gold—a kind of miniature piñata—as well as several tiny figurines of bears in clothes, a rubber widemouthed hippo, and an alphabet block that reads S. Lincoln Logs lean like buttresses against the structure at various points, although their function seems mainly decorative. The entire construct abuts a table covered with woven Bedouin cloths from the Old City of Jerusalem. Three armored knights on horseback, a fuzzy toy armadillo from Texas, and an elephant have been organized into a posse, at right angles to which Adam has positioned a jaunty little Air France teddy bear. Propped at the other end on a platform consisting of two miniature Babar books, a tiny giraffe surveys the scene. Adam's father is heard now, calling down to tell him it's time to go, but Adam is loath to stop. As he painfully extricates himself from his immersion in the creative flow, he looks at me and commands in a tone of artistic authority: "DON'T move anything! It isn't finished."

A Treasure Chest Under the Bed

An object may gain in stature not only because of what a child can do with it but because of the stories that are associated with it. My enduring relationship with Raggedy Ann, for example, may be owing in part to the mischievous Johnny Gruelle adventure stories that are associated with that character and to her romantic origins; she was accidentally found, as it happens, in her grandmother's attic by a proper little girl called Marcella.

Jamaica Kincaid, in her intensely vivid coming-of-age novel, *Annie John*, evokes the pleasures, oft renewable, that children glean from treasures that are linked with stories especially about their own life histories and with the people they love. Kincaid describes a wooden trunk placed under her title character's bed filled with objects relevant to the little girl's life and dating back to the time just before she was born. Painted yellow and green and lined with cream-colored wallpaper covered with roses, this trunk had been brought by Annie's mother from the island of Dominica to Antigua years before the child's birth, and on special occasions it would be taken out. Annie's mother would open the trunk, air it out, and change its camphor balls. She would pick up each object in turn, hold it in her hands, and, sitting on the floor with the little girl crouched on her knees behind her and leaning over her shoulder, tell her a story about it.

Among the trunk's treasures were a pair of white wool infant booties, Annie's crib sheets and hemstitched diapers, her first birthday dress in yellow cotton with green smocking, her first pair of earrings and first pair of shoes, her report cards and certificates of merit from Sunday school. To review these objects and to hear the familiar tales about them was to feel—in Annie's words—that "No small part of my life was so unimportant that [my mother] hadn't made a note of it . . . She smelled sometimes of lemons, sometimes of sage, sometimes of roses, sometimes of bay leaf . . . How terrible it must be for all the people who had no one to love them so and no one whom they loved so, I thought."

Later on in the novel, when Annie reaches puberty, a dramatic reversal occurs. The precious trunk, heretofore the source of so much joy, turns alien. Along with the changes that have taken place in Annie's body, the trunk has altered. Suddenly, it no longer belongs to her or to her mother and herself together but *only* to her mother. Its contents seem filled with objects selected not for their significance to her but for their significance to her mother. Rejecting it, Annie turns to her father and asks him to make her a new trunk, a trunk of her own. This request, however, feels like a betrayal. It causes her to watch her mother warily out of the corner of her eye. She describes a huge shadow cast on the wall by her mother's body as she watches, and Kincaid writes stunningly: "I could not be sure whether for the rest of my life I would be able to tell when it was really my mother and when it was really her shadow standing between me and the rest of the world."

Tokens of Affection

Objects may take on significance for children because of their association with the person who gave them, and parents often help children form and preserve such associations. I am thinking of a miniature silver-turbaned Carmen Miranda doll mailed to me one holiday by my paternal grandmother, a snowbird who wintered in Miami Beach. The exotic figurine survives intact, even though, throughout my childhood, I never had the faintest idea who Carmen Miranda was or even whether she was a fictional character or a real human being. What mattered about her—*my* Carmen Miranda—was her signifance as a tangible reminder of the faraway person who had given her to me. A regal doll, she was treated almost like an iconic representation of my adoring grandmother. According appropriate excesses of affection and respect to her, I arranged an exalted place for her to live, unlike Raggedy, high on a shelf in my bedroom where she could be admired but rarely touched, which is why she continues, even today, to radiate her glamour.

Children, however, must and do learn that meanings survive objects. Beloved treasures from childhood live on in our minds long after we can hold or behold them. Dominique repeated to me that her memory of her lost rag doll continues to haunt her. *The Bracelet,* an exceptional picture book by Yoshiko Uchida and Joanna Yardley, treats this theme against a backdrop of America's internment of our Japanese American citizens during World War II. Emi and Laurie, second-graders in Berkeley, California, are best friends, neighbors, and classmates. When the story begins, Emi's family has been ordered away to a prison camp because America is at war with Japan, and everything in Emi's house has been packed into boxes. The little girl is standing on the stairs of her empty home looking around at the unprecedented nothingness, when she hears the doorbell ring. Her friend Laurie has come to say good-bye and has brought her a gift, a delicate gold bracelet with a tiny pendant heart. Emi promises to wear it at all times and never to take it off, even in the shower.

Watercolor illustrations portray the contrast between Emi's family's bright California home and the objectionable dank horse barn where her cohort of Japanese Americans has been assigned to live out the war. Suddenly, in the midst of the moving, with its attendant chaos, shocks, and confusion, Emi realizes she has lost her bracelet. With her mother's help, she searches the stalls of the stable and even a racetrack surrounded by barbed wire that lies adjacent to the building they have been condemned to inhabit. The bracelet cannot be found.

Feeling that she has lost the one meaningful possession she has brought with her, Emi slowly unpacks her bag. She takes out a red school sweater and remembers that Laurie has one just like it and a lunch box that matches hers as well. A man comes by their stall and nails up a shelf. On it, Emi's mother immediately places a photo of Emi's father, who was taken away earlier to a prison camp in a different state. While arranging the picture, Emi's mother remarks gently that, in fact, they really don't need a photo to remind themselves of him, for he is carried with them in their hearts. Emi understands these words, and slowly she realizes that they are true not only of her father but also of her lost bracelet and her enduring ties of friendship with Laurie. On the last page, we find her sitting alone on some flat stones outside the stable wearing her red sweater, minus her bracelet, knowing that what matters is not the token itself but what the token stands for.

Mending

Not only are treasures sometimes lost; they can be broken, ripped, or cracked, and by intention as well as by accident. All children are at times impulsively and designedly destructive. Clare Winnicott, the good doctor's widow, in a short biographical sketch, recounts a story about her late husband's youth. In notes that were meant to become an auto-biography had he lived long enough, Winnicott wrote that, as a three-year-old, he once took a croquet mallet and smashed the nose of a wax doll belonging to his older sister. This doll was called Rosie, and he was angry at it because his father had been in the habit of teasing him by using its name and his together and singing a verse he could still repeat. Throughout the rest of Winnicott's life, he declared, he continued to be troubled by the fact that, at such a tender age, he had not only wanted to commit a violent act but had actually planned it and carried it out. He had done the deed.

What happened next, however, was both extraordinary and exemplary. His father, instead of reprimanding him, seized the opportunity to teach him an entirely different lesson. Lighting up a series of matches, he was able to warm up the wax nose of the doll that had been deformed by the mallet. As the small boy watched, his father reshaped and remolded it until the doll's face became quite normal in appearance. "This early demonstration," Winnicott wrote, "of the restitutive and reparative act certainly made an impression on me." It enabled him, as he said, to accept rather than to flee in terror the reality of his own aggressive impulses and to acknowledge his frightening ability to act on them. Best of all, it brought into his awareness, in the most dramatic way, his father's good-naturedness and lack of spite. Finally, it taught him that a bad act can sometimes be remedied if one makes the effort to do so.

Saving and Giving Away

Five-year-old Sandy is an only child who dwells in a rustic cottage-in-the-clouds in the Berkeley hills of California with his physicist father and museum-curator mother. The house, deck, and pathways teem with his possessions—toys of every shape, size, and color. Some are intact but others are broken; many form a happy played-with disarray. One day, however, after mulling over this accumulation that seems to have grown exponentially from year to year without respite, Sandy's mother decides it's time to do a weeding out, and she calls him over. "Come, Sandy," she proposes, "let's go through your toys and pick out the ones you don't need anymore so we can give them away."

To her astonishment, the project fails. Each time she picks something up, Sandy looks at it, takes it in his hands, and uncannily recalls some anecdote related to it, some vignette that reanimates it, and then he refuses to part with it. He cannot relinquish it because it has repossessed its value. He remembers exactly what each toy once meant to him, what he traded it for and with which child, whose birthday party it came from, who gave it to him and at which holiday, when and where he lost it and how he found it again. Finally, in a state of combined admiration, exasperation, and amusement, his mother gives up and agrees to keep everything but simply to reorganize the articles and to stow some of them temporarily away.

A picture book called *Arthur's Honey Bear* by Lillian Hoban recounts a similar situation. Two little monkeys, a brother and sister called Arthur and Violet, have decided to do their spring cleaning and hold a tag sale. Emptying their toy chest, they gather their old possessions and display them on the back steps. Arthur makes a sign with arrows and price tags for all his Noah's ark animals, marbles, pail and shovel, yo-yo, and hula hoop, but as Violet points out to him, he puts no price tag on his Honey Bear. Arthur counters that Honey Bear is in good condition with only one eye missing and that maybe he should sell him only for a lot of money. "Father gave me Honey Bear when I had the chicken pox," said Arthur. "Honey Bear always tasted my medicine for me when I was sick."

Arthur places Honey Bear behind another toy, and the children wait for their friends to arrive. When a little girl named Wilma notices Honey Bear hiding behind the stuffed gorilla, she asks why he has no price, and Arthur quickly replies that he costs a lot. Wilma gives Arthur fifty cents, saying she wants Honey Bear as a birthday present for her baby sister, and Arthur reluctantly parts with him. Wilma, however, returns a moment later and gives back the bear because she has no more money for wrapping paper. Gratefully, Arthur hugs Honey Bear.

Nobody else comes to buy, and the children sit on the back steps eating cupcakes, wishing someone would appear to make a purchase. Eventually, Violet says: "I will buy something, Arthur. I will buy your Honey Bear." Bargaining with her brother, she offers him her last thirty-one cents along with a coloring book, some crayons, and even a half-full box of Cracker Jack, but Arthur clutches his bear.

"Honey Bear has been my bear for a long time . . . He wants me to take care of him."

At last the entrepreneurial instinct grows irresistible, and Arthur agrees to sell. All by himself now, he puts everything away, drops the thirty-one cents into his bank, and eats a few pieces of Cracker Jack. Violet appears at his door with Honey Bear dressed in a tutu and bonnet.

"Honey Bear is a *boy!*" Arthur protests.

Violet reminds him that Honey Bear belongs to *her* now and that she can dress him any way she wants. Arthur thinks it over: Since Violet is his sister, he reasons, and since Honey Bear now belongs to her, surely he must be Honey Bear's *uncle*. Picking Honey Bear up for a hug—bonnet and all—he announces that uncles are for taking everyone out for treats. He, Violet, and Honey Bear walk over to the nearest candy store, where Arthur spends his thirty-one cents on chocolate ice cream cones for three.

Material Culture and Contemporary Childhood

In mulling over the role of objects in the lives of children growing up today, I would underscore the unpredictability of what constitutes a treasure. That notwithstanding, I would, in my own way with children, accord a high priority to the value of objects that are made and found and given and received and fixed and fashioned and worked on, at least partially, rather than simply store-bought. I would try, whenever possible, to privilege objects for children that are unique "one-ofs" for whatever reason, rather than monotonous manufactured replicas. Objects that have a life history, such as hand-me-downs. Objects, importantly, that can also be admired and enjoyed and imaginatively manipulated *without being purchased or possessed.* Objects of nature, artifacts in a museum, treasures that belong to other people.

Walt Whitman wrote in *Leaves of Grass* that children *become* the objects they look upon. It is up to us as adults to notice what is occurring in the fertile negotiations that take place from moment to moment between children's souls and the material culture that surrounds us all.

Chapter Seven

Today Is My Birthday

When I was one I'd just begun,
When I was two I was nearly new,
When I was three I was hardly me,
When I was four I was not much more,
When I was five I was barely alive,
But now I am six! As clever as clever!
And I think I'll stay six now forever and ever.

—A. A. Milne

A child's birthday is the central organizing event of his year, often superceding all major holidays, national and religious. By celebrating a child's birthday each year, parents reaffirm the joy of that child's advent as well as mark his progress—physical, psychological, social, and intellectual—on the path from babyhood to adulthood. Birthdays also provide untold opportunities for aesthetic experience.

Homemade Paper Flowers and a Pool of Tears

My special love of birthday parties came, not surprisingly, from my mother, who orchestrated superlative celebrations year after year on the occasion of her children's birthdays. One, in particular, endures in my memory. For my tenth birthday, she took the theme of *Alice's Adventures in Wonderland,* which she and I both loved, and created an event of legendary proportions. Although we were living at that time in an apartment with limited space, she managed to transform it into an enchanted realm. The invitations requested that all my friends arrive in costume, and I later found out that my irrepressible mother had actually possessed the temerity (a quality never in short supply where she was concerned) as well as the maternal prescience to telephone each mother to say that the birthday girl and *only* the birthday girl would come dressed as Alice.

I can still remember my thrill, surprise, and delight as we opened the door and each child entered in masquerade. Some of my friends had been transformed almost beyond recognition. My mother's invitation had placed a covert demand on the other mothers and children to become inventive, and they truly responded. Although some may have felt it a burden, the quality of the results would seem to affirm that dreaming up those costumes was a great deal of fun for all concerned. One blond friend named Carlyn came as the Duchess. Appropriately coiffed and stuffed with an enormous pillow, she wore a handmade habit sewn of stiff fabric that hung to the floor. Several other girls came as the Queen of Hearts, but each had conceived her costume differently. A little boy (my then-current beau, named Jonathan) came as the entire pack of cards, wearing them pinned from top to toe all over his leotard-like costume. I welcomed also a natty Mad Hatter, a Cheshire Cat, and even a Tweedledum and Tweedledee (although technically they must have been crashers from *Through the Looking Glass*). My younger sister, garbed in white from top to toe, with stand-up ears, a fluffy tail, an enormous wristwatch, and bright red lipstick (her own idea, I'm sure), was a spiffy White Rabbit. Others, I can no longer remember. As for me, my mother dressed me in pale blue with a white apron. She brushed out my long hair, which she then uncharacteristically left unbraided, and transformed me into an unmistakable Alice.

How my mother must have reveled in the pleasure of turning our apartment into Wonderland! I can still remember the chaotic mess we made beforehand and how we were working right up to the day of the party. She taught my sister and me how to make brilliantly colored iridescent flowers of various sizes and shapes by taking rainbow-colored tissue and crepe paper and carefully cutting, folding, twisting, pressing, and tying, then gathering our blooms into many-splendored bouquets, which we attached to every available object and surface throughout the apartment. On the party table my mother had placed little cups labeled *Drink me* and cakes that said *Eat me.* There were ornamental signs directing children *To the Pool of Tears,* which turned out to be our bathtub filled with water, in which amazing lilies and strange aquatic toy creatures were swimming about. A tiny key opened a door to a make-believe garden, and somehow Rabbit's house had also been constructed. We went outside for part of the time (the apartment building had walkways, bushes, and manicured gardens) to participate in a caucus race in which all of us ran about until we were exhausted, and everybody, of course, was given a prize (treats for the guests and a silver thimble for me). The experience as I recall it today was one of utter joy. Metamorphosis. Theater. Normal everyday reality had completely receded during those precious hours while the party lasted. My friends simply became the characters they represented, and all of us had entered an enchanted realm.

I suppose I grew up with the wish to repeat this experience somehow and, if possible, to give it one day to my own children. So, later on, there were others: a circus clown party; a *Peter Pan* party replete with Tinkerbell, the Lost Boys, Nana, the crocodile, Captain Hook, Smee, and a treasure hunt that involved finding Peter's shadow; a *Wizard of Oz* party for which the basement was entirely remodeled to resemble the Emerald City; a Raggedy Ann party with a cake in the shape of the giant doll herself with her carrot-colored hair, red-and-white striped stockings, and candy heart that said I LOVE YOU; a storybook party to which each child came as a character from his or her favorite book; and a nurse party where—instead of playing the usual pin-the-tail-on-the-donkey—ten blindfolded children were given Band-Aids to stick on the bruised knee of a blown-up little girl with tears I had painted beforehand on an enormous piece of posterboard. For that party, we also fashioned little first-aid kits filled with special treats instead of the usual birthday party goody bags. In each case, I think it fair to say, the majority of invited children seemed eager to plunge in, and these parties were, for them, a source of active pleasure. (I often wondered afterward what stories were taken home and told to parents.)

To my own family, of course, the parties have always meant far more. The occasion of a child's birthday has necessarily entailed a large expenditure of time and effort, as well as negotiation and cooperation, not all of which ever goes smoothly. There are always differences of opinion and disagreements. But even the rough spots are a crucial element in the learning process because they form an integral part of any creative effort. Children gradually realize this. Some of their ideas, for example, have to be rejected because they are impractical; in such cases, the children are initially disappointed, but then, when an acceptable compromise is found, they discover that the solution can prove surprisingly satisfying.

Each party, importantly, occurs in three temporal phases, and this is one of its most salient features. John Dewey also differentiated the aesthetic from other forms of experience with a triadic analysis. I referred to this in regard to preparing children for events in the performing arts. He speaks first of anticipation, then of the actual event itself, and finally of recall or recapitulation, which, he says, becomes a source, spur, and stimulus for ongoing aesthetic engagement in the future. The aesthetic entails what he calls "consummated experience," by which he means that which involves all of these three phases. Percolating in us over time, aesthetic experience is that to which we attend on many levels—the emotional as well as the perceptual and the rational—and that in which we *actively* participate rather than *passively* undergo. This latter is an especially important point for Dewey. Unconsummated experiences are, by contrast, for him, those that simply happen to us and are, without reflection, abandoned by us for whatever comes along next. They involve no processing over time, no internalization, no strong emotional, physical, or intellectual investment, and no conscious reflection. They can, indeed, hardly be called experiences. They use up time but add little richness to our lives.

Making, Not Buying, the Party

It is sad that so many American parents celebrate their children's birthdays in commercial venues—at fast-food restaurants, for example, or amusement parks—where everything is standardized and predictable, because the practice seems to lend itself to just the sort of "unconsummated experience" Dewey decries. These events, after a while, bore even the children who attend them. They seem a lost opportunity for imagination and creativity. After all, a birthday is a celebration of the existence in this world of a particular *individual*. Shouldn't that celebration logically reflect the current interests, accomplishments, tastes, or predilections of that individual? Unlike nearly all other holidays, which concern groups of persons, a child's birthday is really all about honoring just one. To stamp the party somehow, even in small ways, with the uniqueness of that birthday child is to endow it with important meaning, not only for the child but also for all the other children who attend.

Parents need not be especially gifted artistically or have vast financial resources to help children come up with ideas for games, homemade invitations, and simple decorations, all of which can be pursued together in advance. Even the youngest child can take part. I remember a first-birthday celebration for a baby in Rhode Island. The grandparents and neighbors were invited to a celebratory clambake, and the baby's not-yet-three-year-old sister was so excited by the prospect of a party and her mother's preparations that she wanted to be consulted about the prettiest napkins and even choose the color scheme; on the day of the party, she insisted on helping to set the table. In another family, a little boy who played the recorder was willingly conscripted to provide accompaniment for all the musical games at his older and younger sisters' birthday parties.

Fathers, grandparents, uncles, and aunts also often prove ingenious at these times. They can help hang streamers and balloons in high places. They can clown and act and draw and sing and perform amateur magic tricks. They sometimes come up with the cleverest ideas for charades or treasure hunts and lend their talents to construction. What matters is not how elaborate the results are but the involvement in the preparation of everyone who wants to participate. Homemade parties are inexpensive. One year, by contrast, we departed from our usual practice and took a small group of boys to the Hayden Planetarium in New York City for a birthday celebration; the cost that year was considerably higher than other years. The party was enjoyable, but it seemed a bit lackluster. Without a real preparation phase, it receded into being one of those experiences one lives through without its making a deep impression. It might have worked better and proved more meaningful for those little boys if they had been, at the same time, studying astronomy in school so that they could have looked forward to the party more concretely, followed through with activities afterward, and discovered connections between the birthday excursion and another quadrant of their lives.

What counts most, it seems to me, is that the child being honored be encouraged to express herself in the choices that are made with respect to her party and that parents regard birthdays as annual opportunities to afford rich and meaningful aesthetic experiences. On a child's birthday, she is fully present and attentive. She cares. What occurs matters to her. When, on these special days, parents collaborate with their children to imagine, construct, and perform together, the pleasures that accrue are, as I have learned by watching the results in my own family, readily passed on from one generation to the next.

The Frances Books

Have you ever met Frances the badger? Frances is one of the most delightful, appealing, and psychologically well-crafted characters in twentieth-century American literature for young children. She is the title character and heroine of a series of picture books created between 1960 and 1970 by Russell and Lillian Hoban—"the Frances books," as my older daughter affectionately called them when she asked to have them read over and over again. Why did the Hobans choose a female striped badger for their six wise tales? Perhaps in part because this animal's name, shifted from noun to verb, means "to pester or worry"—something young children often do to their parents and that parents do to their children. In any case, the innuendos are there, and, starting out at about age four in the first book (*Bedtime for Frances,* originally published in 1960), this furry little character grows to about seven years old in the last one (*A Bargain for Frances,* which appeared a decade later). In between, in 1968, comes *A Birthday for Frances,* which is the one I want to refer to here.

Frances is, like all small children, uncannily inventive. Her special mode of expressing unacceptable feelings is to make up spontaneous little rhyming songs about them and sing them softly to herself. Pictured as an animal, she comes across persuasively as a real child. Her intense responsiveness to everyday life, her fervor and passion, her imaginative and expressive openness, give her an authenticity far beyond that of many characters that inhabit children's books. Not, in other words, a mere tabula rasa for readings-in, not passive in the slightest, Frances is a character who actively shapes her environment. Her behavior matches that of the real children who encounter her on the pages of their picture books, but she offers them new twists and flourishes that suggest the possibility of innovative adaptive strategies. She is, in other words, both a reflection and a model.

Like most young children, Frances makes very little effort, initially, to hide or modulate her dysphoric feelings. As her badger mother and father cope with her and respond to her developmental needs, their parenting experiments constitute emulable models. They demonstrate love, patience, and tolerance, as well as frustration and irritation. Children see themselves and their lives faithfully reflected, and adults stand to gain a cross-generational perspective as well as a bit of implicit guidance.

Broomsticks and Chompo Bars

A Birthday for Frances underlines the enormous emotional implications of children's birthdays. Despite the book's title, this story is not about Frances's birthday at all but about her little sister Gloria's. This brilliant choice underscores the supervening significance of the event, even when it belongs to someone else. Gloria will turn two in the story, but because of all the strong feelings the occasion brings out in Frances, it is *she*, above all, who will learn important lessons about jealousy, greed, generosity, kindness, and the meaning of birthdays. Hence, the title: *A Birthday for Frances.*

The first scene takes place on the day before Gloria's birthday, which happens to be a Friday. The children's mother is sitting at the table with Gloria making place cards for the party. Frances, however, is on the floor of the broom closet all by herself among the pails and dust brushes, like a forlorn Cinderella. She sings: "Happy Thursday to you, / Happy Thursday to you" to someone named Alice.

When her mother asks her who Alice is, Frances replies that Alice is invisible and therefore does not have a birthday. Alice will not have cake or candy either. Thus Frances creates for herself an alter ego, an imaginary child who, like herself, is *not* being focused on at the moment, *not* being paid attention to, *not* the center of things, just a poor waif who has no hope of treats.

Her mother, however, understanding perfectly well what is going on, contradicts her daughter flatly by declaring that, even if nobody can see Alice, Alice must still have *one birthday a year* just like everyone else. She reminds Frances that her own birthday will be coming along in a couple of months and that tomorrow will be Gloria's birthday.

Frances responds to her imaginary friend: "That is how it is, Alice. Your birthday is always the one that is not now."

Mother tries in vain to temper her daughter's resentment by eliciting some "big sister" feelings. She invites Frances and Alice to come out of the broom closet and help decorate the place cards. Frances comes to the table, but instead of drawing flowers on the cards, she upsets her baby sister by singing that she will draw "three-legged cats and caterpillars with ugly hats." Then, having achieved her goal of disturbing the formerly serene little birthday-girl-to-be, she gets down from the table and leaves, riding off witchlike on one of the brooms saying she'll be out of town for a couple of weeks visiting Alice but be back in time for dinner.

As the story goes on, Frances announces that she is not going to give Gloria a birthday present. When her mother says that this is all right (an unusually sensitive parenting response), Frances is immediately consumed with guilt and begins to weep, saying: "Everybody is giving Gloria a present but me." Mother then asks her gently whether she would like to give Gloria a present. When Frances now says yes, Mother agrees to give her her allowance in advance so that she can buy the gift. Frances's father walks with her to a nearby store, where Frances spends all her advance allowance to buy Gloria four balls of bubble gum and a Chompo bar.

Their walk home is unforgettable. As she marches along with her father, Frances clutches the sweets and begins to think about the delicious taste of the chewy caramel-and-chocolate Chompo bar. She absentmindedly puts two of the gumballs into her mouth. Next, she thinks about having spent her future allowance on Gloria, and she inadvertently pops the other two balls in. At this point, she starts squeezing the soft Chompo bar in its wrapper. At last her father realizes what's happening and offers to carry the Chompo bar the rest of the way home for her.

At the party, Frances sits with her best friend, Albert, and complains to him about the irritating nature of little sisters (the parents have allowed both Gloria and Frances to invite one friend each). When Mother brings in the candles and cake, everybody else sings "Happy Birthday" to Gloria, but Frances is singing sotto voce to herself: "Happy Chompo to me / Is how it ought to be." Gloria blows out her candles and makes a hopeful wish that Frances will be nice to her in the future and forgive her for a former misdeed.

Gloria has received presents from everyone but Frances. Frances has wrapped up the Chompo bar and tied it with a ribbon. Before giving it, however, she tells Gloria that she wants to sing "Happy Birthday" to her now because she hadn't really sung it before with everyone else. She starts to sing but trails off after each verse. Gloria prompts: "You can have a bite when I get it." Finally Frances finishes and, after giving the Chompo bar one last squeeze, hands it over to her sister. She tells Gloria that she can eat it *all* because *she* is the birthday girl. Gloria says it is a good present, and then she eats it all by herself "because she was the birthday girl."

The celebration of a child's birthday reverberates for all the children in the family and of course for the parents as well. This is made manifest in the story by the sensitive and kindly treatment accorded to Frances by her mother and father. They manage to help her make it through to a good ending without squelching her feelings at any point and without sacrificing the primacy of their younger child, whose day it is. Birthdays, as we know (but do not always like to remember), bring up a host of feelings that may lie at least partially dormant during other times of the year. Children remind us of this somehow, even when we fail to pay attention. Therefore, to take birthdays as occasions for creative and aesthetic exploration seems highly adaptive and auspicious. Here are a few examples.

An International Birthday Party

"*Achat—shtayim—shalosh—rutz!*" (Hebrew for "Ready—get set—go!") was my repetitive script at the most challenging birthday party I ever gave. It took place on Mount Scopus in Jerusalem when I was a visiting professor at the Hebrew University and my daughter Rivi was ten. She insisted on having a birthday party, and none of the obstacles I presented could deter her. I pointed out that we were living five thousand miles from home in a cramped university apartment with no living room, no dining room, no oven, not even a telephone, and that her birthday was falling in the middle of a two-week religious and national holiday. I warned her that she had befriended a group of children who spoke either Hebrew or Arabic but not both, and in most cases only a few words of English, so that communication among them would be extremely difficult. Stubbornly, she countered my objections one by one, and what resulted was a unique social and cultural event.

It took place both indoors, in our apartment, and outdoors in an adjacent dormitory parking lot in the French Hill section of the city. Although Rivi had invited several more children than her age (my rule of thumb has always been to let the number of guests only slightly exceed the age of the child), the event was attended by just eight children ranging in age from seven to eleven, all girls, each representing one of three different native languages and cultures. Homemade invitations decorated with clowns and written in both Hebrew and English (English for the Arabic children, since unfortunately we could not write in their language) were hand-delivered to the invited guests the week before the party, which took place on Rivi's "real birthday" (as she loved to say), which, as it was also a religious and a school holiday, meant not only that there were severe restrictions on what could be served but also that the invitations could not be distributed in school, which is the normal custom in Israel. Since we had no phone, it was necessary for Rivi to go around to each child's apartment with an Israeli friend who knew where everyone lived.

Our own apartment consisted of a kitchen into which you passed when you first entered, two bedrooms equipped with simple desks and bookshelves, and otherwise nothing more than a bath and a toilet. Where was the party to take place? We improvised. We taped balloons to the door and walls, decorated our one kitchen shelf with bright streamers, made a colorful Happy Birthday poster for the wall, and set out goodies on the kitchen table. Because of the holiday, those edibles consisted of candies and nuts, sunflower seeds, fruits, and chocolate-covered matzohs. We might have had one or two other acceptable items, but the choice was strictly limited, and I had discovered, earlier that week even before shopping for the party, that, in our local market, all shelves containing nonkosher items—those unacceptable during Passover—were hidden from view, covered over, and therefore inaccessible in any case.

Israeli birthday parties are informal affairs that normally include a child's whole class, and, since children frequently don't know where their classmates live, their practice, at least in the school Rivi attended, was for everyone to rendezvous at the local Supersol (food market) and then all walk together with the birthday child to his or her home. Rivi and her closest Israeli friend, Miri, who had come over before the party to help set up, decorate, and contribute a few indispensable items (including a tape deck to provide background music for one of the games), departed for the market at about 2:30 p.m. on the day of the big event.

In the meantime, I gathered two little plastic bags of agorot (Israeli pennies, one hundred of which make a shekel, equivalent in American dollars at that time to about sixty-six cents) and went outside to scatter these coins in the dry, sparsely growing grass for one of the games we had planned, an "agorot treasure hunt."

For weeks beforehand, Rivi and I had held lengthy discussions about games for this party. Israeli parties, she informed me (by this time, she had attended three or four), are generally unstructured, with few, if any, organized games. The children her age, she reported authoritatively, mostly play, eat, sing, dance, and after a while become highly rambunctious. In our American home, as I have indicated, the parties have tended to be highly organized affairs, with an overarching theme to which everything—food, games, prizes, decorations, and possibly costumes—are linked. Rivi realized that the cultural and linguistic differences here would preclude many of the games she might have wanted to play, such as charades, but she felt she could not do without games and prizes. She came up with several ideas, which I merely amended, encouraged, and subsequently helped to execute.

Chattering and laughing could be heard from the open windows of the *me'onot*, or apartment house, as Rivi and her friends approached and then came bounding up the stairs. Before the first game was under way, two more little girls—Rivi's friends from the nearby Arab village—had arrived and joined the party. Eight noisy girls now filled the apartment, and there was barely space in Rivi's room to form a circle. Each child offered her a gift. The Arab children, Muna and Nuha, came bearing sacks filled with treasures—small plastic figurines and bracelets—which they proudly handed over. I was deeply moved by this gesture and by the fact that their mothers had allowed them to attend the party. They looked adorable, clearly having taken great care with their appearance; whereas the Israeli children were, as ever, informally attired.

Before playing any active games, we showed everyone a jar filled with sunflower seeds that I had patiently counted out in advance. As each child entered the apartment, I asked her to guess how many seeds were in the jar. Because of the language barrier, we had prepared some paper in advance and asked each girl to write down her number with her name. Prizes were awarded to the closest and second-closest guesses. Interestingly, the guesses were quite wide of the mark. Perhaps this is simply because children of this age are unaccustomed to thinking in terms of extremely high numbers. Most guessed in the hundreds or below. Only Miri picked a high number; she said, "Over two thousand." I can vouch for the fact that the jar contained precisely 1,036 sunflower seeds.

As for indoor games, everyone sat in a circle on the floor in Rivi's bedroom, knee to knee on a colorful handwoven rug I had purchased in Jerusalem's Old City. They played a game called "unwrap the present," which has been a staple of birthday parties in my family for as long as anyone can remember. This involves a small gift or prize that has been wrapped in many layers of brightly colored paper, each successive layer tied in turn with a ribbon. Thus, the treasure lies hidden under the first layer, which, of course, once the game is under way, becomes the last layer of wrapping. The treasure in this case was a paper pad from America in the shape and size of a hamburger, with a highly realistic-looking illustration of a hamburger on the cover. Using pantomime, I was able to convey the rules of the game to the children. They were to pass the present around the circle while music was playing (Madonna on Miri's "box") and then stop whenever the music stopped. Whichever child happened to be holding the package at that moment had the right to unwrap the topmost layer of paper and untie the ribbon. She was then supposed to leave the circle, and the music would start again, with the gift circulating now among the remaining children until the tape stopped again and one more layer could be unwrapped, and so on until only one child was left, the winner, who would unwrap the last layer and receive the prize. To dull the competitive edge of the game, each child after unwrapping a layer and exiting the circle was handed a little gift of her own. This meant that everyone could return home with some small memento from the party. The final layer was, as it turned out, opened by one of the Arab children, Nuha, who was thrilled to acquire her first American "hamburger."

We went outside for some relay races, including one that involved licorice wands that the children had to use to transfer marshmallows into a receptacle and another one in which they had to run to a pile of funny clothes and hats (principally mine), get all dressed up in them, and then return to their team, taking everything off as quickly as possible before tagging the next team member, who had to repeat this process—a hilarious event. At length, I gave each girl a small striped bag and announced that it was time for the agorot hunt. This game was slightly marred by the fact that Miri had forgotten to bring her eyeglasses and therefore began to cry when she realized she would not be able to see the agorot, which are very tiny (less than half the size of an American dime). Another problem arose when two of the girls developed sudden rashes due to biting insects or poisonous plants they must have touched while searching for the coins. First- and second-prize winners of this game, which, despite the hazards, the children wanted to go on playing, were an Israeli girl named Sarit and Rivi herself, who was thrilled to be a winner at her own party.

By now the party girls were no longer alone. Their excited voices had attracted a small crowd of Arab boys from the neighboring village who gathered to watch them at their games. These boys, roughly the same age as Rivi and her friends, settled in a row along the curbside. They looked so entranced and wistful that I was reminded of a page from Munro Leaf's classic picture book, *Wee Gillis*, where the protagonist wants to play the bagpipes but dares not ask his disputatious uncles for permission. Not knowing quite what to do because I wanted the boys not to feel left out but knew at the same time that Rivi would not take kindly to their crashing her party, I finally went over to them and passed out colorful candy sticks. This proved a great solution. I still see them now in my mind's eye, intently sucking on their candy, their eyes fastened on Rivi and her friends at play.

The Birthday Puppet Show

How does a party get started? Where do the ideas come from? In one case, a mother noticed that her almost-two-year-old daughter possessed a mushrooming vocabulary replete with animal words. This little girl loved all picture books that featured animal characters and illustrations of animals, and she adored visiting the nearby zoo. Her mother, who was a bit of an artist, decided to follow up on this theme by painting an enormous mural filled with animals. She hung her painting, wild with elephants and rhinoceroses, toucans and turtles, along the wall of their apartment and used it as a backdrop for the birthday-party table, which was also decorated along the lines of this animal theme. The little girl was delighted and enjoyed pointing to each animal and naming it. The party itself, consisting of just four other children with their parents, featured ice cream and a cake with candles and some very simple games in which the children pretended to be animals, ran around, and made the appropriate noises and movements. Afterward, the painted mural hung in the family's apartment for a while and then got rolled up and was eventually donated to a local nursery school. In this example, therefore, it was the child's current interest that sparked the theme for her party. In another situation, it was the architecture of a child's home that unexpectedly inspired a special birthday party.

Jody sat cross-legged on her living room floor in Newton, Massachusetts, surrounded by a multicolored assemblage of wooden blocks, trains, stuffed animals, and cardboard books. Gazing at these well-loved toys, she mused fondly on her sleeping son, Ben, and his approaching third birthday. Suddenly, she glanced up at the rectangular opening cut into the wall separating her from her kitchen, and a flash of inspiration burst upon her. "David," she asked her husband, pointing, "what does that opening look like to you?"

"I don't know," David replied absentmindedly, looking up from a medical journal to follow her finger.

"Don't you think it looks a little bit like a puppet theater?" she asked excitedly. "Like a little stage, I mean?"

"Hmmm," he replied. "Well, maybe . . ."

"Listen, I have an idea. Why don't we make it into one and rig up a puppet show for Ben's birthday party? I think that would be so great. The kids could sit right here—where I'm sitting now, on the carpet—and we could stand in the kitchen, right behind the kitchen sink, and put up a curtain maybe and move the puppets right along that ledge. Do you think that would work? Mom and Rachel will be here for the party, and they could help us; they're both so dramatic, and Ben already has two hand puppets—a toucan and a giraffe. We could buy a couple more. What do you think?"

"Sounds great."

Jody set off to find an idea for a story script. After flipping through dozens of Ben's picture books over several days and feeling nearly defeated, she finally found a solution. She decided on an old Golden Book from her childhood called *The Saggy Baggy Elephant*, which tells the tale of a kindly pachyderm who is ostracized and teased by others in the jungle on account of his funny looks but who nevertheless helps each of them in turn when they get into trouble and then is helped by all of them when he falls into a trap and has to be extricated. She gave the script considerable thought and decided on this story for a number of reasons. First of all, she knew that an animal theme would have irresistible appeal to the three- and four-year-old guests. Second, she felt this story would be suspenseful and therefore hold the children's interest but would not be too frightening. It had plenty of dialogue and distinct characterizations so as to make it suitable for puppetry, and she felt that it would work for both genders. Finally, she felt that the story conveyed an important message to children about the value of helping others and taught that what one *does* matters more than how one *looks*. And from a practical standpoint, the story would enable her to make use of a colorful puppet Ben already had and loved, his toucan (who, animated by his grandmother, became the narrator in the show), and of several of his favorite stuffed animals including a gray elephant, who served as the title character. Three other toys—a stuffed giraffe, a monkey puppet, and a soft lion (animated by Ben's aunt)—also became characters.

Jody and David decided to make the puppet show a surprise for Ben, but I can imagine other families in which even a three-year-old birthday child might be invited to participate in advance. Age and personality are relevant factors here, and, after all, surprises can be delightful. Ben was told that there would be a puppet show at his party, but he didn't know any of the details beforehand. David rigged the curtain, set up the props, and animated one of the puppets, as did Ben's other relatives. On the day of the party, the invited children sat in a rapt group on the living room carpet, exactly as Jody had imagined the scene weeks before. The production went on after just three or four rehearsals and was clearly what the French call a *succès fou*. Ben and his friends were spellbound. Ben himself simply could not get enough of it, and he and the others clamored for a repeat performance. They didn't want the show to end. Instead of performing an encore, however, Jody, David, and the other puppeteers did something even better: They handed out their puppet characters to the children themselves, who began spontaneously to make them talk and to create their own impromptu dialogues. This was truly a wonderful sight to behold. For weeks afterward, Ben was begging anyone who would humor him to be in a puppet show with him, and virtually every one of his toys got in on the act. For all the children who attended, I think it fair to say, the party proved a powerful spur to imaginative activity.

The Space Party

Among other sources of party themes are suggestions by parents with special interests of their own or unique memories they want to share and make palpable for their child. This was the case when a little boy named Henry was on the verge of becoming five. He had been taken by his father several times to see space exhibits at a nearby science center, and when his birthday approached, his father suggested the idea of a space party to him; he brightened at the thought, and the theme was immediately adopted.

The preparations followed a cooperative creative process in which each person's ideas spawned another's. Henry's mother and his visiting aunt proceeded first to decorate the main floor of the house with dozens of stars cut from shiny gold posterboard that they hung about the house from threads. Henry's mother found some star garlands in a neighborhood party shop and some golden gauze that she suspended from the ceiling, using blue crepe paper to suggest the sky. Henry contributed by making a paper chain of colored stars with his aunt, while his father created space-rocket invitations on the computer. With Henry's help, he also constructed a large-scale model of the solar system, beginning with the planet Mercury, which they hung from the ceiling of the breakfast room at one end of the house, and ending with Pluto, which they suspended from the ceiling of the study at the other end. To traverse the width of the house, therefore, was to experience the entire solar system! To complete the decorations, Henry's aunt, a graduate student who loves both art and theater, created a magnificent six-foot-by-four-foot space station that was placed on the living room floor and used for one of the games. Outdoors there was to be a rocketship piñata.

Nine children attended the party—eight who had been invited plus an unexpected younger sibling of one of the boys from Henry's class. Only one little girl came, but she was able to hold her own. As stated earlier, I believe it is best to limit the number of children asked, so that each child receives individual attention and does not get lost in the crowd, so to speak. Birthday parties are, after all, significant early social experiences for young children, and one wants them to be enjoyable so that each guest leaves with positive feelings, especially since, at someone else's birthday party, the primary focus is and should be on that someone else rather than on any individual little guest.

Among the actitivites and games, the first was an art project conceived by Henry's mother. She had the children make their own rocket ships with cardboard paper-towel rolls, construction paper, markers, glitter glue, and stickers. The children enjoyed this activity so much, gleefully flying their rockets around the house, that they could hardly bear to be separated from their creations long enough to eat. As to the party food, Henry had informed his mother in advance that all birthday parties require pizza with pepperoni, so this is what was served for lunch. Next, in the living room where the large "space station" was located, the children played a sort of musical-chairs game, floating their rocket ships around the space station looking for a place to dock. After this, a game of "unwrap the present" ensued (like the one at Rivi's party in Israel), with the final treasure being a book about the solar system. The children all trooped outdoors to bat the rocket-ship piñata—specially requested by the birthday boy—then returned indoors for a dress-up moonwalk race, where two teams had to put on space suits and take giant steps from one end of the house to the other. Finally, the birthday cake arrived. Baked by Henry's father, it was chocolate with vanilla frosting, which Henry's mom had decorated by drawing—after her husband had found her a photo from the Internet to copy—a blue-and-purple space shuttle blasting off.

By common consent, the family decided to keep the space decorations up around the house for a several weeks. By way of follow-up, Henry's grandmother arrived from overseas the following week to see them and to hear Henry's tales of the festivities. He announced unbidden that his favorite moment occurred out-of-doors when they were whacking at the piñata, but from his parents' report, he seems to have enjoyed the whole experience and to be replaying it still.

Polar Bears and Crab Walks

How can you be an imaginative party giver when your child is an energetic boy with a winter birthday—a second-grader who wants to invite only other boys—and you live in a small house in the cold Northeast of the United States? After weeks of struggling with this question because her son's seventh birthday was fast approaching, Jill was at a loss as to how to celebrate. She was firmly opposed to taking them to what she deemed a hackneyed commercial spot. She discussed the problem with her husband, Rob, and they put their heads together and brainstormed. A not especially athletic child, Sam, they suddenly thought with excitement, had always loved swimming. Ever since he'd splashed about in his fish-shaped baby bath, water had held a special appeal for him. With this in mind, his parents dreamt up a scheme for a party that would, in fact, need to take place in a commercial venue but that would also represent one of their child's greatest loves. Furthermore, Jill determined to make it a genuinely aesthetic experience.

Once Sam had been consulted and had expressed enormous enthusiasm, laughing uproariously at what struck him as the incongruous idea of a swimming party in wintertime, Jill researched the possibilities and discovered a local facility called Kids First Swim School, which would allow them to rent the space for two hours on a Sunday afternoon. Visiting the spot, she was delighted to find that the walls had been hand-painted with vibrant murals depicting castles and mermaids and other fanciful images and that there were, adjacent to the pool itself, two spacious rooms with ample tables, chairs, storage cubicles, and changing facilities. The establishment was ready to provide a registered lifeguard and even a person to clean up after the party. A one-way glass wall would permit lingering concerned parents to observe their children in the water.

For the party invitation, Sam and his parents considered images of various aquatic creatures including whales and fish, and Rob turned up photographs of each on the Internet. Apparently preferring warm- to cold-blooded species, Sam ultimately chose a photo of three or four animated polar bears who looked, he thought, like a group of friends getting ready to have some fun together. Rob masterminded the invitation on the computer, a simple sheet with the question: "Feel like a swim?" printed in blue over the heads of the bears, who appeared to be on the verge of plunging into the sea. Below the bears two other large-type lines announced Sam's birthday and invited each recipient to a pool party.

Jill realized worriedly that not having the party in her own home meant she would have to think of absolutely everything in advance.

Since cutting a birthday cake requires a special knife and forks, she asked Sam what he thought about the notion of ornamented cupcakes; he was pleased. They even bought Gummi fish—in keeping with their theme—to place on top. Jill filled several large bags with all the necessary paraphernalia: tablecloth, party napkins, plates, cups, blowers, goody bags, a candle shaped like a 7, matches, and prizes for games. Sam's grandmother, the official photographer, supplied the centerpiece, a traditional gumdrop tree that Sam himself decorated, consuming approximately one gumdrop for every five or so he stuck to its translucent branches.

The establishment told Jill she could have one hour of pool time and one hour of party time outside the pool for celebrating, eating, and singing. They decided to let the children swim first so they could express their high spirits and enjoy the promised water. Rob, a first-rate swimmer, sported a whistle around his neck and spent this first hour in the water with the ten boys. He gave them an initial period of free swim in order to observe their individual levels of ability and to determine whether the games they had dreamt up needed to be played in the pool's shallow end. After watching the boys cavort, he began surreptitiously to drop dozens of pennies to the floor of the pool; then, blowing his whistle, he called them over and announced that an underwater treasure hunt was about to take place. With that, he distributed plastic sandwich bags and directed the boys to dive down and retrieve pennies; the boy with the most pennies in his bag at whistle time would be the winner. Except for one child who felt uncomfortable about submerging his head, everyone loved this game, and the one left out rejoined the others later. Another game involved an octopus and some minnows. Rob called the boys to one side of the pool and told them to make believe they were minnows. He was to be the octopus! The minnows' task was to swim to the opposite side of the pool without being tagged by the octopus. As each child was tagged, he became a new tentacle of the octopus, thus acquiring the ability to tag someone else. The last child to be tagged, of course, won the prize. The participants laughed gleefully as they experienced the growing reach of the strange composite creature they were generating in the water.

When Sam had been asked in advance what game he especially wanted to play, he had asked for his favorite, Capture the Flag; Jill and Rob cleverly accommodated his wish by creating an aquatic version renamed Capture the Duck. This involved dividing the boys into two teams, which had to strategize about how much effort to spend on offensive and defensive maneuvers, in other words, whether to concentrate on capturing the other team's rubber duck that had been placed on the opposite ledge of the pool or to focus on protecting their own duck, which was resting on the near ledge. From the viewpoint offered by the parental one-way window, this game appeared to be less successful than the others and far more chaotic, but in fact to the children themselves it was the most challenging and compelling, and it ended only because their pool time eventually ran out. Watching closely was a parent who happened to be a professor of English literature. Recently having taught Shakespeare's *Julius Caesar*, he remarked that the boys' deliberations reminded him of act 4, scene 3 of the play, in which the conspirators Cassius and Brutus are debating whether to hold their ground and wait for the avenging forces of Mark Antony and Octavius (Cassius's preference) or to take the offensive and march boldly forward to meet the enemy at Philippi (Brutus's preference). We all know the outcome, of course. How marvelous that here, in this birthday party, a group of six- and seven-year-old boys clad in bathing trunks could become just as passionately engaged as those noble (and ignoble) Romans—proposing their tactics, offering their reasons, judging the possible consequences.

After the swimming and singing and candlelit cupcakes came another game Jill had prepared, a land-based one, and Rob blew his whistle to gather the troops once more. He explained that each boy was going to receive, from Jill, a lettered sign that would be attached to his back telling what sort of water creature he was. No one would be able to see his own sign, of course, but everyone else would. Without trying to look behind himself, each person was to guess what animal he was by asking helpful questions of others who could read the sign on his back, and the first person to know what he was would receive a prize. The animals included a seahorse, starfish, sea turtle, lobster, crab, alligator, penguin, seal, and duck. Shortly, a winner was proclaimed—a little boy named Daniel, who had had the prescience to ask whether he had a big shell and then guessed he must surely be a sea turtle. The final party game involved a crab-walk race, which was hilarious but extremely difficult for the children to sustain, as they kept breaking out of their crab walks into normal running steps in their zeal to get ahead.

Sam, when it was all over, looked exhausted and happy, as were both of his parents and probably the rest of the crew as well. Aesthetically speaking, the event called upon each child to be fully present in many ways, to be attentive, active, innovative, and persuasive; to interact, listen and respond, to move and cooperate, and to practice learned skills. This party seems to me the very opposite of the passive repetitive experience all too often made available for children on their birthdays.

Five Cups of Coffee

Educators sometimes speak of "windows of opportunity," and psychologists refer to "critical stage theories." My purpose in this chapter has been to indicate, by analogy, that children's birthday celebrations can serve as key occasions for aesthetic learning. Children are so alive at these times, so eager and enthusiastic, so ready to fantasize and participate. Parents who capitalize on this excitement can give their children and themselves enhanced experiences that will live in memory. Here is a final case to demonstrate the way a child's birthday can inhabit his fantasy life without his even realizing it. A coffee-loving uncle of a little boy who had just turned five was traveling abroad for several weeks and had, consequently, missed the child's birthday. He telephoned his nephew one day to say hello and to announce that he would soon be returning to the United States and would pay the child a visit. He did not specifically mention the child's birthday. Nevertheless, he was charmed and delighted (and slightly embarrassed) when the little boy said excitedly to him at the end of the call, "And Uncle, when you come back, we will make you *five* cups of coffee!"

Chapter Eight

Imagination as a Key to the Future

We are not here to do what has already been done.
—Robert Henri, *The Art Spirit*

By now, with your imagination, you have joined me in "observing" children using theirs in myriad ways. We have watched them transform mashed potatoes into turtles, mayonnaise jars into persons, the clicking of tongues into showers of rain, a feeling of momentary loss into a crayon drawing of a storm, a wedding into an uncanny site where dinosaurs lurk, a space under a bed into a secret hiding place, an apartment into Wonderland, and a house into the solar system. What, if any, is the future of such transformative acts?

In all I have written here, I have taken for granted the advantages of fostering in the present the imaginative and aesthetic lives of children. But what about the future? What benefits, if any, might accrue later in life to individual children from having had a wealth of such experiences early on? Do we know? Can we tell?

My hunch is that the advantages are abundant. After an imaginative childhood, one does not want to stop conjuring up possibilities; one wants to go on enjoying mental adventures. Moreover, since imagination and disciplined perception are germane to nearly all major disciplines, it is not only a child with artistic proclivities who can profit from being given opportunities of the sort described in the preceding chapters. Every child can benefit.

Before elaborating, however, let's envision a scene in which a group of adults have gathered . . .

The Board Meeting

The setting is midtown Manhattan in winter. The advisory board of a charitable arts foundation is holding its first meeting. Seated at arm's length around a massive burnished oval table, its conservatively attired members sip their coffee. People seem reserved, blasé; most are strangers to one another. The chairman, who has been intoning a rather dull introductory speech, suddenly wakes everyone up by proposing a warm-up exercise: "Think back to childhood and tell us about your first experience in the arts. What was it like? What can you come up with?"

Linseed Oil and Alizarin Crimson

An awkward silence follows. A heavyset man seated at the chairman's end of the table begins to smile slowly as though he is reliving something. "Mine," he offers, breaking the ice, "was frankly sensuous." It involved the rich, strong smells of oil paint—the scent of linseed oil mingling with turpentine. His mother had been a painter, and her medium had permeated every aspect of his early life. Sensations of her were inextricable, he says, from studio smells, from fragrances and odors that seemed to emanate from her body as if they were a part of her. The intoxicating aromas she exuded formed an essential element of his experience of her.

In the brief silence following his description, I, seated at the opposite end of the table, begin to recall my own first box of oil paints and how exhilarating it was to squeeze those hard metal tubes, their exotic labels printed with names euphonious to pronounce: burnt sienna, cadmium yellow, alizarin crimson, Prussian blue. When I was about seven, my parents left me with relatives over the winter holidays, and the stay was memorable because, whereas our family did not celebrate Christmas, these cousins did, and I was allowed to help decorate their fragrant evergreen tree with fragile bulbs and tinsel. On Christmas morning, a large, elegantly wrapped present under the tree bore my name attached with golden string to its shiny bow; inside was a varnished wooden box containing oil paints, brushes, small tin containers for linseed oil and turpentine, and even some canvas boards of various dimensions. No child could have been more thrilled. The rest of my day was spent painting, and a couple of years later, when my parents acquired a house with servants' quarters, I commandeered the unused space to offer free oil-painting lessons to all the neighborhood children who wanted to "study" with me.

Mozart for Children

"For me," confessed a southern gentleman, "it was hearing Mozart's fourth horn concerto." He could no longer remember the specific circumstances of the performance but just the visceral thrill of his first encounter with the music and his knowledge, even then, that the experience would be with him forever. The sounds he heard that day had such clarity and brilliance that, although years passed before he came to listen seriously to Mozart's music and had become familiar with the canon—the great orchestral pieces, the chamber works, and the operas—and had heard inspired performances by artists of renown, nothing equaled the impact of that first childhood rapture at the notes of the horn concerto.

As he spoke and in the silence that followed, I was taken back to a modest Presbyterian church in Oakland, California. The young choir director had introduced a small orchestra for the Christmas service— a rare treat because ordinarily, in this church, the choir sings a cappella or accompanied only by a piano. After the final hymn and the minister's dismissal, the congregation rose to leave the sanctuary, but having assembled the orchestra, the conductor wanted to make the most of its presence and began leading a postlude—an exquisite Mozart church sonata—previously unannounced. Most of the adults continued to make their way, greeting one another as usual, to the back of the church. Two little girls, however, their blond pigtails tied up with ribbons for the holiday, did not rise. Rapt, they remained glued to their pew as the music rose and fell, enveloping them with its rich harmonies. I can still see them, riveted; neither child moved a muscle. They sat in perfect silence following every glorious note of the Mozart. Only when it was over and the conductor turned around did they shyly disappear.

> She hummed one of the tunes, and after a while in the hot, empty house by herself she felt the tears come in her eyes. Her throat got tight and rough and she couldn't sing any more. Quickly she wrote the fellow's name at the very top of the list—MOTSART.
>
> —Carson McCullers, *The Heart Is a Lonely Hunter*

The Many-Headed Princess and a Caged Canary

A smallish woman with large eyeglasses was next to speak. She described her first experience in the arts as literary and clandestine. As a child, she huddled day after day on the floor of her big sister's bedroom closet amidst piles of clothes and sneakers. In the dark, with a flashlight, her sister read to her in whispers from the Oz books by L. Frank Baum while, outside the closet, their mother yelled suspiciously at them: "What *are* you girls doing in there? Are you doing your homework?"

The anecdote gave me special pleasure because the Oz books adorned my family's bookshelves, and I still revel in their cleverness and in the whimsical population of their pages—Glinda, Ozma, Dorothy, Tik-tok, the Patchwork Girl, the Wheelers (who had no hands or feet but simply hard round wheels that rolled them over the ground), and above all, the vainglorious peremptory Princess Langwidere, my favorite character, with her thirty heads all kept in separate velvet-lined jewel-framed mirrored cupboards with numbers so she could choose the perfect one for every occasion. I remember an awful moment when Princess Langwidere ordered Dorothy to exchange *her* head for head number twenty-something and then locked the little heroine up in a tower when she refused to comply. And what about the Deadly Desert, which became my childhood metaphor for places where I didn't want to put down my feet?

Finally, an art professor from a midwestern university told a story she could not be entirely sure she actually remembered herself but that had attained legendary status in her family. At the age of three, she had been sent to a nursery school where one especially enticing play area was filled with wooden easels, and large sheets of newsprint, jars of tempera paint, and brushes had been set out for the children to try. Every morning, she was told, she would stand quietly watching as other children approached the easels. Dipping their brushes into the viscous paint, they would draw the stiff hairs of their brushes across the paper, leaving sweeping streaks of red, yellow, black, and blue. With intense and unspoken desire, she would watch them. Concerned after a while that she was secretly longing to paint but afraid to try, her teacher approached her one day, tied an apron around her neck and waist, took her by the hand, and led her over to an unoccupied easel. Placing a brush into her hand, the teacher then stepped back to see what she would do. The little girl did not hesitate. Confidently dipping her brush into the yellow paint, she formed—dead center on her paper—two adjacent round shapes that looked for all the world like a head and a body. Next, she overpainted these conjoined forms with vertical parallel black lines. When she was finished, the image seemed to coalesce into the picture of a caged yellow bird, a canary perhaps—symbolic, as the teacher interpreted it later to her mother, of the child herself—timid, fenced in, unable to fly. Unable, that is, until a sensitive adult who was carefully watching came over to her and unlocked the door.

Gargantua, Penelope, and Hanuman

The last person to speak was a middle-aged lady from the south of France, near Marseille. She spoke to us about her grandmother, an austere personage who, by the most inventive and circuitous routes, introduced her, when she was a small girl, to literature. When the family was at the dinner table, her grandmother would chastise her and warn her that she should not eat too rapidly, or she would turn into a Gargantua. Of course, she, hadn't the slightest idea at the time what a Gargantua could be, but she was duly chastened, and her grandmother offered no clarification. Likewise, this grandmother would criticize her severely when she dropped a stitch in her knitting and refused to undo the subsequent stitches in order to go back to correct her mistake. Again without explanation, her grandmother would say: "Don't forget Penelope! You must take out your stitches, Louise, and be just like Penelope."

What happened later, this woman explained, struck me as wonderful. For, eventually, of course, she went off to school and read Rabelais and Homer. When she did so, she experienced a thrill of recognition as she realized that some of their characters—Gargantua and Penelope and others—were already well-known to her; they were, in fact, figures from her childhood. Her grandmother had introduced them to her and thus had made them and the literature from which they came an integral part of her life from the start. In such interchanges, a wise adult, without resorting to prescription, persuasion, or dogma, passes on a tradition in which she is deeply invested but does so subtly, planting seeds of aesthetic knowledge and preparing a young child for a life in the arts.

This story reminded me of another one relayed to me by the father of Govinda, whose mother in Chennai had told him stories when he was a child, tales she now retells to her four-year-old grandson. One of his favorites—which the family occasionally acts out—and one that has remained with his father over the years because it impressed him so greatly is the Monkey's Tail story from the *Mahābhārata*, a story that,

Govinda's father explained to me, can expand and contract according to the size of the meal the child is supposed to be eating while listening.

Bhima, mightiest of the five Pandava princes, is walking through the jungle when he comes upon an old monkey lying across the footpath. Since it is improper to step over a living body, Bhima haughtily commands the monkey to get up and clear the path for him. The monkey, however, pretends to be asleep, and Bhima becomes increasingly impatient. Finally the monkey opens its eyes, looks up at Bhima, and pleads with him: "You are a mighty warrior, but I am just an old enfeebled monkey; I can't even get up. Please, why don't you just lift up my tail and put it to one side and walk along?" Bhima, proud of his strength, thinks this will be just fine, and with one hand he tries to lift the monkey's tail. This does not seem easy to do, however, and he puts his mace down; with both hands now he struggles to lift the old monkey's tail. Gradually, it dawns on him that this is no ordinary monkey. Humbled, he immediately realizes his folly, and he greets the monkey with great humility and seeks its forgiveness. The old monkey reveals himself now by transforming himself into the mighty Hanuman—who, incidentally, is a half brother of Bhima—and promises to help Bhima in the future.

"When this story is told to a child," Govinda's father explained to me, "there is not much moralizing, but nevertheless there is a powerful and lasting impact."

What About You?

Suppose *you* had been a member of the board of that arts foundation and had been at the meeting that day? How would you have answered the question about the dawn of your early aesthetic sensibilities? What can you remember? And what has happened to your own first experiences in the arts?

Now let's turn from the past and the present to consider the future. I promised to try to persuade you that these experiences *can* matter in the future and that they have potential value for every child.

The Imaginative Mathematician

"God thinks in numbers," Auntie Len used to say. "Numbers are the way the world is put together."
—Oliver Sacks, *Uncle Tungsten*

Let's suppose your child is destined to become a mathematician. Would early cultural and aesthetic experiences matter to her? If this destiny were known to you in advance, might that serve as all the more reason to enrich her girlhood and to privilege her imaginative play? For imagination figures prominently in mathematics. This is because the discourse of mathematics—unlike everyday parlance, which is referential in nature—concerns itself principally with inner consistency and with patterns of coherence rather than with correspondence to the external world, and therefore, it relies heavily on speculative thinking. Remember how little Govinda "discovered infinity" by envisioning a long line of zeroes that stretched to the sky? He is, as we have seen, a child who enjoys a particularly close relationship with a devoted grandmother who sits with him daily in his home in southern India and regales him with ancient Hindu legends and magical stories of her own.

The relation of imagination to mathematical thought can be traced historically to the ancient world, where mathematical and mythical thought commingled. People fancied that their lives and actions could be explained by reference to cosmic phenomena, and there has long been an association between magic and numbers. We speak of *numeri ficti* or imaginary numbers, and of mathematics itself as an a priori mental activity—an imagining, a conjuring, and a creating. Heuristic in the development of mathematical thought has long been associated with intuition, dreams, and flashes of insight. Mathematics involves the necessity for quite unreal conceptions and for wondering *if.*

In considering the role of the imagination in mathematics, E. T. Bell, in his *Men of Mathematics*, refers to Henri Poincaré and quotes the famous passage in which Poincaré, stepping onto a bus at Coutances, suddenly experiences a flash of insight into the nature of Fuchsian functions, with which he had been unsuccessfully struggling. Apropos the enigma of mathematical invention, Poincaré elaborates a theory in which he holds that "sudden illumination [is] a manifest sign of previous long subconscious work." He actually equates the mathematician with the artist: "The scientist worthy of the name, above all a mathematician, experiences in his work the same impression as an artist; his pleasure is as great and of the same nature." German mathematician Carl Friedrich Gauss made a similar analogy; he compared his theoretical work to the building of a cathedral after which, when the last scaffolding has come down and the completed structure is beheld in all its glory, one cannot tell how it came into being. As with Gauss's own mathematical proofs, one cannot tell where his reasoning in fact began. In this Gaussian analogy, the privileged aesthetic of mathematics seems to resemble that of a masterwork of northern Renaissance painting, such as the *Ghent Altarpiece* by Jan van Eyck or a seventeenth-century Dutch genre scene by Gerard Terborch, in which all brushstrokes have vanished, and what the eye sees are surfaces that evoke the tactile values of the objects portrayed but do not reveal the artist's secrets.

Parenthetically, not being a mathematician myself, I am indebted for the foregoing to mathematician John S. Lew, formerly of the Thomas J. Watson Research Labs, IBM (personal communication), who grew up in a literary home with a father who read Marcel Proust habitually and uninhibitedly while soaking for hours in the bathtub and who was a connoisseur of French wines. Well versed in classical music and poetry, Lew became a tenor soloist in college and wrote poetry privately for many years in addition to his mathematical texts. We might think also of the eminent polymath Charles Dodgson and his varied literary, visual, and mathematical inclinations. Thus, we *could* perhaps advocate persuasively for the value of an aesthetic childhood even for a budding mathematician.

Imagination and Music

What about music—that most abstract of arts—the sister, as the ancient Greeks saw her, to mathematics? Suppose your child wants to go into some form of music later on. What might be the role of the imagination here, especially since music comes to us in concrete form, as a performance? One answer, strange as it might at first seem, lies partly in the very fact that music presents itself to us as a phenomenon that we are meant to experience with full attention in the present moment, as was demonstrated by the two little girls who remained behind after a church service to listen to Mozart. Musicologist Nicholas Cook quotes philosopher R. G. Collingwood and reminds us of little Chloe's answer to her aunt after the concert at Tanglewood:

> A piece of music is not something audible, but something which may exist solely in the musician's head. To some extent it must exist solely in the musician's head (including, of course, the audience as well as the composer under that name), for his imagination is always supplementing, correcting and expurgating what he actually hears.

The American composer Aaron Copland, in *The Gifted Listener*, explains the connection as follows:

> The more I live the life of music the more I am convinced that it is the freely imaginative mind that is at the core of all vital music making and music listening. . . . An imaginative mind is essential to the creation of art in any medium, but it is even more essential in music precisely because music provides the broadest possible vista for the imagination since it is the freest, the most abstract, the least fettered of all the arts . . . no strict limitation of frame need hamper the intuitive functioning of the imaginative mind.

Music, furthermore, offers us an example of a paradox characteristic of the imagination, a paradox that we touched on earlier with respect to children's play and to which Copland alludes when he says: "There is something about music that keeps its distance even at the moment it engulfs us. In one sense it dwarfs us, and in another we master it. We are led on and on and yet in some strange way we never lose control." In other words, in the imaginative and the aesthetic mode, experiences can be overwhelming without being truly dangerous. Although we speak of the imagination as free and unfettered, we do in fact retain mastery over it. We can always return from it to the world of everyday reality. Children learn this best, as little Hannah did in her make-believe game with the mayonnaise jar, when the adults who participate with them in these experiences model it for them.

This paradox of being fully transported within a musical experience but also remaining outside it at the same time leads to the question of the nature of emotion in music. How, for example, when we have enjoyed no recent success of any kind, can we speak of experiencing "triumph" at the final chords of Liszt's *Les Preludes* or at the musical finale of *Hansel and Gretel* (although this of course is an easier question because we have characters and a story with which to identify)? How can we speak of ominous foreboding, of anguish or transcendent joy, while listening to music? Are these emotions real or illusory? Philosopher Susanne Langer's answer focuses not on the experience of the composer or the performer or the listener but on the musical work per se. She makes an analogy between the qualities of its form and the feelings it evokes:

> The tonal structures we call "music" bear a close logical similarity to the forms of human feeling—forms of growth and attenuation, flowing and stowing, conflict and resolution, speed, arrest, terrific excitement, calm or subtle activation and dreamy lapses—not joy and sorrow perhaps, but the poignancy of either and both—the greatness and brevity and eternal passing of everything vitally felt. Such is the pattern, or logical form, of sentience; and the pattern of music is that same form worked out in pure, measured sound and silence. Music is a tonal analogue of the emotive life.

Thus, in relating feeling to form, the philosopher uses her own imagination. Stressing this idea of the resemblance between music and emotion, she goes on to describe the meaning of music specifically as a "semblance of vital, experiential *time*. . . . Music makes *time* audible and its form and continuity sensible." But Langer's idea does not, as far as I can see, fully settle the question of real versus imaginary feelings in the aesthetic realm, a question that continues to puzzle philosophers. I will comment on this later when we ask about the role of the imagination in the visual arts.

Because music is such a complex interpretive art involving composers, scores, performers, and listeners, it raises many puzzles as to just how we ought to think about it. Earlier, I mentioned a segment of *Mister Rogers' Neighborhood* where the first page of the score of Brahms's Symphony no. 2 is shown to the audience, and Rogers plays a recording of the music. But *which* is the music? Is it the notes on the paper, or is it that performance of those notes? His puppet, Lady Elaine Fairchilde, isolates the two aspects and then reunites them. Using the score in a highly original way—presumably because it consists of written marks that *are*, in a way, a set of directions—she takes it as a blueprint for building a new castle. Langer offers a resolution to this puzzle by conceiving of every musical performance as a *completion* of a musical score. By saying that, she is able to honor the imagination of the performer and that of the composer. The "real performance," she says, "is as creative an act as composition . . . a logical continuation of the composition, carrying creation through from thought to physical expression." By putting it this way, she gives full homage to the "sonorous imagination" of a musician who, as she eloquently puts it, gives "utterance" to the "conceptual imagination" of a composer.

The most musical child I ever knew grew up telling tales of dreams he claimed to have had (and no doubt at least partly embroidered), fantastically elaborated dreams that trailed off into the empyrean after intricate labyrinthine sequences that others could scarcely follow. He spent hours reading fantasy literature and science fiction. At the age of five, he produced a small painting his mother treasured for years, a picture of summertime, which he had been asked to make in kindergarten. This painting, otherwise unremarkable for its typical childish clumsiness, included a strange dark shape in the air and another one on the ground. When his mother received confirmation that she had correctly identified his dizzying representations of sun, tree, bird, and flower, she asked him curiously what *those* other marks were meant to represent. He replied nonchalantly: "Oh, that's a bumblebee, and that's a doggy's doo." Clearly, *these* were features just as germane to his vision of summer as all the other aspects, and, unlike a more conventionally minded child, he had included them. Having imagined them, he did not censor them in keeping with a prematurely internalized propriety. Parenthetically, apropos of conventionality and its viselike grip on children, Alan Lightman, in *A Sense of the Mysterious*, quotes a three-year-old girl who is already so indoctrinated to associate nurses exclusively with women and doctors with men that when her uncle suggests *she* be doctor and *he* be nurse so as to cure her sick toy rabbit, she retorts: "Boys can't be girls." In the case of the musical child's painting, his mother suppressed a giggle at its honesty, saved it in a cardboard box, and wondered how it might relate to his music, for she was sure that, in some quite circuitous way within his inner life, it must.

Thus, we can see that a life in music, from whatever vantage point, involves the imaginative faculties.

Artists and Beholders

Pretend you are dancing or singing a picture . . .
Rather paint the flying spirit of the bird
than its feathers . . .

The wrinkles of a child's dress are full of the history of the day.
—Robert Henri, *The Art Spirit*

Your child, however, does not want to be a musician. She wants to be an artist. Here the connection is virtually transparent because the visual

214

arts are often referred to as "the *image-making* arts" and thus they relate even etymologically to the *imagination*. To paint a picture or carve a piece of wood or model with clay is to create an image, to make an object for contemplation. Once again, but first from the side of the beholder of art, we can foreground the imagination. Think of Leonardo's *Last Supper*, where the pigment has deteriorated and nearly vanished from the wall of the refectory to which it was originally applied so that now all we have is the illusion of the picture. Still, we *have* the illusion. And, with our own imaginative powers, we can mentally supply what is missing. *Where*, then, is the art? Is it on the wall, or in our minds? Surely, the answer must be both. An analogy here would be to the carver who, looking at a block of marble or wood, can already *see* within it the shape he will endeavor to bring out.

With regard to the process of making art, we know that artistic possibilities come into being for an artist as she creates, so that it makes sense to speak of art-making as having both mental and physical components rather than as a primarily physical activity rooted in craftsmanship and technique or as a purely mental activity. We observed this earlier *in statu nascendi* with the story of little Peter and his drawing of the "someone's going away" pain. As modes of representation and methods are invented and practiced and as workmanship progresses, the imaginative powers are simultaneously developed. In this way, the realms of the imagination and aesthetic experience grow together. As the American painter and revered teacher Robert Henri wrote: "An artist who does not use his imagination is a mechanic."

Turning to the observer of visual art—and it is important to recall that every artist is first and foremost an observer—she must learn to discover meanings not sequentially, as in logical discourse, but through the grasping of totalities, as in a gestalt. An artist's own growing ability to do this matters deeply, for as Henri reminds us, "It is harder to see than to express. The whole value of art rests in the artist's ability to see well into what is before him." To me, this intuitive grasping of totalities relates to the way visual symbols embody paradox and ambiguities that cannot be fully unraveled. In aesthetic experience we often come to know (in the sense of *connaître*) that which cannot be experienced discursively and categorically—a richly embroidered quilt of differing sensations, feelings, wishes, and values. In an earlier chapter, we "witnessed" something analogous to this with respect to the operatic form of *Hansel and Gretel*, where I wrote about the fact that some children may be bothered at first by the mismatch between their known version of the fairy tale and what they encounter onstage, or with the fact that Hansel is sung by a woman dressed as a boy, as well as by other elements that must be stitched together during the course of the performance so that the opera can be experienced as a whole. In undergoing that process, the children in question are—all unknowingly—recapitulating aspects of the creative process of the composer and the librettist, who likewise had to integrate what they originally knew with what they wanted to bring into being. Of course, in *Hansel and Gretel*, we have a temporal dimension that is missing in the same way from experiences in the visual arts, but the analogy holds. The coexistence and silent unstable resolution of seeming contradictions is fundamental to imaginative creation and re-creation. And it is not principally intellectual.

Safety, strange to say, counts as a factor, too, both for artist and beholder. No matter how threatening, disquieting, or bizarre a work of art is, it must leave its maker and its beholder at least physically intact; to make the point more cogently, we could reverse these terms and say that an artist and a beholder must always be able to depart intact after being with a work of art, whether that work is in progress or completed. This issue of safety may seem an obvious point, but it has important psychological consequences and constitutes an integral aspect of aesthetic experience. I touched on it earlier with the reference to *la belle dame sans merci*. Perhaps, in fact, our awareness of our personal safety as a background for experiences in the arts provides a key to the question raised earlier about distinctions between emotions experienced in art and in life. In life, we are not safe. Therefore, paradoxically, we may be not more but actually less free to express our emotions openly. Art, by giving us more freedom to feel strongly without risk of negative consequences, possesses great liberating powers—for both its makers and its beholders. Safety matters also when art and politics, and art and social issues, overlap, as we discussed briefly in the chapter "What Is Too Scary?" Adults who as children had chances to live out some of their fantasies—by creating scenarios with toys and stuffed animals in their play spaces, by making believe, by constructing secret spaces, by hearing imaginative literature and poetry, by attending musical and dramatic performances, or by looking at the art of others—may, because of this preparation, feel safer later on, less threatened, and more confident in the face of experimentation both in the creation of their own works and in confrontation with new art by others.

As we have seen, however, the issue of safety is an open one for young children. *They* cannot feel entirely safe as long as the realms of fantasy and reality continue to merge. This is why the little boy in the San Bernardino hills was on the lookout for dinosaurs and why I felt it important to stress how sensitively a good teacher must work with parents and toddlers together in an early music class. As for art-making, this, too, often requires empathy and encouragement—remember the little girl who so longed to paint but was unable to do so until her nursery school teacher tied an apron on her and led her gently over to an easel?

I Want to Be a Writer When I Grow Up

You could find in them Bengal lights, magic boxes, the stamps of long-forgotten countries, Chinese decals, indigo, calaphony from Malabar, the eggs of exotic insects, parrots, toucans, live salamanders and basilisks, mandrake roots, mechanical toys from Nuremberg, homunculi in jars, microscopes, binoculars, and, most especially, strange and rare books, old folio volumes full of astonishing engravings and amazing stories.

—Bruno Schulz, "Cinnamon Shops"

Suppose you have a child you think might become a poet, a novelist, or a playwright. Literature raises similar but also new questions about the relationship between mental activities and finished products.

In discussing his own working processes, the American poet Richard Wilbur brings imagination and craftsmanship together by writing: "*I think inside my lines* and the thought must get where it can amongst the moods and sounds and gravitating particulars which are appearing there" (my emphasis). This sentence, slightly altered, could surely apply to the absorbed play of a child.

Intensity must count as a special element in the aesthetic experience of literature. A good book, Kafka said, should strike like a pickax at the ice within our brains. But as we lend ourselves to illusion and to fiction, we experience tension, and the writer feels this as well. The art of fiction, when it succeeds, takes writers *and* readers out of themselves. Temporarily, we lose touch with our surroundings, and yet literature cannot succeed for very long in achieving this. Except perhaps in childhood. Which explains the force of my mother's envy when she saw me reading *The Magic Mountain* for the first time, and also a memory recorded by the French philosopher Sarah Kofman, who, as a little girl, became so absorbed in reading *Merlin the Magician* that she fell over backward into the fireplace and kept right on turning the pages. For us as adults it is the opposite: We must exert effort, pulled away as we are by the powerful countervailing forces of self-consciousness, to sustain the fiction. One moment we are in touch and the next out of touch with the work. We must bracket out mnemonic irrelevancies, sustain attention, and discipline our imagination to focus. Shakespeare dallies, in *A Midsummer Night's Dream*, act 5, scene 1, with the tensions of this tuning in and out, as audience members give themselves over to a work of drama and then pull back from it:

> THESEUS: The best in this kind are but shadows; and the worst are no worse, if imagination amend them.
> HIPPOLYTA: It must be your imagination then, and not theirs.
> THESEUS: If we imagine no worse of them than they of themselves, they may pass for excellent men.

The adult, however, who has been an imaginative child, already has, in this game, a running start. Concentration has become a habit of mind.

Because literature takes ordinary language as its medium, it gives rise to a unique practice in that (as I have just demonstrated by quoting Shakespeare) its works are frequently taken apart and pulled out of context. Its ideas, characters, and situations are treated sui generis rather than kept within the fabric of a total composition. Readers become captivated by, say, the philosophical arguments of a character like Settembrini or Naphta from Thomas Mann's *Magic Mountain* and treat them as if they were more than speeches written for imaginary characters imbedded in works of fiction. Yet, in fact, it is the supreme test of a writer's imagination to be able to *make* us do just that. A writer of fiction or drama wants to transport us bodily into another time-space and make us care about the characters she has invented. To do this she must discern how human beings different from her would think and how they might speak and act in whatever situations she concocts for them. She can do this only by drawing on the resources of a rich inner life.

But writers also call directly on their own childhoods, as mentioned earlier with respect to Hans Christian Andersen. Polish Jewish writer Bruno Schulz describes his childhood in stories studded with word pictures such as that conveyed by the following sentence: "Thus my mother and I ambled along the two sunny sides of Market Square, guiding our broken shadows along the houses as over a keyboard." Pablo Neruda, the Chilean-born poet, describes his first literary efforts as love letters written to a blacksmith's daughter for another lad who, smitten, had asked Neruda to write to her for him à la Cyrano. And who can forget Maxim Gorky's recounting of his father's agonizing death, which he witnessed when he was a small boy, his horror and pity for the helpless frogs trapped under the coffin, and his fateful boat ride up the dark Volga with two grieving women, his mother and long-haired grandmother?

In a recent autobiographical novel, *The Museum of Unconditional Surrender*, exiled Croatian writer Dubravka Ugrešić evocatively recalls the peekaboo games of her infancy. Baby games were followed, in protean forms, by dramas of hide-and-seek, and she compares these to her life as an exile from Zagreb in a progression: First, in her Yugoslav girlhood, she would cover her eyes with her hands, calling out "I've gone away" until the family squealed their delight at her "reappearance." Later on, she and her friends curled their fingers into telescopes and peered through their hands at one another, crying out "I see you!" and imagining—as before—that they were hidden from one another while staring out from inside their handmade spyglasses. Still later, she and her friends replaced their hands with paper tubes that not only "hid" the beholder but also served to reduce the field of vision so that it could be framed according to choice.

Ugrešić relates how, years later, after leaving her homeland and wandering about Europe in an emotionally torpid state devoid of all energy and enthusiasm, she arrived finally in New York City, where she hoped she might once again be able to feel some pleasure and recover a sense of belonging. New York had been a fabled city for her as she was growing up, a place she had read and heard about while living in Eastern Europe. Sadly, however, even here, walking the unfamiliar streets, she feels nothing. Her lifelessness persists. One day, however, she enters a taxi in which a radio is blaring loud music. The cab speeds down a hectic avenue, and crowds whiz by. She stares straight ahead through the windshield. In a flash, she is, excitedly, *in* New York! Suddenly, she begins to experience the thrill of the city. Why at that precise moment? What has happened to her? The taxi window, she realizes, is just like the magic tube of her childhood—a tunnel through which she can finally recognize New York and feel herself authentically inside the city. She is, at that moment, home.

Other childhood moments connect with authors' later lives, real and fictional, especially, perhaps, those moments that involve uncanny admixtures of familiarity and strangeness, states of identification and disjunction (believing, for example, that one is both here and not here). From their vivid descriptions of such states, we can see some of the ways in which children who grow up to create fiction are, in their play, already embarked on their imaginary adventures. In a famous essay, "The Creative Writer and Daydreaming," Sigmund Freud deliberates on the relations between children's play and imaginative literature. But while admiring the theme of his essay, which was a groundbreaker in its day, I would prefer a more circumspect, less dogmatic approach. Freud's conclusions seem to require qualification. I doubt, for example, that all literature can be derived from erotic or ambitious wishes (although obviously these play leading roles in many texts) and that "happy people never make phantasies, only unsatisfied ones." In fact, despite all that I have written here, I would deem it simplistic to assume, as Freud does, that literature can be derived in a direct line of causation from childhood. While it is true that, for many a writer, childhood experience counts as an invaluable source, the rivers of literary creativity feed on multiple currents far beyond childhood before reaching, if ever, their final destination in an enduring work of poetry, drama, or fiction.

The Scientist's Imagination

I, at least, needed to smell and touch and feel, to place myself, my senses, in the middle of the perceptual world.
—Oliver Sacks, *Uncle Tungsten*

But, you protest, my little fellow doesn't *want* to be a writer or a musician or an artist. He wants to be a scientist. He takes everything apart and tries to find out how it works. Nevertheless, hear philosopher Stephen Toulmin, who, in his book on the philosophy of science, makes exciting parallels between notions of creation in the arts and in science. If we accept Toulmin as one of our temporary mentors, we may end up believing that, even in the physical sciences, imagination can play a starring role.

One of Toulmin's ideas is that "the novelty of the conclusion [in physics] comes, not from the data, but from the inference; by [which] we are led to look at familiar phenomena in a new way, not at new phenomena in a familiar way." He takes examples from the science of optics to show that new ways of knowing lead to knowing what is new. He puts it this way: "The heart of all major discoveries in the physical sciences is the discovery of novel methods of representation, and so of fresh techniques by which inferences can be drawn—and drawn in ways which fit the phenomena under investigation." The way you say it, show it, and represent it, in other words, counts.

Language being, after all, the medium for expressing our understanding of the physical world, Toulmin points out ways in which we can be trapped by its conventions. Take: "His eyes swept the horizon." Clearly, this descriptive phrase does not match reality. If, however, we were to take it literally, it might prevent us from exploring further such pertinent questions as, for instance, the nature of light. Toulmin shows therefore that it is necessary to change the way we think and speak about phenomena in order to advance scientifically. We must in our explanations use words in novel and extended ways so that we can ask questions that formerly would have been unintelligible. These ideas should by now, in the terms of this book, have a familiar ring, for they connect with what the poet says about thinking inside his lines and with the philosopher's insistence on the inseparability of technique from conceptual content in the visual arts.

If we go on to consider the views of Albert Einstein on the subject of the imagination, we find further parallels between descriptions of artistic and of scientific creation. Einstein speaks of "physical theories as 'free products' of the human imagination" and says that novel ways of regarding phenomena "cannot be abstracted from experience but must be freely invented." Toulmin's gloss on this is that one cannot make discoveries in the physical sciences with an untutored imagination and that only a trained mind can exercise the sort of imagination that counts in this field. Likewise, rigorous training, though of a different type, is equally necessary for the success of a pianist, painter, composer, or poet. In each discipline, one must proceed with a mind that is perpetually in a state of preparation.

Oliver Sacks, the distinguished neurologist, insists that a blend of sensuous, aesthetic, and imaginative elements fed his own earliest scientific explorations. Capturing his first tries at making sense of physical phenomena, he tells us: "As a child I thought that light had form and size, the flower-like shapes of candle flames, like unopened magnolias, the luminous polygons in my uncle's tungsten bulbs." With respect to metals, he writes of his fondness for gold with its weight and rich yellow hue and how, as he played with his mother's wedding ring, she explained its properties to him, its softness and heaviness relative to other metals. He writes of his fascination with his family's cast-iron lawn mower and the brass menorahs that were lit for Hanukah and of how, when he admired the diamond in his mother's engagement ring, she explained to him that it was just another form of carbon like the coal they burned in winter. He puzzled mightily, he remembers, trying hard to imagine how such a flaky black substance could in any way relate to the icy sparkling jewel she wore on her finger.

Growing up in London during World War II, Sacks had his budding scientific interests nourished in the bosom of a large, closely knit family of impressive intellectuals—parents, aunts, and uncles variously trained in chemistry, botany, and medicine. Science, however, was never separated from the arts. His family owned two pianos, Bechsteins, and his brothers played the flute and the clarinet as well. Sacks writes: "The house was full of music . . . a veritable aquarium of sound." In a stunning summation of the afterlife of this extraordinary childhood, he reveals, at the very end of his memoir, a favorite dream. He is going to the opera as an element! He is Hafnium, and he is "sharing a box at the Met with the other heavy transition metals—my old and valued friends—Tantalum, Rhenium, Osmium, Iridium, Platinum, Gold, and Tungsten."

And yet, to argue for the primacy of imagination in scientific thinking is perhaps too much. After all, physicist Max Planck once defined the task of physics as measuring all measurable things and rendering all unmeasurable things measurable. Such a view may accord less prominence to the imagination. We might, however, put forth the notion that, in the sciences, once imagination *does* make its leap—as in biology, for example, when Darwin first conceived of all distinct species as being linked through time—then much of the subsequent work, the testing, comparing, verifying, et cetera, belongs to other powers of the mind.

If we imagine science as a theater, it would seem as though imagination might play the part of a character of rare and astonishing gifts on whom the plot hinges but a character who appears onstage infrequently albeit commandingly. On that basis alone, however, we could surely argue for the aesthetic education of a little scientist-to-be.

Moral Imagination

Whatever our children grow up to do in terms of a career, we hope they will be kind and just to themselves and to other human beings and to the world of all living creatures and nonliving things. Ethics presupposes the freedom to make choices. One must choose to be good, and to make an ethical choice, one must transcend the actual, the existing, and the merely appropriate. One must enter the realm of possibility, and in precisely that sense, ethics requires imagination. Since moral frontiers are never given but are always being declared, a social or a political reformer has to treat the impossible as if it were possible.

Some years ago, when I was reading William Frankena's *Ethics* in graduate school, my then-four-year-old daughter asked: "Mommy, why are there thieves in the world?"

Delighted with this unexpected opportunity to apply my esoteric knowledge, I immediately asked her what she would do if she wanted something that belonged to somebody else. She said right away that she would ask for it.

"But suppose the person said no," I countered.

She said she would ask again.

I pressed her, and finally, after I had pushed her very hard, she reluctantly admitted that she might "just take it."

"Okay," I returned, "so now you can *imagine* how thieves come into the world and how a thief might feel."

As she pondered this in silence, I put the obvious next question to her. "Rivi," I asked, "how would you feel if someone took something of *yours* when you said they couldn't have it?"

"Bad," she said, looking very serious and undoubtedly imagining something awful.

"Well, Rivi," I said, "maybe a person who could *imagine* how you would feel about that and who understood how bad you would feel would not steal anything from you. Maybe thieves are people who have trouble imagining other people's feelings."

What happened next was that Rivi, who takes after her grandfather in being—then as now—quite as down-to-earth as she is philosophical, ran swiftly off to her room to check up on all her most prized possessions. *What* was she imagining?

Historical Imagination

Even history requires imagination. The Latin word *historia* suggests that we actually conceptualize history not as the totality of our past actions, *res gestae,* but as stories, in other words, as the accounts we construct of those actions in the present. Children begin to learn history by retelling the stories of their day at bedtime. Their stories and replays and re-creations of experiences are the antecedents of history writing in a more formal sense. It is also, as noted above, especially pleasurable for them to hear episodes of family history passed on by older relatives. History, of course, must not merely tell stories but tell *true* stories. Let's think, however, of great histories where attempts have been made to portray transcendent panoramas of particular epochs—for example, Jacob Burckhardt's celebrated volumes on the Italian Renaissance. In works such as this, the role of the imagination looms large. Burckhardt himself writes: "What I construct historically is not the result of criticism or speculation but of imagination seeking to fill the gaps in observation. To me history is still in large measure poetry; it is a series of the most beautiful and picturesque compositions."

Questions about imagination and memory and imagination as freedom from the limitations of the present are supremely relevant to history, which tries to organize the chaos of the past and help us "remember" that which occurred outside the scope of our own personal past. The historian's task is to bring former times to life, and in so doing, he must, to paraphrase Goethe on Herder, not simply sift gold out of the rubbish but regenerate the rubbish itself into a living plant; he must "fuse together all these *disjecta membra,* the scattered limbs of the past and synthesize them and mold them into a new shape."

But just as imagination is essential to the writing of history, so, likewise, is a cultivated sense of history a boon to the working of the imagination. By understanding something of the complexity of our human past, we can better project our consciousness into the unknown and conceive of human potentiality—not in the narrow sense of prediction but in a creative sense, as in the Leibnizian maxim *"Reculer pour mieux sauter,"* which restates Virgil's description of Aeneas's descent into Avernus in the *Aeneid* and which fits also with Freud's notion of delving into the recesses of the forgotten past in order to proceed more rationally with life in the here and now. Was it not Santayana who said that unless we can remember the past, we might be doomed to repeat it?

Embracing the World

Children are on the move; physically as well as metaphorically, they bounce and wiggle and climb and jump and sometimes fall. They are relational creatures, and, growing themselves, they insist on our mobility as well. Pushing us away as hard as they can, they need us—at the same time—to be with them. Dragging us over to a window to marvel at the evening sky, or showing us the insides of their hearts by means of crude paintbrushes and some yellow tempera paint, withdrawing to a shady hillside after a concert, getting down on the ground with us to watch the russet-colored leaves dance by, or begging for a birthday party in a country where children speak different languages and are being taught to distrust one another, they are also paying close attention to us. They are noticing our responses. As Stephen Sondheim writes in the lyrics of one of his best songs from *Into the Woods,* "Children will listen."

But in turn, we must listen to their small voices rather than drowning them out. When we listen, we will find that we are not only promoting their growth but also rediscovering the world through their eyes. Their enlarging gaze, as Bachelard puts it, will magnify our own.

When we refrain from insisting preemptively that they see it through ours (remember the Henry Moore sculpture series), we will sustain their inner growth, and we will simultaneously refresh the sources of our own imaginative lives.

Against the grain of current educational fetishes for testing children's cognitive abilities, measuring their factual knowledge, and quantifying their skills acquisition, I plead for the according of a higher priority to children's inner lives. I ask us to uphold their birthright to wonder and to question and to make up their *own* "superheroes." Let them experiment and be wrong but in their own terms so that it is they who want to find better answers (this is how Socrates does it in the *Meno*).

Raising Children, Not Rhinoceroses

Products of contemporary mass culture, even when ostensibly targeted for children, rarely have their best interests at heart. Seldom do the profit-making interests that fuel these products mesh with the needs and priorities of developing young minds. Seldom do the electronic media spawn programs designed for young people that give priority to goals such as stimulating children's ingenuity; fostering in them the passionate curiosity that takes them beyond an assigned task; encouraging critical reflection and the patience it inevitably requires; revealing how much pleasure there can be in variety and diversity rather than in sameness; identifying, depicting, and valorizing a broad spectrum of emotions rather than limiting the emotional palette to aggression, sentimentality, and eroticism; raising children's ethical awareness and probing its conundrums; demonstrating that the first try is rarely the last when the goal is to perform up to a pinnacle of excellence; and offering children examples of quality in the arts as templates for their future lives.

My undertaking in these pages constitutes an effort not only to describe and interpret but also to advocate. I want to encourage you, my reader, to endorse the importance, in our time, of raising aesthetic rather than anesthetic children. Young people who can remain sensitive and alert, responsive, discriminating, and playful claim access to a repertoire of creative possibilities with which to vitalize their own lives, those of others, and of the societies in which they partake. On the other hand, children who ingest only a diet of cultural rubbish are less able to do so. Suffering the repression of their wondrously variegated selves, they cannot but be more vulnerable to domination, to a debased cultural uniformity, and to whatever sort of political control might go along with it. I conjure for you the mental images and anguished sounds of Ionesco's thundering rhinoceroses!

Through the realms of the aesthetic, young people's inner lives can flourish and be protected from endless violation. Through aesthetic experiences, there exists the exquisite chance to discover the world, again and again, for the first time. Children can practice their inborn proclivities to imagine, select, reject, taste, try, make new patterns, search with feeling for what matters in their lives.

In every culture, the most precious achievements have been linked with aesthetic and not merely practical goals. Ceaselessly, we symbolize, represent, and elaborate our everyday tools and necessities. Children have the right to come to know and learn to appreciate the finest of these achievements in many different cultures and thus to enrich the course of their future lives. Those who grow up with a range of such experiences in the musical, visual, theatrical, and literary arts may learn to communicate and to respond with a wider range of expressive possibilities than those who do not.

Furthermore, as Hegel points out in his *Aesthetics*, experiences in the arts even enhance our appreciation of natural beauty. We love nature, he argues, because, when it seems to imitate art, we perceive in it reflections of artistic order and design. In earliest childhood, nature can seem a mere extension of the body and the self, and children produce, as we know, hilarious examples of this mode of interpretation, such as the case of the Hungarian child who, upon seeing the Danube for the first time, said, "What a lot of spit!" Later on, aesthetic experiences, whether within the arts directly or in natural settings, carry us both into and radically out of ourselves. Whereas for young children art functions as an extension of the play that occupies them, for us the aesthetic involves a restoration of what we have, too soon and at too great a cost, relinquished.

"Behind dark curtains," as Bachelard writes, "the snow seems whiter. Indeed, everything comes alive when contradictions accumulate."

Children, with the freshness of their perceptions, return us to the origins of our own aesthetic moments, to sensuous joys, and to almost forgotten hurts. When we play with them, they redeem us by refusing to allow us to remain anesthetized. They reanimate us by generously including us—at least sometimes—in their passionate love affairs with the world.

Selected Bibliography

The following list of references consists of works consulted and may be seen as a complement to the preceding chapters.

In addition to the works that follow, I wish to endorse the many fine ubiquitously available practical manuals devoted to formal instruction for children in the various arts. Equally pertinent and recommended to readers who seek a rigorous, academic approach to topics adumbrated in these pages are works by researchers and pioneers in the fields of psychology and art education who scientifically study the aesthetic responses of children. Working within various social science disciplines and paradigms, such investigators deploy theories of cognitive development and sophisticated statistical methodologies to conduct large- and small-scale empirical research projects. They study how children perceive aesthetically at different stages of growth. Articles on research of this kind can readily be found in academic journals of early-childhood education, art education, and child psychology. I regard them as worthy supplements to the informal, personal approach I have adopted in this volume.

America's Childhood. 1993. *Daedalus* (Proceedings of the American Academy of Arts and Sciences), vol. 122, no. 1, ed. Stephen R. Graubard.

Anzieu, Didier. 1986. *Freud's Self-Analysis.* Trans. Peter Graham. Madison, Conn.: International Universities Press.

Apfel, Roberta, and Bennett Simon. 1996. *Minefields in Their Hearts.* New Haven: Yale University Press.

Ariès, Philippe. 1960. *L'Enfant et la vie familiale sous l'Ancien Régime.* Paris: Libraire Plon.

Arnheim, Rudolf. 1969. *Visual Thinking.* Berkeley: University of California Press.

————. 1974. *Art and Visual Perception.* Berkeley: University of California Press.

Axline, Virginia. 1969. *Play Therapy.* New York: Ballantine Books.

Bachelard, Gaston. 1964. *The Poetics of Space.* Trans. Maria Jolas. Boston: Beacon Press.

Bell, E. T. [1937] 1961. *Men of Mathematics.* Reprint, New York: Simon and Schuster.

Benjamin, Walter. 1968. *Illuminations.* Trans. Harry Zohn. Ed. Hannah Arendt. New York: Schocken Books.

Berg, Michael, Michael J. Wilson, and Peter Ackerman. 2002. *Ice Age.* Twentieth Century Fox. Animated film.

Bergman, Ingmar. 1982. *Fanny and Alexander.* Co-production Sweden-France-Germany: Svenska Filminstitutet / Sveriges TV1 / Personafilm / Gaumont. Film.

Berliner, Alain. 1997. *Ma vie en rose.* Haut et court. Sony Pictures Classics. Film.

Bettelheim, Bruno. 1991. *Freud's Vienna and Other Essays.* New York: Vintage Books.

Blake, William. [1789, 1794] 1971. *Songs of Innocence; Songs of Experience.* Reprint, Mineola, N.Y.: Dover.

Bower, T. G. R. 1977. *The Perceptual World of the Child.* Cambridge, Mass.: Harvard University Press.

Brody, Jane. 2004. "TV's Toll on Young Minds and Bodies." *New York Times,* August 3, 2004.

Brooks, Ellen. 1999–ongoing. *Overthere Somewhere.* Unpublished photographs.

Brown, Margaret Wise, and Clement Hurd. 1942. *The Runaway Bunny.* New York: Harper & Row.

Bruner, Jerome, Alison Jolley, and Kathy Sylva, eds. 1976. *Play: Its Role in Development and Evolution.* New York: Basic Books.

Brunhoff, Jean de. [1933] 1961. *The Story of Babar.* Trans. Merle S. Haas. Reprint, New York: Random House.

Burckhardt, Jacob. 2002. *The Civilization of the Renaissance in Italy.* New York: Modern Library.

Calvino, Italo. 1983. *Mr. Palomar.* Trans. William Weaver. New York: Harcourt Brace Jovanovich.

Cassirer, Ernst. [1944] 1962. *Essay on Man.* Reprint, New Haven: Yale University Press.

Cole, Michael. 1996. *Cultural Psychology: A Once and Future Discipline.* Cambridge, Mass.: Belknap Press of Harvard University Press.

Coles, Robert. 1997. *The Moral Intelligence of Children.* New York: Random House.

Collins, Mark, and Margaret Mary Kimmel, eds. 1996. *Mister Rogers' Neighborhood: Children, Television, and Fred Rogers.* Pittsburgh: University of Pittsburgh Press.

Cook, Nicholas. 1990. *Music, Imagination, and Culture.* Oxford: Clarendon Press.

Copland, Aaron. 1952. "The Gifted Listener." In *Music and Imagination.* Cambridge, Mass.: Harvard University Press.

Csikszentmihalyi, Mihaly. 1990. *Flow: The Psychology of Optimal Experience.* New York: Harper & Row.

Dewey, John. [1934] 1979. *Art as Experience.* Reprint, New York: Paragon Books.

Edelman, Marian Wright. 1992. *The Measure of Our Success: A Letter to My Children and Yours.* Boston: Beacon Press.

Edwards, Betty. 1979. *Drawing on the Right Side of the Brain.* Los Angeles: J. P. Tarcher.

Egoyan, Atom. 1997. *The Sweet Hereafter.* New Line Studio. Film.

Eisner, Elliott. 2002. *The Arts and the Creation of Mind.* New Haven: Yale University Press.

Eisner, Elliott, ed. 1976. *The Arts, Human Development, and Education.* Berkeley, Calif.: McCutchan.

Erikson, Erik H. 1950. *Childhood and Society.* New York: W. W. Norton.

Fraiberg, Selma H. 1959. *The Magic Years.* New York: Charles Scribner's Sons.

Freud, Anna. [1936] 1966. *The Ego and the Mechanisms of Defense.* Reprint, New York: International Universities Press.

Freud, Sigmund. 1901. "Childhood Memories and Screen Memories." Chapter 4 of *The Psychopathology of Everyday Life.* Vol. 6 of *The Standard Edition of the Complete Psychological Works of Sigmund Freud.* Ed. and trans. James Strachey. 24 vols. London: Hogarth Press, 1953–74.

―――. 1908. "The Creative Writer and Daydreaming." *Standard Edition,* 9:142–53.

―――. 1909. "Family Romances." *Standard Edition,* 9:236–41.

Gardner, Howard. 1973. *The Arts and Human Development.* New York: John Wiley and Sons.

Gershon, Karen. 1989. *We Came as Children.* London: Macmillan Papermac.

Golomb, Claire. 1992. *The Child's Creation of a Pictorial World.* Berkeley: University of California Press.

Gombrich, E. H. 1963. *Meditations on a Hobby Horse and Other Essays on the Theory of Art.* New York: Phaidon Press.

Gombrich, E. H., Julian Hochberg, and Max Black. 1972. *Art, Perception, and Reality.* Baltimore: Johns Hopkins University Press.

Goodenough, Elizabeth, ed. 2000. *Secret Spaces of Childhood* (Part Two). Special issue of *Michigan Quarterly Review,* vol. 39, no. 3 (Summer).

Gorky, Maxim. [1913] 1966. *My Childhood.* Trans. Ronald Wilks. Reprint, London: Penguin.

Greenacre, Phyllis. [1957] 1971. "The Childhood of the Artist." In *Emotional Growth.* Reprint, New York: International Universities Press.

Greene, Maxine. 1995. *Releasing the Imagination.* San Francisco: Jossey-Bass.

Hamilton, Jane. 2000. *Disobedience.* New York: Doubleday.

Hegel, G. W. F. [1820–29] 1993. *Introductory Lectures on Aesthetics.* Hotho Compilations (1835, 1842). Trans. Bernard Bosanquet. London: Penguin.

Henri, Robert. [1923] 1960. *The Art Spirit.* Reprint, Philadelphia: J. B. Lippincott.

Herrington, Susan. 1997. "The Received View of Play and the Subculture of Infants." *Landscape Journal* 16, no. 2: 149–60.

Hoban, Lillian. 1974. *Arthur's Honey Bear.* New York: Harper & Row.

Hoban, Russell, and Lillian Hoban. 1968. *A Birthday for Frances.* New York: Harper & Row.

Hopkins, Gerard Manley. 1979. *Poems and Prose.* Ed. W. H. Gardner. Harmondsworth, England: Penguin.

Hrabal, Bohumil. 1976. *Too Loud a Solitude.* Trans. Michael Henry Heim. New York: Harcourt Brace Jovanovich.

Ionesco, Eugene. 1960. *Rhinoceros and Other Plays.* Trans. Derek Prouse. New York: Grove Press.

Jackson, Philip W. 1998. *John Dewey and the Lessons of Art.* New Haven: Yale University Press.

Jones, Ernest. 1957. *The Life and Work of Sigmund Freud.* New York: Basic Books.

Kagan, Jerome. 1984. *The Nature of the Child.* New York: Basic Books.

Keats, John. 1819. "La Belle Dame sans merci: A Ballad." In *John Keats: Selected Poems.* Ed. John Barnard. London: Penguin, 1988.

Kerman, Joseph. 1956. *Opera as Drama.* Berkeley: University of California Press.

Kincaid, Jamaica. 1986. *Annie John.* New York: Penguin.

Klein, Melanie. [1932] 1975. *The Psychoanalysis of Children.* Reprint, London: Hogarth Press.

Kofman, Sarah. 1994. *Rue Ordener, Rue Labat.* Paris: Éditions Galilée.

Lacan, Jacques. 1966. *Écrits.* Paris: Éditions du Seuil.

Langer, Susanne. 1953. *Feeling and Form.* New York: Charles Scribner's Sons.

Levi, Primo. 1986. *The Periodic Table.* Trans. Raymond Rosenthal. London: Abacus.

Lightman, Alan. 2005. *A Sense of the Mysterious.* New York: Pantheon Books.

Lobel, Arnold. 1969. *Small Pig.* New York: Harper & Row.

Locke, John. 1964. *John Locke on Education.* Ed. Peter Gay. New York: Teachers College Press.

Lowenfeld, Viktor. 1960. *Creative and Mental Growth.* 3rd ed. New York: Macmillan.

Lurie, Alison. 1990. *Don't Tell the Grown-ups: The Subversive Power of Children's Literature.* Boston: Little, Brown.

Manguel, Alberto. 2000. *Reading Pictures.* New York: Random House.

Matthews, Gareth B. 1980. *Philosophy and the Young Child.* Cambridge, Mass.: Harvard University Press.

McCloskey, Robert. 1963. *Burt Dow, Deep Water Man.* New York: Viking Press.

McCullers, Carson. 1940. *The Heart Is a Lonely Hunter.* New York: Houghton Mifflin.

Mead, Margaret, and Martha Wolfenstein, eds. 1955. *Childhood in Contemporary Cultures.* Chicago: University of Chicago Press.

Milne, A. A. [1927] 1955. *Now We Are Six.* Reprint, New York: Dell.

Minow, Newton, and Craig Lamay. 1995. *Abandoned in the Wasteland: Children, Television, and the First Amendment.* New York: Hill and Wang.

Montello, Louise. 2002. *Essential Musical Intelligence.* Wheaton, Ill.: Quest Books.

Moore, G. E. [1903] 2005. *Principia Ethica.* Reprint, New York: Barnes and Noble Books.

Moore, Ronald, ed. 1995. *Aesthetics for Young People.* Reston, Va.: National Art Education Association.

Morrison, Toni. 1970. *The Bluest Eye.* New York: Bantam Books.

Nagel, Thomas. 1974. "What Is It Like to Be a Bat?" In *Mortal Questions.* Cambridge: Cambridge University Press, 1979. (Orig. published in *Philosophical Review* 83 [1974]: 435–50.)

Neiman, Susan. 2002. *Evil in Modern Thought: An Alternative History of Philosophy.* Princeton, N.J.: Princeton University Press.

Neruda, Pablo. 1978. *Memoirs.* Trans. Hardie St. Martin. Harmondsworth, England: Penguin.

Parsons, Michael J. 1987. *How We Understand Art.* Cambridge: Cambridge University Press.

Piaget, Jean. [1929] 1983. *The Child's Conception of the World.* Trans. Joan and Andrew Tomlinson. Reprint, Totowa, N.J.: Rowman & Littlefield.

Plato. 1957. *Meno.* Trans. Benjamin Jowett. Indianapolis: Bobbs-Merrill.

Polanyi, Michael. 1969. *Knowing and Being.* Ed. Marjorie Grene. Chicago: University of Chicago Press.

Polhemus, Robert M. 2005. *Lot's Daughters.* Stanford: Stanford University Press.

Potter, Beatrix. 1918. *The Tale of Johnny Town-Mouse.* London: Frederick Warne.

Project Zero: http://www.pz.harvard.edu.

Riding, Alan. 2001. "Adieu to the Louvre." *New York Times,* April 12, 2001.

Rilke, Rainer Maria. [1934] 1954. *Letters to a Young Poet.* Trans. M. D. Herter Norton. Reprint, New York: W. W. Norton.

Rogers, Fred. 1970. *Mister Rogers' Songbook.* New York: Random House.

Roiphe, Anne Richardson. 1970. *Up the Sandbox.* New York: Simon and Schuster.

Rose, Jacqueline. 1984. *The Case of Peter Pan; or, The Impossibility of Children's Fiction.* London: Macmillan.

Roth, Henry. [1934] 1991. *Call It Sleep.* Reprint, New York: Farrar, Straus and Giroux.

Ryle, Gilbert. 1949. *The Concept of Mind.* Chicago: University of Chicago Press.

Sacks, Oliver. 2001. *Uncle Tungsten: Memories of a Chemical Boyhood.* New York: Vintage Books.

Schack, Juliane. 2000. *Comprendre les dessins d'enfants.* Paris: Marabout.

Schneider, Laurie. 1985. "The Theme of Mother and Child in the Art of Henry Moore." In *Psychoanalytic Perspectives on Art,* ed. Mary Gedo. Hillsdale, N.J.: Analytic Press.

Schulz, Bruno. [1934] 1963. "Cinnamon Shops." In *The Street of Crocodiles.* Trans. Celina Wieniewska. New York: Viking.

Sendak, Maurice. 1963. *Where the Wild Things Are.* New York: Harper & Row.

Shloss, Carol Loeb. 2003. *Lucia Joyce: To Dance in the Wake.* New York: Farrar, Straus and Giroux.

Smith, Ralph A., and Alan Simpson, eds. 1991. *Aesthetics and Arts Education.* Urbana: University of Illinois Press.

Sondheim, Stephen, and James Lapine. 1987. *Into the Woods.* Play. Book, with adaptation and illustrations by Hudson Talbott, New York: Crown, 1988.

Spiegelman, Art. 1986. *Maus: A Survivor's Tale.* New York: Pantheon Books.

Spitz, Ellen Handler. 1989. "Psychoanalysis and the Legacies of Antiquity." In *Freud and Art,* ed. Lynn Gamwell and Richard Wells. New York: Abrams.

———. 1991. *Image and Insight.* New York: Columbia University Press.

———. 1994. *Museums of the Mind.* New Haven: Yale University Press.

———. 1999. *Inside Picture Books.* New Haven: Yale University Press.

Steinberg, Michael. 2000. "Notes on *Luisa Miller.*" *Performing Arts* 78, no. 1 (September).

Stern, Daniel N. 1985. *The Interpersonal World of the Infant.* New York: Basic Books.

Stevenson, Robert Louis. 1905. *A Child's Garden of Verses.* New York: Charles Scribner's Sons.

Suransky, Valerie Polakow. 1982. *The Erosion of Childhood.* Chicago: University of Chicago Press.

Surface, Mary Hall, and David Maddox. 2004. *The Odyssey of Telémaca.* Book by M. H. Surface; lyrics by David Maddox and M. H. Surface; music by David Maddox. Musical theater, libretto and score.

Tatar, Maria. 1987. *The Hard Facts of the Grimms' Fairy Tales.* Princeton: Princeton University Press.

———. 1999. *The Classic Fairy Tales: A Norton Critical Edition.* New York: W. W. Norton.

Tati, Jacques. 1958. *Mon oncle.* Continental. Film.

Thomas, Alexander, and Stella Chess. 1977. *Temperament and Development.* New York: Brunner/Mazel.

Thurber, James. 1943. *Many Moons.* New York: Harcourt Brace.

———. 1953. *The Thurber Carnival.* Harmondsworth, England: Penguin.

Toulmin, Stephen. 1960. *The Philosophy of Science: An Introduction.* New York: Harper & Row.

Twain, Mark. [1876] 2005. *The Adventures of Tom Sawyer.* Reprint, New York: HarperCollins.

Uchida, Yoshiko, and Joanna Yardley. 1993. *The Bracelet.* New York: Putnam and Grosset.

Ugrešić, Dubravka. 1996. *The Museum of Unconditional Surrender.* Trans. Celia Hawkesworth. London: Phoenix House.

Vygotsky, L. S. 1978. *Mind in Society,* ed. Michael Cole et al. Cambridge, Mass.: Harvard University Press.

Warner, Marina. 1994. *Six Myths of Our Time.* New York: Vintage Books.

Watterson, Bill. 1987. *Something Under the Bed Is Drooling.* Kansas City, Mo.: Andrews, McMeel and Parker.

Waxman, Sharon. 2004. "Study Finds Film Ratings Are Growing More Lenient." *New York Times*, July 14, 2004.

Whitman, Walt. 1983. *Leaves of Grass: The 1892 Edition.* New York: Bantam Books.

Wilbur, Richard. 1978. "The Writer." In *The Mind Reader.* New York: Harcourt Brace Jovanovich.

Winner, Ellen. 1982. *Invented Worlds.* Cambridge, Mass.: Harvard University Press.

Winnicott, Clare. 1978. "D.W.W.: A Reflection." In *Between Reality and Fantasy: Transitional Objects and Phenomena,* ed. Simon Grolnick and Leonard Barkin. Northvale, N.J.: Jason Aronson.

Winnicott, D. W. 1966. "The Location of Cultural Experience." *International Journal of Psycho-Analysis* 48:368–72.

———. 1971. *Playing and Reality.* London: Routledge.

Wolfenstein, Martha. [1954] 1978. *Children's Humor: A Psychological Analysis.* Reprint, Bloomington, Ind.: Free Press.

———. 1957. *Disaster, A Psychological Essay.* Glencoe, Ill.: Free Press.

———. 1969. "Loss, Rage, and Repetition." *The Psychoanalytic Study of the Child* 24:432–60.

Wolfenstein, Martha, and Gilbert Kliman, eds. 1965. *Children and the Death of a President.* Garden City, N.Y.: Doubleday.

Woolf, Virginia. 1927. *To the Lighthouse.* London: Harcourt.

Wordsworth, William. 1950. *Selected Poetry.* Ed. Mark Van Doren. New York: Modern Library.

Wullschlager, Jackie. 2001. *Hans Christian Andersen: The Life of a Storyteller.* New York: Knopf.

Acknowledgments

Sometimes it seems that to write a book is to depend, like Blanche DuBois, on the kindness of strangers. Over time, however, some of these kindly strangers morph into cherished friends. And since this book underwent a long gestation followed by a correspondingly protracted labor, it has generated a plethora of wonderful people who deserve my thanks—people old and young, living and no longer alive. Each has helped me in original ways, subtle, direct, ever generous, to bring this book into being. I seek here to acknowledge many who are not mentioned by name in the body of the text. First, my debt to teachers. I want to acknowledge the legendary educator Maxine Greene of Teachers College, Columbia University, and the Lincoln Center Institute. Captivated by her ardor and enthusiasm, I began as a graduate student to dream of writing my own book one day on the aesthetic lives of children. Mary Mothersill, formerly of Barnard College, taught aesthetics with a rigor that has indelibly stamped my intellectual life, even though I doubt I have lived up to her scrupulous standards. During the years devoted directly to the writing of this book, I was privileged to be the recipient of several fellowships that gave me the boons of time, space, and community. I am grateful for having had the chance to read, think, and write in the sequestered, elegantly appointed Camargo Foundation in Cassis, France, under the direction of Michael Pretina; for having participated as a Senior Fellow at the Rutgers Center for Children and Childhood Studies under the aegis of anthropologist Myra Bluebond-Langner; and for sojourning at the Clark Art Institute, under the leadership of art historian Michael Ann Holly, where, in a unique atmosphere of combined scintillation and serenity, I brought the writing of my manuscript to completion.

For the chance to learn, acquire, debate, and parry ideas germane to the subject matter of this book and to receive vital peer criticism, I wish to thank my colleagues at the American Society for Aesthetics, in whose annual meetings I have participated for many years and on whose board I have been proud to serve. To colleagues and friends, my heartfelt gratitude is extended to all who have stimulated my thinking about aesthetics and childhood through lectures and in conversation, or who have held my hand at moments of despair, or who have cheered me, invited me, hosted me, fed me, shared their own trials and triumphs with me, read chapters and given me courage, made fruitful suggestions, or simply stayed with me, so to speak: Knut Aagaard, Judith Aissen, Nina Kivelson Auerbach, Mieke Bal, Martin and Maria Bergmann, Jeanne W. Bernstein, Rebecca Boehling, Sarah Burns, Betty Butler, Mary Ann Caws, Jane Celwyn, Nancy Chodorow, Robert Coles, Wanda Corn, Lucy Daniels, Alla Efimova, Elliott Eisner, Marie-Thérèse Fabre, Yael Feldman, Christine Ford, Jay Freyman, Eleanor Galenson, Sander L. Gilman, Horst Hoheisel, Peter Jelavich, Marjoleine Kars, Jules Kerman, Paulina Kernberg, Norman Kleeblatt, Florence Ladd, Ruth Lax, M. G. Lord, Cindy McLaughlin, Helen and Donald Meyers, Mara Miller, Maria Phillips and Franc Nunoo-Quarcoo, Anne Roiphe, Rachel Rosenblum, Cynthia Rostankowski, Carol Loeb Schloss, Tracy Sharpley-Whiting, the late Albert J. Solnit, Joanna and Peter L. Strauss, Maria Tatar, John Toews, Dubravka Ugrešić, Judith and Robert Wallerstein, Marina Warner, Eleanor Wood.

For graciously sharing their stories with me, both of their own lives and of their children's, I would like to thank Janet Berlo, Betty Butler, Antonia Handler Chayes and the late Abram Chayes, Alla Efimova, Annie and Marie-Thérèse Fabre, Gilles Fabre, Constance Greenspan, Deborah and Horst Hoheisel, Olivier Levieil, Andrew Lewis, Keith Moxey, Annie Rouzoul, Raman Srinivasan, Roger Stein, and Berbeli Wanning. For special sustenance, both tangible and intangible, at the University of Maryland (UMBC), I wish to express my appreciation to Freeman Hrabowski, Arthur Johnson, and Marilyn Demorest, and also to Lisa Whittle, Lee Tydings, and Elwyn Hickson. My wholehearted appreciation goes without reservation to my entire family, including not only my late parents and grandparents, my children and their families, but also my sister, niece, uncles, aunts, and cousins; without them, this book could not have been written.

My greatest debt of gratitude goes to two people, my superlative agent, Eric Simonoff, of Janklow and Nesbit, and my nonpareil editor, Dan Frank, of Pantheon Books, with whom it has been an unqualified privilege to work. Both expressed their faith in this project right from the start, and even when I seemed to be fluttering or flying off course, neither of them tried to impale me or clip my wings. They simply waited patiently for me to alight and then listened gravely and gave me their sensitive comments and *bon courage*. At Jankow and Nesbit, I also wish to thank Edith Klemm for her sweetness and ever-ready kindness. At Pantheon Books, I am grateful to Fran Bigman, whose warmth and responsiveness have been constant; to Margaret Wimberger for her fine copyediting; to Katie Freeman, who loved this book from the start; to Mark

Melnick, who designed its cover; and to Ellen Feldman, who brought it all together.

My last-but-not-least moment of thanks is reserved for Gilles Fabre, whose benign presence in my life throughout the period when I was writing this book was vital in ways that go deeper than words.

To all the children—wise, silly, naughty, and bashful—my love.

Index

About the Author

A native of New York, Ellen Handler Spitz was educated at Barnard College and at Harvard and Columbia universities. The author of *Inside Picture Books,* she is a professor of visual arts at the University of Maryland, Baltimore County.

A Note on the Type

The text of this book was set in Centaur, the only typeface designed by Bruce Rogers (1870–1957), the well-known American book designer. A celebrated penman, Rogers based his design on the roman face cut by Nicolas Jenson in 1470 for his Eusebius. Jenson's roman surpassed all of its forerunners and even today, in modern recuttings, remains one of the most popular and attractive of all typefaces. The italic used to accompany Centaur is Arrighi, designed by another American, Frederic Warde, and based on the chancery face used by Lodovico degli Arrighi in 1524.

Composed by Creative Graphics, Allentown, Pennsylvania
Printed and bound by Berryville Graphics, Berryville, Virginia
Designed by M. Kristen Bearse